Mystic Union

Cornell Studies in the Philosophy of Religion

EDITED BY WILLIAM P. ALSTON

Nelson Pike

Mystic Union

An Essay in the
Phenomenology of Mysticism

Cornell University Press, *Ithaca and London*

First published 1992 by Cornell University Press.

Library of Congress Cataloging-in-Publication Data

Pike, Nelson.
  Mystic union : an essay in the phenomenology of mysticism / Nelson Pike.
    p. cm. — (Cornell studies in the philosophy of religion)
  Includes bibliographical references and index.
  ISBN 0-8014-2684-7 (alk. paper). — ISBN 0-8014-9969-0 (pbk. : alk. paper)
  1. Mystical union. I. Title. II. Series.
BT767.7.P55 1992
248.2'2—dc20   91-55553

Printed in the United States of America

♾ The paper in this book meets the minimum requirements of the American National Standard for Information Sciences—Permanence of Paper for Printed Library Materials, ANSI Z39.48-1984.

To my two sons,
Kevin Allen and
Joel Raymond

Contents

Preface

According to the accounts given in most standard manuals of Christian mystical theology, the phenomena of central importance to the spiritual life of the practicing mystic are the so-called states of infused contemplation—often referred to in more colloquial terms as the "states of mystic union." Tradition has it that although all must be regarded as states in which the mystic experiences union with God, the union class includes three distinct types of experience. Listed in order from "lower" to "higher" they are (1) the Prayer of Quiet—also called the "prayer of silence," (2) the Prayer of Union—called "full," "perfect," or "simple" union when "union" is used to cover all three types of experience, and (3) Rapture—also called "ecstasy" and "flight of spirit." It is important to note that the states of infused contemplation are not the only kinds of experiences Christian mystical theologians count as mystical phenomena. So-called mystic apprehensions (visions and locutions) are also included in the mystical class. Mystic apprehensions, however, are usually classified as "gratuitous graces," indicating that they are special or (as is said) "extraordinary" gifts tailored to meet the particular needs of particular individuals at particular times and are not to be thought of as regular parts of the contemplative life. By contrast, the states of infused contemplation are taken to be essential ingredients in the spiritual life of the developing mystic. In fact, the occurrence of these states is regularly used as a way of measuring the experiencing mystic's progress along the mystic path. If what makes a mystical tradition specifically *mystical* is its connection with mystical phenomena, those speaking from within the Christian mystical tradition would insist that the states of infused contemplation constitute the experiential underpinnings of the tradition as a whole.

What is it to experience union with God? More precisely, what are the experiential or phenomenological features of the various experiences traditionally included in the union class? In an interesting text published in 1975 entitled *Exploring Mysticism,* Frits Staal contends that there is just one way to conduct a serious inquiry aimed at finding an answer to this sort of question. If we are to understand the nature of mystical phenomena we must abandon what he calls the "armchair approach" and strive to attain mystical experiences for ourselves (136). Staal writes:

> If mysticism is to be studied seriously, it should not merely be studied indirectly and from without, but also directly and from within. Mysticism can at least in part be regarded as something affecting the human mind, and it is therefore quite unreasonable to expect that it could be fruitfully explored by confining oneself to literature about or contributed by mystics, or to the behavior and physiological characteristics of mystics and their bodies. No one would willingly impose upon himself such artificial constraints when exploring other phenomena affecting or pertaining to the mind; he would not study perception only by analyzing reports of those who describe what they perceive, or by looking at what happens to people and their bodies when they engage in perceiving. What one would do when studying perception, in addition, if not first of all, is to observe and analyze one's own perception. (123)

Staal concludes that it makes no sense to study mysticism without at least some firsthand exposure to mystical phenomena. One attempting to do so, he says, would be "like a blind man studying vision" (124). The implication is clear as regards the question asked above about the states of union. A serious probe of their phenomenological features would require that we take up a life devoted to the development of what is called "Christian perfection" and attain these experiences for ourselves.

Let us suppose that I set out to have the experiences referred to by Christian mystics as the "states of mystic union." Following prescribed procedures, I slowly develop the meditative techniques and mental dispositions regarded in the Christian mystical community as requisite to the end. Now and again (perhaps with increasing frequency) I am subject to a state of consciousness that is manifestly unusual. Shall I conclude that I am now experiencing one of the states of union? Let's suppose that I believe (rightly or wrongly) that if I have an aptitude for the life of contemplation, then unless I have flouted one of the prescribed meditative procedures, the state I am experiencing probably belongs in the union class. The trouble here is that there are no criteria for determining whether I have the required aptitude or whether I have followed the prescribed procedures, short of determining whether I am experiencing one of the states of union. It is not like traveling to Seattle, where there are ways of telling whether my car is working and whether I am traveling in the right direction that are independent of determining whether I have arrived in the right city. The point is that somewhere along the line descriptive information about the experiential features of the union states will have to come into play. Either I shall have to acquire that information for myself or I shall have to rely on an adviser (perhaps a confessor) who possesses the information and is thus in a position to judge whether the experience I am having is of the desired sort. In the absence of such descriptive information, I shall be unable to tell whether I have reached my goal.

How, then, is the requisite information to be acquired either by me or by my adviser? Of course, there are scholarly sources—texts put together by students of mysticism such as Augustin Poulain (*The Graces of Interior Prayer*), Evelyn Underhill (*Mysticism*), Albert Fargas (*Mystical Phenomena*), and the like. These works at least purport to be instructive on the topic. But the accounts given in these scholarly texts are, themselves, derived from other sources, namely, the writings of great Christian mystics such as Teresa of Avila, John of the Cross, Jan van Ruysbroeck, and Bernard of

Clairvaux. What are called "experiences of union" in these last-mentioned sources constitute the extension of this phrase as it is used both by scholars and by practitioners of the contemplative life. So here is the touchstone. In the end, whether I am in a position to launch what Staal would regard as a "serious" study of the several states of union will depend on whether I am having experiences of a kind that primary mystics call by that name. We are thus brought back to the "armchair approach" in our study of mysticism. The study "from within" presupposes the study "from without." Although I think Staal is right in insisting that *full* understanding of mystical phenomena requires *more* than a study of mystical literature (and I shall return to this point in Section 2 of Chapter 8 below), Staal's program seems clearly to require at least some sustained attention to the reports delivered in primary mystical texts.

What, then, do we find when we turn to the primary literature? At this point I shall make only two very general remarks in answer to this question. First, comments about the states of union are often embedded in contexts in which mystics are less concerned to describe the features of mystical phenomena than to extol the majesty of God, decry the sinful status of the soul, warn against the dangers of deception, etc. A workbook of relevant primary descriptions would thus be difficult to compile. It would look more like a collection of isolated excerpts than a set of sustained and organized essays. Second—and restricting attention to just those passages that appear to be focused on experiences of union—almost always the burden of description is carried by one or more of a number of seemingly disparate images. So, for example, at the center of attention will be the soul of the mystic described as a "bird," a "sponge," a "broken vessel," a "castle," or a "tortoise." God is then characterized as a "cauter," a "sickle," a "pilgrim," or a "mother," who meets the soul "in the wine cellar," "in the palace," "in the kingdom," or "in second heaven." The language, in other words, is heavily metaphorical. One senses very quickly that if one is to read the primary literature with any degree of understanding, one will have to make ready to "read" the pictures. It is thus not surprising that even as treated in the best of the scholarly sources, the materials appear sketchy, disorganized, and oblique. If there is a message contained concerning the phenomenological features of the various states of union, it is not one that the primary discourse is wearing on its sleeve.

The primary aim of the present book is to provide phenomenological analyses of the several states of union as these states are described and explained in the classical primary literature of the Christian mystical tradition. The first four chapters constitute a data-gathering effort on my part. Here I attempt to arrange the pictures of union provided in the primary mystical texts into a single complex collage. In the next four chapters, I assume a more critical posture and strive to emerge with a phenomenological account that fits the data assembled in the first half of the book. Along the way I probe several of the more important theses that have been advanced in the contemporary philosophical literature on union—for example, the theory defended by Walter Stace concerning the way in which the phrase "union with God" is used in traditional Christian mystical sources. And in three separate essays attached at the end of the text, I attempt to broaden this aspect of my work by discussing some claims put forward by contemporary scholars of Christian mysticism that are mentioned but not examined earlier in the book. Let me add that because these last-mentioned essays make no direct contribution to the main argument of the book, I include them as what I shall call "supplementary studies" rather than giving them status as regular chapters. Concerning matters of methodology, I address a selection of meta-issues in the last two sections of Chapter 8. There they emerge as natural preliminaries to my argument for the claim that the phenomenological account I propose in Section 2 of that chapter is probably correct. I proceed in this way rather than offering an isolated discussion of methodological issues because when considered apart from a concrete application, matters of methodology strike me as singularly uninteresting topics.

My primary aim in undertaking this study has been to seek for its own sake a clear understanding of the phenomenological message contained in the primary Christian mystical literature on union. However, I have also been prompted by a correlated concern, to wit, that the message in question should be accurately and sympathetically represented in the contemporary philosophical dialogue now under way in the general area of comparative mysticism. Relevant, too, has been the abiding respect I have acquired over the years for the deeply religious sensitivities of prominent Christian mystics, such as Teresa of Avila, as well as the subtle and yet powerful ways in which these sensitivities are expressed in their various mystical writings. Although I hope my book will be received as a successful study in the phenomenology of religion, even if it isn't I shall count myself amply rewarded if it proves to be a vehicle by which even a few of its readers are brought to the beginnings of a similar appreciation.

In the summer of 1970 I began planning a book that would bear the title "Mysticism: Its Phenomenological and Epistemological Foundations." Though I now shudder when reflecting on the magnitude of the ambition expressed in that title, I recall with gratitude a number of friends and colleagues whose encouragement at the outset and whose repeated inquiries over the years have helped to sustain the effort necessary to bring this small part of the original undertaking to fruition. Thus I thank Marilyn McCord Adams and Robert Merrihew Adams of the University of California at Los Angeles as well as Margaret Pabst Battin of the University of Utah. Later, in the fall of 1987, I asked both Marilyn Adams and Linda Peterson of the University of San Diego to examine an early draft of the present book. I also asked William Forgie of the University of California at Santa Barbara to comment on the argument developed in Chapter 7. I am profoundly grateful to each of these philosophers for thoughtful suggestions and penetrating criticisms that helped me see ways of both filtering and expanding the materials then included in the text. As regards the present version of the book, in the spring of 1990 I was encouraged by William P. Alston of Syracuse University to foreshorten further deliberation about its content and to hasten the manuscript into finished form. I am indebted to Alston for these promptings. I am also grateful to Alston as well as to William J. Wainwright of the University of Wisconsin at Milwaukee for valuable criticisms and suggestions offered in their respective reviews of the text for Cornell University Press.

NELSON PIKE

Irvine, California

Mystic Union

[1]

Varieties of
Spiritual Closeness

In this chapter I shall introduce my discussion of the states of infused contemplation by distilling from the writings of Saint Teresa of Avila three verbal pictures offered in her texts as descriptive of the Prayer of Quiet, the Prayer of Full Union, and Rapture, respectively. I have chosen to use Teresa's accounts as a point of departure in part to acknowledge the prominence she enjoys within the Christian mystical community, but primarily because her portrayals are, for the most part, more precise than those provided by other mystics. I should add that in the discussion to follow I shall make no effort to interpret the verbal pictures Teresa provides. Whether they might be translated into some other more literal way of talking (and if so, how) is a question I shall not attempt to answer—at least not here.

1. The Prayer of Quiet

The term "Recollection" is used in Christian mystical literature as the name of a kind of prayer.[1] For most, to pray is to speak, either audibly or silently, to some unseen listener. It is thus a

---

1. Teresa refers to Recollection sometimes as "the Prayer of Recollection" and sometimes as "inward recollection." See *The Way of Perfection*, 232 (chap. 35).

verbal, discursive activity. By contrast, Recollection is a nonverbal, nondiscursive activity; it is a form of what is more widely referred to as "meditation." One starts by dwelling on a single item. As for the item in question, it might be almost anything—one's navel or one's name. In the Christian mystical tradition, it is usually some passage from Scripture or some scene from the life of Christ—Teresa suggested "an image or a picture of [the] Lord—one that you like."[2] The task is not so much to think about a single subject as to sink deeply and without interruption into it. The idea is to bring the mind into tight focus—to *collect*, or *re-collect*, the usually scattered and diversified mental contents that make up the mind. As anyone who has attempted to pray in this way can testify, it is not something easily accomplished. Clearing the mind of distraction requires considerable effort and a good deal of diligent practice.

Recollection is something one *does*—the effort is one's own. Those skilled at the doing, however, tell us that there comes a point where a state of Recollection can be sustained without effort on the part of the one who is at prayer. In the Christian mystical community, this is sometimes referred to as "affective prayer." It is at this point that one is subject to an experience in which one feels oneself taken over by an outside force, pulled (as it were) into a dark, deep, and peaceful space. A sense of quiet falls over the mind. One is suspended in a region where everything is still. This is what mystics in the Christian community have come to call (following Teresa) the Prayer of Quiet. The appropriateness of the name is evident.

Teresa characterized the Prayer of Quiet as a "supernatural" state. The term marks the idea that it is not a state achieved by one's own effort. Recollection would thus not count as supernatural in this sense because it is a state initiated (and generally sustained) by the effort of the one at prayer. By contrast, the Prayer of Quiet (so it is claimed) is imposed by another—a supernatural being.[3] It is thus a state that Christian mystical theologians, following John of the Cross, have come to characterize as "in-

2. Teresa, *The Way of Perfection*, 177 (chap. 26).
3. This distinction between the Prayer of Quiet and Recollection is stressed by Teresa in Fourth Mansions, chap. II, of *Interior Castle*.

fused" by God.[4] If we think of the preparation for the Prayer of Quiet (Recollection) as an *achievement*, Christian mystics insist that we must think of the state itself as a *gift*.[5]

The following paragraph is taken from chapter 31 of Teresa's *Way of Perfection*. It is often taken to be the definitive description of the Prayer of Quiet.

> This is a supernatural state, and, however hard we try, we cannot reach it for ourselves; for it is a state in which the soul enters into peace, or, rather, in which the Lord gives it peace through His presence, as He did that just man Simeon. In this state, all the faculties are stilled. The soul, in a way which has nothing to do with the outward senses, realizes that it is now very close to its God, and that, if it were but a little closer, it would become one with Him through union. This is not because it sees Him either with its bodily or with its spiritual eyes. The just man Simeon saw no more than the glorious Infant—a poor Child, Who, to judge from the swaddling-clothes in which He was wrapped and from the small number of the people whom He had *as a retinue* to take Him up to the Temple, might well have been the son of these poor people rather than the Son of his Heavenly Father. But the Child Himself revealed to him Who He was. Just so, though less clearly, does the soul know Who He is. It cannot understand how it knows Him, yet it sees that it is in the Kingdom (or at least is near the King Who will give it the Kingdom), and it feels such reverence that it dares ask for nothing. It is, as it were, in a swoon, both inwardly and outwardly, so that the outward man (let me call it the "body", and then you will understand me better) does not wish to move, but rests, like one who has almost reached the end of his journey, so that it may the better start again upon its way, with redoubled strength for its task. (200–201)

The central message is clear enough. In this state, Teresa says, the soul finds itself "close to its God" but not so close as to preclude

<hr>

4. John, *Living Flame of Love*, 113 (stanza III).
5. The materials presented in the preceding three paragraphs are a digest of Teresa's discussions in chaps. 25–31 of *The Way of Perfection*, and Fourth Mansions, chaps. II and III, of *Interior Castle*. See also John of the Cross, *Living Flame of Love*, stanza III. I should add that I have also used some interpretative materials from pt. 2, chap. 6, of Underhill's *Mysticism*.

coming closer. The soul is "near the King," but it anticipates the moment when it will come even nearer and will then be "one with Him through union." This point is also repeated several times in the paragraphs immediately following the one just quoted. Some details, however, require clarification. Not everything is here, and some of what is here needs to be expanded.

Mystics of the Christian tradition generally make a distinction between God "in his Humanity" (as they say; sometimes, "in his *sacred* Humanity") and God "in his Divinity." "God in his Humanity" is a phrase used to identify Christ, that is, the *man* Jesus—God incarnate. God in his Humanity is thus a human being possessed of body. By contrast, "God in his Divinity" refers to a purely spiritual being. Unlike God in his Humanity, God in his Divinity has no body. Now, although it is not made clear in the passage we are studying, Teresa elsewhere tells us that it is God *in his Divinity* and *not* God in his Humanity that the mystic encounters in the Prayer of Quiet.[6] The objects related are thus both noncorporeal in nature. They are, as Teresa says, the "soul" of the mystic and God considered as a purely spiritual being. In Section 6 of Chapter 7 and again in Section 3 of Supplementary Study 2, we shall see that it is important to be clear about this somewhat technical point of mystical theology.

Teresa says that in the Prayer of Quiet, although the soul is directly aware of God, it does not see him "either with its bodily or with its spiritual eyes." For Teresa, to see something with "spiritual eyes" is to see something with the mind's eye—to see something imaginatively or in the imagination. It is to see in a sense of "see" that involves imaginative visual imagery.[7] Thus, what is being claimed here, I think, is that in the Prayer of Quiet one is directly aware of God but that this awareness does not consist of regular visual images gained via the physical eyes, nor does it consist of imaginative visual images such as are involved when one "sees" something in the imagination. Teresa says that although the

6. Teresa, *Life*, 250 (chap. xxvii).
7. Teresa sometimes uses the phrase "eyes of the soul" and sometimes "inward sense" instead of "spiritual eyes." In chaps. xxviii and xxix of her *Life*, Teresa discusses a number of visions in which various objects were seen with "spiritual eyes."

soul knows it is in the presence of God, it does not know *how* it knows it. Whatever perceptions may be involved in this experience (and I shall return to this topic in Chapter 3), God is not detected via visual imagery of any kind.

God and the soul are close to each other. So far we have their relative positions pretty well established. But it is not yet clear *where* this encounter takes place. Where are they? No answer to this question is provided in the passage quoted—unless the phrase "in the Kingdom" is taken as a clue. We must look elsewhere—specifically in Teresa's last major work, *Interior Castle*. Here it is made abundantly clear that in the Prayer of Quiet the encounter between God and the soul takes place *in the soul* of the experiencing mystic. But how could this be? How could the encounter take place *in* the soul unless God and the soul were, themselves, *in* the soul? But what would it be for the soul to be *in* the soul?[8] And how could one say that God and the soul are only *close* (and not so close as to preclude coming closer) if God, himself, were *in* the soul. If an apple is *in* the pie, how could it be said to be only *close to* the pie, let alone that it might even get closer still? The imagery appears to be muddled. We must straighten it out if we are to proceed any further.

In her text *Interior Castle*, Teresa speaks of the soul as if it were an enclosure of some sort. It is, in her words, "spacious, ample and lofty."[9] The enclosure is within the body—Teresa says that it is in the upper part of the head.[10] Using the dominant metaphor at work in the text: the soul *is* the interior castle—the body is its "outer wall."[11] Now, the castle is made up of seven compartments, each of which is made up of many rooms, or "mansions." The compartments are arranged in such a way that as one moves in sequence from the first to the sixth, one encircles and, at the same time, comes closer to the seventh, which is located at the center of the edifice. The castle thus has an inward-spiraling floor plan. It winds in upon itself like, for example, the shell of a snail. Further,

8. Teresa recognizes this seeming paradox in *Interior Castle*, 31 (First Mansions, chap. I).

9. Teresa, *Interior Castle*, 37 (First Mansions, chap. II).

10. Teresa, *Interior Castle*, 77–78 (Fourth Mansions, chap. I).

11. Teresa, *Interior Castle*, 29 (First Mansions, chap. I).

according to the imagery developed in the text, the castle normally
has two occupants. One is God: He dwells in the innermost
compartment—the (so-called) Seventh Mansions. The other, surprisingly, is what Teresa refers to simply as "the soul." Teresa says
that on some occasions this second occupant hovers in the outer
reaches of the interior castle—staying in the outer courtyards.
Sometimes, too, it enters into the rooms. She says that it "roams"
through the enclosure, or, like a bird, flies through the various
chambers. What emerges, then, is that Teresa uses the term "soul"
in two quite different senses—what I shall call "soul*" and
"soul+." Soul* is the name of a region or domain. Teresa sometimes speaks of it as "an interior world," "an abiding place," or "a
dwelling place."[12] Since this interior world is, in part, the dwelling
place of God, she also refers to it as "the Tabernacle of God" and as
"second Heaven."[13] On the other hand, soul+ is the name of an
entity, that is, a thing rather than a place or domain. Teresa sometimes refers to this as "the essential part of the soul."[14] This is what
Saint John called "the substance of the soul"—the same "substance," I suspect, that Descartes later identified as the self: that
which thinks (perceives, doubts) and animates the body.[15] According to standard Christian doctrine, this is the entity that departs the
body at death and remains elsewhere forever more. If we look
again at the floor plan of the interior castle, the snail image begins
to take on more significance. In a sense, the snail can be said to live
within itself: the soft body dwells within the shell though both are
parts of the animal as a whole. I think I would get the drift of the
comment if someone were to say that the snail is more deeply
within itself on some occasions than on others. In *Interior Castle*
(Fourth Mansions, chapter III), Teresa makes this very point, using
the tortoise as a model (87).

Given the distinction between soul* and soul+ I think we can
now make better sense of the picture Teresa gives of the Prayer of
Quiet. In the paragraph following the one quoted above from
chapter 31 of *The Way of Perfection*, Teresa says that God and the

12. Teresa, *Interior Castle*, 207 and 211 (Seventh Mansions, chap. I).
13. Teresa, *Interior Castle*, 224, 207 (Seventh Mansions, chaps. III and I).
14. E.g., Teresa, *Interior Castle*, 211 (Seventh Mansions, chap. I).
15. John, *Living Flame of Love*, 62 and 70 (stanza II).

soul are "in the palace." This, I am sure, is a reference back to the imagery of *Interior Castle*. Using the latter: God is within soul*— he is in the seventh compartment at the very center of the interior domain. Further, soul$^+$ is also within soul*. It is within the abiding-place that constitutes its normal place of residence. In the Prayer of Quiet, soul$^+$ has penetrated its domain through to one of the intermediate compartments. Thus, at this juncture, it is relatively *close* to God but is not so close as to preclude its coming closer. Soul$^+$ anticipates the time when it will penetrate even more deeply into soul*. It yearns to reach the Seventh Mansions—there to enjoy union with God.

2. The Prayer of Full Union

In Fifth Mansions, chapter 1, of *Interior Castle*, Teresa writes as follows concerning the state of Full Union:

> Here is this soul which God has made, as it were, completely foolish in order the better to impress upon it true wisdom. For as long as such a soul is in this state, it can neither see nor hear nor understand: the period is always short and seems to the soul even shorter than it really is. God implants Himself in the interior of that soul in such a way that, when it returns to itself, it cannot possibly doubt that God has been in it and it has been in God; so firmly does this truth remain within it that, although for years God may never grant it that favor again, it can neither forget it nor doubt that it has received it (and this quite apart from the effects which remain within it, and of which I will speak later). This certainty of the soul is very material. (101)

The soul herein mentioned must be soul$^+$—that which normally (but not in this state) sees, hears, and understands. In fact, several paragraphs earlier Teresa explicitly identifies it as "the essence of the soul" (99). As for God, again Teresa specifies clearly that it is God in "his Divinity" rather than God in bodily form—rather than "our Lord Jesus Christ" (102). So now let us ask, Where are they? Where does this meeting between God in his Divinity and the essence of the soul take place? Three paragraphs after the passage just quoted, Teresa says that the meeting takes place in "the wine

cellar"—the one mentioned in the Song of Songs, the place where
the king put his bride prior to their embrace. The wine cellar is
then identified as the "center of the soul," where God first "puts
us" and then "must enter there Himself" (102–3). Thus, the elements of the picture are the same as they were in the Prayer of
Quiet. God (in noncorporeal form) and soul$^+$ are both within
soul*. As for the rest of the picture, I'll come in on it a bit more
slowly. It constitutes the point of *contrast* between the Prayer of
Quiet and the Prayer of Full Union.

Consider, first of all, the following two passages. The first is
from book VII, chapter III, of Saint Francis de Sales's *Treatise on the
Love of God* and the second is from chapter 12 of Venerable
Blosius's *Book of Spiritual Instruction*.

> But when the union of the soul with God is most especially strict
> and close, it is called by theologians inhesion or adhesion, because
> by it the soul is caught up, fastened, glued and affixed to the divine
> majesty, so that she cannot easily loose or draw herself back again.
> (291)

> In very truth the soul, immersed in God and absorbed into Him,
> swims, as it were, to and fro in the Godhead, and abounds with
> unspeakable joy which even overflows plenteously into the body.
> Now does the soul, itself, even in this exile, enjoy a foretaste of
> eternal life. (96)

In the first of these descriptions, the picture is one of two objects
whose surfaces are in contact. They are "fastened," "glued," and
"affixed" together in such a way that they cannot easily come
apart. In the second account, however, the suggestion is that the
connection between God and the soul is more intimate than this.
Here, it is not just that contact has been made. God has come to
contain the soul: the soul is immersed in and absorbed by God—
that is, submerged in or enwrapped by him. Saint John of the
Cross once said that in union, God has the soul in his mouth.[16]
That is the picture here being given via the image of the soul
swimming to and fro in the Godhead.

16. John, *Living Flame of Love*, 122 (stanza III). See also p. 123 for the fish image.

In stanza 1 of *Living Flame of Love*, John of the Cross tells us that in the state of Full Union, the soul is "wounded," as he says, "in its deepest center" (38). This is described in numbered paragraph 13 as "substantial union" of the soul with God. Focusing for a moment on the notion of "the deepest center," John makes clear in numbered paragraph 11 that this is a location concept. The deepest center of something (x) is the center of what he calls the "sphere," which constitutes x's natural place or habitat—that place to which x moves if unimpaired. Thus, to use his example, when a stone is in the earth, it is in its center. It is in its "deepest center" when it is in the center of the earth. It is clear, then, that when John says that the soul is wounded in its deepest center, he is indicating the place where the soul is located when the "wound" involved in substantial union is inflicted. Now, where is the place John supposes to be the "deepest center" of the soul? John's direct answer is "God" (39). But as the discussion continues, he brings the imagery more in line with that used in Teresa's *Interior Castle*. He finally identifies the deepest center of the soul as the deepest of the "many mansions" that are "in his (the soul's) Father's house" (40). Teresa (I am sure) would equate this with the most interior of the Seventh Mansions. This is the most inward part of what we are calling "soul*."

What then is wounded? John says that it is "the substance of the soul"—in our language, soul⁺. And what about the wound itself? It is, in fact, a *burn*—God is a *cauter*. God "dost pierce the substance of my soul and cauterize it with [his] heat" (57). Elaborating further on the encounter in the first four stanzas of *Living Flame of Love*, John says that when God assails the substance of the soul, his assaults are encounters "wherewith He penetrates the soul continually, deifying its substance and making it Divine. Herein He absorbs the soul, above all being, in the Being of God, for He has encountered it and pierced it to the quick in the Holy Spirit, Whose communications are impetuous when they are full of fervor, as is this communication" (56).[17] The substance of the soul is *absorbed* in God. This is the way it was pictured when Blosius characterized the soul as swimming to and fro in God. But more than this, the substance of the soul is also *penetrated* by God. This is a new

17. See also pp. 62–63, 67, and 146–47.

element in the picture. Prior to this point, God was within soul*
and has engulfed soul⁺. But now, God has also pierced and penetrated soul⁺. This is to say that God is not only within the soul's *domain* but is within the entity itself. To use the metaphor of the snail:
God is not only within the shell, he has invaded the soft body as
well.

I think we may now be in position to speculate about how the
passage quoted at the beginning of this section from Fifth Mansions, chapter 1, of *Interior Castle* should be understood. As we
have already noted, Teresa locates the encounter between God and
soul⁺ in the "wine cellar," that is, in soul*. But then she says that
in the encounter, the soul (meaning soul⁺) "dwelt in" God
(Blosius's fish image) and that God was also "within it." What we
have here is what might be called a "double-inclusion" relationship
between the two principals involved in the encounter. God and
soul⁺ each contains and is contained by the other. And now, of
course, we can readily distinguish between the picture Teresa provides of the Prayer of Quiet and the one she sketches of the Prayer
of Full Union. In each case, the encounter takes place in the Castle
(soul*), but in the Prayer of Quiet, God and the essence of the soul
(soul⁺) are only *close,* whereas in Full Union the gap between them
has been closed. Further, on Teresa's account, Full Union is not
just a case in which God and soul⁺ are stuck together (Francis), nor
is it only a case of soul⁺ immersed in God (Blosius). As Teresa
notes twice in her writings, in Full Union the soul is less like a fish
than like a *sponge* in water. The soul is not just submerged, it is also
sopped with God.[18] This is to say that soul⁺ has been absorbed
into God and that God has also been absorbed into soul⁺. Commenting on the Prayer of Full Union in his Opuscule 65, Saint
Thomas Aquinas frames the same idea in the following words:
"The soul, in the preceding degrees, loves and is loved in return;
she seeks and she is sought; she calls and is called. But in this, in an
admirable and ineffable way, she lifts and is lifted up; *she holds and
is herself held*; she clasps and she is *closely embraced*, and by the bond
of love she unites herself with God, one with one, alone with

18. See Teresa's Relation III, para. 9, and Relation IX, para. 10, in Teresa,
Relations, 376 and 412.

Him."[19] Full Union is double inclusion. Deep in the recesses of the interior castle, God and the soul—one on one—hold each other in mutual embrace.

3. Rapture

I turn now to the state of Rapture—alternately referred to by Teresa as "elevation," "flight of spirit," "transport," and "ecstasy."[20] Teresa devotes the whole of chapter xx of her *Life* to this topic. What follows is based mostly on the account given in this source.

In the second paragraph of the above-mentioned text, Teresa begins her account of Rapture with a vivid description of the soul in flight. Referring to a "blessing" described in the preceding chapter, which I shall not here relate, she writes as follows:

> But as we are giving Him thanks for this great blessing and doing our utmost to draw near to Him in a practical way, the Lord gathers up the soul just (we might say) as a cloud gathers up the vapors from the earth, and raises it up till it is right out of itself (I have heard that it is in this way that the clouds or the sun gather up the vapors) and the cloud rises to Heaven and takes the soul with it, and begins to reveal to it things concerning the Kingdom that He has prepared for it. I do not know if the comparison is an exact one, but that is the way it actually happens.
>
> In these raptures the soul seems no longer to animate the body, and thus the natural heat of the body is felt to be very sensibly diminished: it gradually becomes colder, though conscious of the greatest sweetness and delight. No means of resistance is possible, whereas in union, where we are on our own home ground, such a means exists: resistance may be painful and violent but it can almost always be effected. But with rapture, as a rule, there is no such possibility: often it comes like a strong, swift impulse, before your thought can forewarn you of it or you can do anything to help yourself; you see and feel this cloud, or this powerful eagle, rising and bearing you up with it on its wings. (190)

19. Quoted in Poulain, *Graces of Interior Prayer*, 109 (pt. II, chap. IV, extracts).
20. See the opening two sentences of chap. XX of Teresa's *Life*, 189.

In Rapture, the soul feels itself to be in upward motion. Teresa emphasizes this point in all of her various writings on this topic. For example, a little later in chapter xx she says, "The soul, then, seems to be, not in itself at all, but on the house-top, or the roof, of its own house, and raised above all created things; I think it is far above even its own very high part" (194). And picturing soul* as a "basin" and soul+ as a "little ship," in *Interior Castle*, Sixth Mansions, chapter v, she says again, "But now this great God, Who controls the sources of the waters and forbids the sea to move beyond its bounds, has loosed the sources whence water has been coming into this basin; and with tremendous force there rises up so powerful a wave that this little ship—our soul—is lifted up on high" (158). Further, interspersed in this discussion are a number of passages in which Teresa makes clear that the soul is not the only thing that rises. Almost always, she says, the body or some part of the body is also raised into the air. In her *Life* Teresa writes, "My soul has been borne away, and indeed, as a rule my head also, without being able to prevent it: sometimes my whole body has been affected, to the point of being raised up off the ground" (191). Teresa says that it is as if there were a great force beneath her feet lifting her into the air (191). This, she tells us, gave her great fear. "Indeed, I confess that in me it produced great fear—at first a terrible fear. One sees one's body being lifted up from the ground; and although the spirit draws it after itself, and if no resistance is offered does so very gently, one does not lose consciousness—at least, I myself have had sufficient to enable me to realize that I was being lifted up" (192). Teresa adds that even after the Rapture state is over, the body often feels buoyant, "as if all weight had left it" (197).

When the soul takes flight, where is it going? Teresa gives the first hint in the seventh paragraph of chapter xx of her *Life*, where she says that God is "literally drawing the soul to Himself" (192). This point is expanded (though only briefly) a few pages later. Here, Teresa tells us that when Rapture reaches its "highest point" the soul is "united closely with God." She continues, "The soul is often engulfed—or, to put it better, the Lord engulfs it in Himself—and, when He has kept it in this state for a short time, He retains the will alone" (197). The soul takes flight and is then drawn toward and, ultimately, engulfed by God. That, in outline, is Teresa's portrait of Rapture. I want now to expand a bit on each of the two items that appear to constitute the essence of the Rapture experience.[21]

1. Beginning with a sense of upward motion, Teresa says that the soul is "borne away" to the "house-tops." It is, she tells us, "out of itself," or "not in itself." As a first probe for more detail concerning the state of Rapture, let's pause here for a moment and inquire about these last couple of phrases. What is it for the soul be to "out of itself" in the sense herein intended?

There are many places in Teresa's writings where this phrase is used to communicate the idea that one is no longer attending to the body nor to the physical environment. The sense faculties are dysfunctional. In the account given in *Interior Castle*, Sixth Mansions, chapters IV and V, Teresa makes clear that this is at least part of the meaning intended in the present case. Here she says that in Rapture, the soul is "out of its senses"—not in possession of its ordinary sense faculties (149). This point is made more carefully in the account contained in chapter XX of her *Life*. Here Teresa claims that if Rapture is not resisted, the sense faculties generally (though not always) remain in operation, though sense perceptions are dim and distorted. She adds, however, that at the height of Rapture the sense faculties are always completely suspended for the brief moment in which the soul is "closely united with God" (197).[22]

There is clearly, however, a second theme conveyed in Teresa's claim that in Rapture the soul is "out of itself" or, as she sometimes

21. In chap. XX of her *Life*, Teresa spends eight full paragraphs describing a kind of experience that she distinguishes from Rapture but that came as a kind of aftermath to Rapture more and more frequently during the time she was writing her autobiography (192–97). Like Rapture, these were apparently out-of-body experiences. Unlike Rapture, however, these experiences involved great suffering, estrangement, and loneliness. As regards these aftermath states, Teresa says that she valued them even more than she did Rapture experiences because through them she came to learn "the way of the cross" (196). I have not included these aftermath states in the above account for two reasons. First, Teresa herself distinguishes them from Rapture (197). Second, though obviously of great significance to Teresa, such states are not generally reported in the Christian mystical literature on Rapture and thus cannot be regarded as standard accompaniments of the Rapture state.

22. See also pp. 177–78 (chap. XVIII).

says, "above itself." In *Interior Castle*, both of these phrases are
used in connection with what Teresa says about the relationship
between the soul and the body during the Rapture experience.
Here she says that in Rapture, "the soul really seems to have left
the body" (160). This theme is conveyed elsewhere in Teresa's
various discussions of Rapture—for example, in chapter xxxviii of
her *Life*, where she reports a Rapture state in which her spirit
"became so completely transported that it seemed to have departed
almost wholly from the body: or, at least, there was no way of
telling that it was in the body" (368). She makes the same point at
least three times in Relation viii, where, for example, she says,
"This little bird of the spirit seems to have escaped out of this
wretchedness of the flesh, out of the prison of this body, and now,
disentangled therefrom, is able to be more intent on that which the
Lord is giving it."[23] Although in Rapture both the soul and the
body are felt to rise in the air, the idea seems to be that they rise
separately. The soul is disconnected from the body. This point was
already implicit in the passage cited above in which Teresa said that
when the soul rises, it draws the body *after* it. Concerning the
physical body, itself, in another passage already cited, Teresa says
that during the interval in which the mystic is enwrapped "the soul
seems no longer to animate the body, and thus the natural heat of
the body is felt to be sensibly diminished." Later she says that the
pulse slows and sometimes seems to stop altogether. The bones
"are all disjointed, and my hands are so stiff that sometimes I
cannot clasp them together."[24] From the moment Rapture begins
until the time it ends, which may be several hours, the body does
not change position. During Rapture, in other words, the body
is—in Teresa's words—"as if dead."[25]

Is Teresa saying that in Rapture the soul really does leave the
body? The straightforward answer to this question is no. In the
passages quoted above and elsewhere as well, Teresa says only that
in Rapture it "seems" or "feels" to the experiencing mystic that the
soul is out of the body.[26] Using more contemporary language, we

23. Teresa, *Relations*, 405.
24. Teresa, *Life*, 195.
25. Teresa, *Life*, 197.
26. See, for example, *Interior Castle*, 160 (Sixth Mansions, chap. v).

can say that *phenomenologically*, Rapture is an out-of-body experience. This entails nothing as regards the metaphysical question of whether the soul does or does not, in fact, depart the body. Still, Teresa has some things to say about the metaphysics of the matter. I'll pause here for a moment to make sure we are clear about this part of her thinking.

According to common Christian understanding death is the state that results when the soul leaves the body. But, of course, in Rapture the body is not, in fact, dead—it is only (in Teresa's words) "*as if* dead" (my italics). One would thus expect that Christian mystics generally (Teresa included) would hold that the sense of flight from the body during Rapture is a kind of illusion. To claim that the soul really does leave the body would appear to conflict with the obvious fact that the mystic does not suffer physical death in the process. Speaking of his own Rapture experience in Corinthians II (1:12), however, Saint Paul said: "Whether [the soul] is in the body or out of the body I know not. God knows." And commenting on this passage from Corinthians in book 12, chapters 1–6, of *A Literal Commentary on Genesis*, Augustine allowed that it could be either way but expressed the guarded opinion that at least some part of the soul does leave the body during Rapture. Working with Plato's notion of the tri-part soul, Augustine saw no reason why the highest (intellectual) part of the soul could not depart the body leaving the other (lower) parts behind to animate the body.[27] Interesting to note in this connection is that in *Summa Theologica*, II–II, Q. 175, a. 5 and 6, Thomas displayed reluctance to accept Augustine's metaphysical suggestion on this point.[28] Though he doesn't say so, I suspect that his reluctance stemmed from the fact that Thomas held an Aristotelian view concerning the nature of the soul. As the "substantial form" of the body, the soul does not have parts. There was thus no easy way of understanding how the soul might depart the body in Rapture while still allowing for the fact that the body does not die. Still, Thomas does not deny that this could happen. Like Augustine's, his discussion ends in agnostic posture. What we have here, then, is a rather

27. See Augustine's *A Literal Commentary on Genesis*, bk. 12, chap. 5, para. 14.
28. See esp. a. 6 reply to obj. 1.

substantial theological tradition of what might be called "flexible agnosticism" with respect to the question of whether the soul leaves the body in Rapture. Though metaphysical preferences differ, out of deference to Saint Paul the received opinion concerning the metaphysics of Rapture seems to be, in effect, "God knows."

In Relation VIII Teresa entertains what looks to be a variation on Augustine's theory of flight. Here she says that if we think of the soul as a "fire burning rapidly," we can suppose that in Rapture it "sends up a flame" while, at the same time, remaining within the body as its animating principle. She continues, "The flame ascends on high, but the fire thereof is the same as that below, nor does the flame cease to be fire because it ascends: so here, in the soul, something so subtle and so swift seems to issue from it, that it ascends to the higher part and goes thither whither our Lord wills."[29] After relating her variation on the flame theory in Sixth Mansions, chapter V, of *Interior Castle*, however, Teresa admits that she does not really know whether this makes any sense. With respect to her own speculations on the matter, she says, "Really, I hardly know what I am saying" (161). She then expresses her final position on the metaphysical question. "If the soul is in the body or not while all this is happening, I cannot say: I would not myself swear that the soul is in the body, nor that the body is bereft of soul." Though the phenomenological facts are clear, the metaphysical question is open. Given the theological tradition to which she was subject, that is probably just what we should have expected Teresa to say.

Let us return now to Teresa's claim that in Rapture the soul is "out of itself" or "above itself," that is, "not in itself." Given Teresa's metaphysical agnosticism, we cannot interpret this as meaning that the soul is in fact out of the body. We are thus left with just two messages. In part, Teresa is saying that the sense faculties cease to operate normally; and in part she is saying that phenomenologically—though not, for all we know, metaphysically—Rapture is an out-of-body experience. When used to convey this second theme, the term "itself" in "out of *itself*" should be read as referring to what I have been calling soul*, that is, the domain

29. Teresa, *Relations*, 405.

or place in the body where soul$^+$ is normally located. Read "The soul is felt to be out of itself" as "the soul is felt to be out of the soul," which, in turn, means, "the conscious self is felt to be out of its normal domain within the body." This use of the pronoun "itself" reflects the double meaning of "soul," also evident in Teresa's descriptions of the Prayer of Quiet and the Prayer of Full Union.

That the sense faculties fail and that the soul (or some part of the soul) departs the body are different claims. Similarly, and more important in the present context, that one is *aware of* the senses failing and that one *feels* the self departing the body are different claims as well. Still, there is one place in Teresa's discussion of this matter where she suggests that although these last-mentioned phenomena are different, they are nonetheless intimately connected. At the end of Sixth Mansions, chapter v, of *Interior Castle* she says, "For the soul really feels that it is leaving the body when it sees the senses leaving it and has no idea why they are going" (162). When one "sees" that the sense faculties are failing, one "feels" that the soul is leaving the body. Here it looks as if the first of these experiences is the cause or occasion for the second. Perhaps this is why the same phrases ("out of itself" and "above itself") are used in Teresa's discussion to cover both of these experiential elements of Rapture.

2. After the onset of Rapture, the soul is transported to what Teresa calls "another world" (160), and at the "highest point" it is "united with"—that is, "engulfed by"—God. In chapter xxxviii of her *Life* Teresa adds that the highest point is one in which the soul finds itself "in the Bosom of the Father" (369), and in Relation viii she speaks of the soul in flight as throwing itself "into the arms of our Lord."[30] Of course, these last descriptions add little (if anything) to what we already had. And since Teresa nowhere elaborates further than this on the culmination point of the Rapture encounter, I want here to supplement her remarks on this topic with the following passage from volume 1, book 3, chapter 1, of Marina Escobar's *The Divine Darkness*.[31] In this passage Escobar

---

30. Teresa, *Relations*, 404.
31. Marina Escobar was a friend and colleague of Saint Teresa's in the convent at Avila.

provides considerable detail concerning what she experienced at
the height of one of her Rapture experiences.

The holy angels surrounded me, and preceded by the Lord of all
Majesty, they bore me to a very great height, traversing, so to
speak, the whole vault of heaven. They placed me on the shore of a
kind of immense ocean, which was the vastness of God Himself,
His goodness, His Wisdom, and His Essence. In the presence of
Jesus Christ they cast me suddenly into this vast sea of the divine
obscurity and of the essence of the unknown and incomprehensible
God. I was submerged in it and lost. No language can describe the
secret marvels that are there wrought between God and the soul, or
the grandeur of God which is there manifested. No created intelli-
gence can speak of it adequately. . . .

For the space of a time, which seemed to me shorter than it really
was, I remained plunged in this ocean. Afterwards the angels carried
me back to the shore. By this I mean that they drew me forth from
this immensity, and not that there was really a sea, a shore, or any
material image.

I rested a short time on this shore so as to again regain my
strength. Then the angels cast me in again, with more force than the
first time, so that I was submerged and lost in the divine essence
more profoundly than before. Again they brought me back to the
shore. I was in even greater danger, as it seemed to me, of losing my
life, if God had not upheld me. When I had rested for a few minutes
they cast me for the third time. By the word cast I would express a
certain admirable way employed by God and the angels to bring the
soul into the immensity of the divine perfections. There is no question here of anything corporeal.

How long I remained in this sea I could not judge. But this last
submersion was slighter than the two previous ones and so I experienced less fatigue. God then gave me His blessing and the angels
bore me back to my cell. When I had come to myself again, I felt
great weakness. I was seized with admiration, and while conform-
ing to the will of God, I raised my eyes toward the angels with great
grief at finding myself thus in this exile.[32]

32. Quoted in Poulain, *Graces of Interior Prayer*, 275 (pt. III, chap. XVIII, extracts).

Like Teresa, Escobar describes herself as being raised into the air. She is then "plunged" into the ocean that is God—she is submerged, enveloped and absorbed; or, as Teresa would have it, "engulfed by"—that is, wrapped "in the bosom" or "in the arms of"—the Lord. This last sounds very much like the description given by Blosius when discussing the Prayer of Full Union. Indeed, the image of being submerged in the Divine Ocean is one that is persistently used by Christian mystics when describing both the Prayer of Full Union and the culmination stage of Rapture. And, of course, the idea of the double-inclusion relationship (Teresa's sponge metaphor) is hardly a pictorial step away. Speaking of the culmination stage of Rapture in chapter 12 of the *Institutions*, the fourteenth-century German mystic John Tauler says: "The spirit is *submerged* and absorbed in the depths of the divine ocean, so that we can exclaim: God is in me, God is outside me, God is everywhere around me. God is everything to me, I see naught but God."[33]

I shall have considerably more to say about Rapture in the next two chapters. Before leaving this initial treatment of the topic, however, I should like to add one observation about this state as it relates to the controlling imagery of Teresa's *Interior Castle*. Recall that in that picture, the castle (soul*) has two residents, namely, (1) soul$^+$, who at any given time may be in one of the outer courtyards, or somewhere in the edifice itself; and (2) God, who resides permanently in the most interior of the Seventh Mansions. This diagram works nicely when one maps the elements of the Prayer of Quiet and Full Union. Referring to Full Union in chapter xx of her *Life*, Teresa says that it "happens interiorly" (189), that is, "on our home ground" (190). The imagery highlights this feature of Full Union and allows Teresa to establish its development out of the Prayer of Quiet. But as Teresa herself emphasizes in this very same passage, the fact that Full Union "happens interiorly" is one of the major points of *contrast* between it and the state of Rapture. In Rapture, soul$^+$ departs soul* (that is, it is "out of itself") and is transported to what Teresa calls "another world." It is in this other

33. Quoted in Poulain, *Graces of Interior Prayer*, 101 (pt. ii, chap. vi, extracts).

world—and not within the recesses of soul*—that God and soul⁺ meet in mutual embrace. The upshot is that the Rapture state strains the format imagery of *Interior Castle*. The description of Rapture requires that God be assigned a new address and that soul⁺ be portrayed not as a miner burrowing more deeply into "home ground" (as in the progression from the Prayer of Quiet to Full Union) but as an astronaut thrust above the vault of seventh heaven by the engines of the Supreme Being. Teresa's reaction to this pictorial hiatus is one of seeming indifference. In that part of *Interior Castle* where she discusses the state referred to in chapter xx of her *Life* as "Rapture" (chapter v of Sixth Mansions), she unceremoniously drops the imagery used pervasively in the rest of the text.[34] This is as it should be. Pictures should be retained only as long as they work. And in her discussion of Rapture, this imagery would surely have been in her way.

4. A Summary Comment

Given the pictures sketched in this chapter, we can distinguish the three states of union from one another using two variables: (1) the relative position of God and the soul of the mystic during the mystical encounter; and (2) the place or domain in which the encounter takes place. Using the first of these variables as a basis for comparison, we find that the Prayer of Quiet is the odd case. Here, God and the soul are only "close," whereas in Full Union and in the culmination stage of Rapture, God and the soul are in direct contact—usually in mutual embrace. Working with the second variable, on the other hand, we can see that Rapture is unique. In the Prayer of Quiet and in Full Union, the encounter between God and the soul takes place (as Teresa says) "on home ground," that is, in the normal domain of the soul. In Rapture, on the other hand, the encounter is elsewhere—in "another world." A pattern

34. In Sixth Mansions, chap. iv, of *Interior Castle*, Teresa discusses a mystical state she refers to as "one kind of rapture" (149), which has some things in common with the state we have been discussing, except that it is portrayed as an interior state and is framed using the pictorial categories of *Interior Castle* (152). This is obviously not the state referred to as "Rapture" in chap. xx of *Life*. I suspect that it is best understood as an especially intense case of what Teresa classified as Full Union in *Life*.

is clearly discernible. Think of Full Union as standing between the Prayer of Quiet and the state of Rapture. It has a feature in common with each, and the feature it shares with one constitutes its point of contrast with the other. Thus, Full Union is similar to the Prayer of Quiet, and both are dissimilar from Rapture as regards the place where the encounter occurs. Full Union is similar to Rapture and both are dissimilar from the Prayer of Quiet as regards the intimacy of the God-soul encounter. Note that although we have three quite distinct pictures, they are not scattered snapshots. Put together in the same frame, they could easily be taken for a kind of family portrait.

[2]

Variations on Full
Union and Rapture

The pictures presented in the preceding chapter will serve in the sequel as standard characterizations of the three states of mystic union. Before proceeding to the next major topic, however, I want to consider some classical mystical writings in which are sketched alternatives to the images already established. In particular, Full Union and Rapture—the two "highest" states of Union—sometimes come in different figures. It is to these variations that I want to call attention in the present chapter.

1. God the Pilgrim

In treatise II, chapter I, of her *Divine Consolations,* Angela of Foligno speaks at some length about times when she has been aware that God has been within her soul. Regarding the ways in which she has known that God was there, she mentions that God instills "a fire and a love and a sweetness" that are not customarily there, and she also says that the soul can "feel God within it." Regarding the latter, Angela says that it is "when the soul doth feel the presence of God more deeply than is customary, then doth it certify unto itself that He is within it." What she feels, she tell us, is "an embrace which He doth give unto the soul." In this way "doth the soul feel that God is mingled with it and hath made companionship with it." The soul then cannot doubt that God is within it—in her words, that the soul does "lodge the Pilgrim, who is God" (24–29). In addition to these ways in which the soul is made aware of the fact that God is within it, however, Angela says that on some occasions she "beholds Him" coming into the soul with something she refers to as "the eyes of the soul." "Further, when God cometh unto the soul, it is sometimes given unto it to behold Him, and it beholdeth Him devoid of any bodily shape or form, and more clearly than doth one man behold another. For the eyes of the soul do behold a spiritual and not a bodily presence, of the which I am not able to speak because words and imagination do fail me" (26). In the next chapter I shall have something to say about the sorts of perceptions that I think Angela is here finding difficult to describe—those attained by "the eyes of the soul."[1] For the moment, however, I want to switch to treatise III of the *Divine Consolations;* here Angela provides some interesting detail of an experience in which she "beheld" God in the way just described.

> Methought one time in Lent that I was exceedingly parched and lacking in devotion, wherefore I prayed God that He would give me something of Himself, because all goodness was dried up within me. Then were the eyes of my soul opened, and I beheld love advancing gently toward me, and I beheld the beginning but not the end. Unto me there seemed only a continuation and eternity there-of, so that I can describe neither likeness nor colour, but imme-diately that this love reached me, I did behold all these things more clearly with the eyes of the soul than I could with the eyes of the body.
>
> This love came toward me after the manner of a sickle. Not that there was any actual and measurable likeness, but when first it appeared unto me it did not give itself unto me in such abundance as I expected, but part of it was withdrawn. Therefore do I say, after

1. In the first section of Chapter 1, I made note of the fact that, for Teresa, to see something with "spiritual eyes" or "with the eyes of the soul" is to see it (as we say) in the imagination. It thus involves an imaginative image, the apprehension of form and/or color. It is reasonably clear from what Angela says in this passage that what she means by seeing "with the eyes of the soul" is not this kind of seeing. Angela here says that what she sees in this mode is a spiritual object having no "bodily shape or form." In the next chapter I shall discuss the kind of mystical seeing that I think is involved in Angela's case.

the manner of a sickle. Then was I filled with love and inestimable
satiety; but although it did well satisfy me, it did generate within me
so great a hunger that all my members were loosened and my soul
fainted with longing to attain unto the remainder. (178)

Angela makes clear in the title attached to this section of her text
that the "love" referred to in this passage is God. It is (as she says)
"God inasmuch as He is love" (178). Thus Angela seems here to be
saying that in this experience she beheld God "advancing gently"
toward her; and the advance, she says, was "after the manner of a
sickle." The suggestion is that the advance had a kind of pulsating
character—God advanced and withdrew in alternating swings as a
sickle advances and withdraws through a field of grass. And what
was the outcome? In the passage before us, the outcome is not
made clear—in fact there is some question as to whether there was
an outcome. In the second sentence Angela says that she perceived
the beginning but not the end of the advance. And in the third
sentence she at least suggests that she perceived only the eternal
"continuation" of the advance. Still, she also affirms that God
finally reached her; and in the closing sentence she says that she
was "filled with" God. I think we can suppose that the outcome
was as it had been described earlier. God and the soul are "mingled"; the soul is "embraced by" and (in this passage) "filled with"
God.

In the opening paragraph of chapter xx of her *Life,* Saint Teresa
is concerned to identify a number of differences between the states
of Full Union and Rapture. She says this:

I should like, with the help of God, to be able to describe the
difference between union and rapture, or elevation, or what they
call flight of spirit, or transport—it is all one. I mean these different
names all refer to the same thing, which is also called ecstasy. It is
much more beneficial than union: the effects it produces are far
more beneficial and it has a great many more operations, for union
gives the impression of being just the same at the beginning, in the
middle and at the end, and it all happens interiorly. (189)

One of the contrasts that Teresa seems to be making here relates to
the fact that Rapture has what might be called a "developmental"

character. As we have seen, on Teresa's account, Rapture begins with an awareness of being swooped out of the body and proceeds to an interval where the soul finds itself in flight far above "all created things." At its "highest point," it culminates in a sense of being submerged in God. It thus has a beginning, a middle, and an end in the sense that it has distinguishable intervals, or stages. But this appears to be what Teresa is *denying* about the state of Full Union. While Full Union involves an awareness of being en-wrapped and penetrated by God (as does the culmination stage of Rapture), that is really all Teresa has to say about the elements of this experience. In particular, on her account, Full Union is not portrayed as unfolding in discernible stages. In fact, in this passage Teresa explicitly tells us that Full Union does *not* have this sort of complex structure.

Returning, then, to the experience that Angela reports in which she beheld God advancing toward her "in the manner of a sickle," I would judge this to be a case of Full Union. It looks as though God advanced into soul* and embraced soul+. But if this is the correct interpretation of the text, it would appear that in this case, at least, Full Union was not "just the same at the beginning, in the middle and at the end." Like an instance of Rapture, it included a discern-ible prelude to the final embrace. Further, the prelude in question is like the early stages of Rapture in that it involved the awareness of a "pilgrim" in motion. Of course, the identity of the pilgrim and the direction of the motion are different in the two cases. In Rap-ture, it is the soul of the mystic that is felt to depart its natural domain and move toward "another world." By contrast, in An-gela's experience, God is the pilgrim, and the motion perceived is an "advance" into, rather than a retreat out of, the domain of the soul. In sermon 74 of his *Sermons on the Canticle of Canticles,* Ber-nard of Clairvaux comments on this topic.

I confess, then, though I say it in my foolishness, that the Word has visited me, and very often. But although He has frequently entered into my soul, I have never at any time been sensible of the precise moment of His coming. I have felt that he was present; I remember that he has been with me; I have sometimes been able even to have a presentiment that He would come; but never to feel His coming or

His departure. From whence He came to enter my soul, or whither
He went on quitting it, by what means He has made entrance or
departure, I confess that I know not even to this day.[2]

Bernard is here speaking of what he calls in another place "the
loving descent of God into the soul." He contrasts this with what
he refers to as "transport of a pure soul into God"—that is, I would
suppose, Rapture.[3] Like Teresa, Bernard apparently never experienced the "descent" itself, that is, the *coming* of the "Word," which,
as he says, "visited" him. Still, I think it would be a mistake to
suppose that this is an invariable feature of Full Union. Angela
seems to have detected the descent. The entrance of the pilgrim,
"in the manner of a sickle" was something that she claims to have
directly "beheld."

2. Ecstasy

But how does this sacred outflowing of the soul into its well-
beloved take place? An extreme complacency of the lover in the
thing beloved begets a certain spiritual powerlessness, which makes
the soul feel herself no longer able to remain in herself. Wherefore,
as melted balm, that no longer has firmness or solidity, she lets
herself pass and flow into what she loves: she does not spring out of
herself as by a sudden leap, nor does she cling as by a joining and
union, but gently glides as a fluid thing, into the divinity whom she
loves. . . . [And] so the soul which, though loving, remained as yet
in herself, goes out by this sacred outflowing and holy liquefaction,
and quits herself, not only to be united with the well-beloved, but
to be entirely mingled with and steeped in him. [This] outflowing
of a soul into her God is a true ecstasy, by which the soul quite
transcends the limits of her natural form of existence [*maintien*]
being wholly mingled with, absorbed and engulfed in, her God.

This passage, from book vi, chapter 12, of Saint Francis de Sales's
Treatise on the Love of God (266–67), contains at least two themes

2. Quoted in Butler, *Western Mysticism,* 101.
3. Sermon 31, quoted in Butler, *Western Mysticism,* 103.

that accord well with what Teresa says in her various accounts of Rapture: (1) the soul "quits herself"; and (2) after quitting herself, the soul is united with its "well-beloved." In the first of these claims, I suspect, the term "herself" in "quits *herself*" refers to the soul's normal domain and that which "quits" this domain is the conscious self. In the language developed in the preceding chapter, this is to say (as in Teresa) that soul$^+$ leaves soul*. On the second point, Francis says that the union in question is one in which the soul is "absorbed and engulfed in her God," that is, one in which the soul is "mingled with and steeped in God." Again the imagery is the same as we found in Teresa—Teresa's sponge analogy comes easily to mind.

One of the themes emphasized in Francis's account contrasts openly, however, with Teresa's description of Rapture. According to the account given in her *Life,* the onset of Rapture is "violent" (193)—it comes upon one as a "strong, swift impulse" (190), which, if one tries to resist, feels as if one is "fighting with a powerful giant" and, in the process, is being "ground to powder" (191). One is swooped into the air as if borne on the back of a "powerful eagle." The import of Francis's description, however, is precisely the reverse. He maintains that in this state, the soul does not "spring out of herself as by a sudden leap." The soul's departure from its normal domain is described as an "outflowing." The liquefaction image governs his description of the final embrace as well. Here he says that the soul "gently glides, as a fluid thing, into the divinity whom she loves." There is a corollary: in all of Teresa's descriptions of Rapture, when soul$^+$ departs soul* it moves in an *upward* direction. This is a more or less standard description—recall Escobar's account in which the soul was borne by angels to the highest vault of heaven. But Francis does not say the motion is upward. He says the soul "quits herself"; but the only direction indicated is *out,* not up. Depending on how far the liquefaction image can be pressed, one might even suppose that the direction of motion might be down.

Regarding the presence or absence of the "violent" element in the experience we are now discussing, Thomas Aquinas suggests that it can be used as a way of distinguishing Rapture as a subspecies of a more general class of experiences, which he calls "ecstasy." He says, "Rapture adds nothing to ecstasy: for ecstasy means simply going out of oneself by being placed outside one's proper order; while rapture denotes a certain violence in addition."[4] Perhaps because she had no experiences of the sort recorded by Francis, this distinction was not made by Teresa. As noted above, she used "ecstasy" and "rapture" interchangeably—both applied to "violent" experiences in which the soul is powered out of its normal domain. Once the peaceful variation of the Rapture state is noted (as in Francis), however, Aquinas's way of talking would seem to me to be a useful classificatory tool. I'm surprised that it did not achieve more currency than it did in the classical, Christian mystical literature on the states of infused contemplation.

3. Union without Distinction

After speaking of the mystical encounter as one in which "enlightened men" are brought to "the summit of their spirits," in chapter xi of *The Book of Supreme Truth,* Jan van Ruysbroeck continues so:

> There, their bare understanding is drenched through by the Eternal Brightness, even as the air is drenched through by sunshine. And the bare, uplifted will is transformed and drenched through by abysmal love, even as iron is by fire. And the bare, uplifted memory feels itself enwrapped and established in an abysmal Absence of Image. And thereby the created image is united above reason in a threefold way with its Eternal Image, which is the origin of its being and its life; and this origin is preserved and possessed essentially and eternally, through a simple seeing in the imageless void; and so a man is lifted up above reason in a threefold manner into the Unity, and in a onefold manner into the Trinity. Yet the creature does not become God, for the union takes place in God and through grace and our homeward turning love; and therefore the creature in its inward contemplation feels a distinction and otherness between itself and God. . . . There (in this union) all is full and overflowing, for the spirit feels itself to be one truth and one richness and one unity with God. Yet even here there is an essential tending forward,

4. Aquinas, *Summa Theologica,* II–II, Q. 175, a. 2, reply to obj. 1.

and therein is an essential distinction between the being of the soul and the Being of God; and this is the highest and finest distinction which we are able to feel.[5]

Commenting on the metaphors of the air and the sunshine and the iron and the heat, in chapter VIII of the same text, Ruysbroeck tells us that "the iron is within the fire and the fire is within the iron; and so also the air is in the sunshine and the sunshine in the air" (236–37). The idea of being "drenched through" thus seems to carry the message of the double-inclusion relation (the double embrace) characteristic of Full Union and Rapture. Again, we are reminded of Teresa's image of the sponge in water. Further, there is at least some evidence (admittedly slender) that we may here be dealing with a case of Rapture rather than Full Union. Not only is the soul "enwrapped"; it is also "*lifted up* above reason in a threefold manner into the Unity, and in a onefold manner into the Trinity" (my italics). This suggestion will be reenforced in the passage next to be quoted. The point to which I want to draw special attention, however, is this: although Ruysbroeck says that the soul is "lifted up" into the Trinity and thus "feels itself to be one truth and one richness and one unity with God," it also "feels a distinction and otherness between itself and God." Although the soul is "enwrapped" and "united above reason" with the "origin of its being," there is still "an essential distinction between the being of the soul and the Being of God." This latter, he adds, is "the highest and finest distinction which we are able to feel."

Using this last theme as a context, I now want to look at the very next thing Ruysbroeck says in *The Book of Supreme Truth*. What follows is almost the whole of chapter XII, which is entitled "Of the Highest Union, without Difference or Distinction."

And after this there follows the union without distinction. For you must apprehend the Love of God not only as an outpouring with all good, and as a drawing back again into Unity; but it is also, above all distinction, an essential fruition of the bare Essence of the Godhead. . . . Behold, this beatitude is so onefold and so wayless that in it every essential gazing, tendency, and creaturely distinction ceases

5. In *John of Ruysbroeck*, 243–44.

and passes away. For by this fruition, all uplifted spirits are melted
and naughted in the Essence of God, Which is the superessence of all
essences. There they fall from themselves into a solitude and an
ignorance which is fathomless; there all light is turned to darkness;
there the three Persons give place to the Essential Unity, and abide
without distinction in fruition of the essential blessedness. This
blessedness is essential to God and superessential to all creatures; for
no created essence can become one with God's essence and pass
away from its own substance. For so the creature would become
God, which is impossible; for the Divine Essence can neither wax
nor wane nor can anything be added to It nor taken from It. Yet all
loving spirits are one fruition and one blessedness with God without
distinction; for that beatific state, which is the fruition of God and of
all His beloved, is so simple and onefold that therein neither Father,
nor Son, nor Holy Ghost is distinct according to Persons, neither is
any creature. But all enlightened spirits are here lifted up above
themselves into a wayless fruition, which is an abundance beyond
all the fullness that any creature has ever received or shall ever
receive. For there all uplifted spirits are, in their superessence, one
fruition and one beatitude with God without distinction; and there
this beatitude is so onefold and no distinction can enter into it.
(244–46)

Though there is a lot in this passage that is difficult to grasp (and
that I do not understand), one point emerges with abundant
clarity. After the union state described in chapter xi, in which the
soul "feels a distinction and otherness between itself and God,"
there occurs an experience in which this felt distinction is lost—
this is why Ruysbroeck describes it as "the union without distinction." In addition to this theme, however, two other supplementary theses are at least suggested. Since both are interesting and will
be of importance in our later discussion, I shall take time here to
expose what I take to be their import.

   1. Ruysbroeck says that in the union without distinction, "uplifted spirits are melted and naughted in the Essence of God." He
adds: "There they fall from themselves into a solitude and an ignorance which is fathomless." I now want to develop what I think is
the most likely interpretation of these lines. I'll begin by sketching
a little theory that may or may not be correct but that will furnish
some principles that may help to guide our thinking.

Consider an ordinary case of sense perception—for example, my visual perception of the chair. What I see (the chair) is experienced as being *other than me*. Of course, this is not to say that if I have a visual perception of a chair, there is something actually out there in the external world that is, in fact, other than me. I mean to be talking only about the chair *as experienced*—the (so-called) "intentional" or "phenomenological" object of the experience. It is perceived as other than me. This remains a fact about the experience even if it is later discovered (or was already known) that I was hallucinating or seeing the chair in a dream. Note, too, that although I perceive the chair as other than me, this does not imply that the perception is not caused or conditioned by some state of my mind or body. The point I am after does not concern the *causes* of the experience. Whatever may be the circumstances under which the experience occurs, the intentional object is experienced as what Gottlieb Fichte once called a "not-me."

If this is right, the implication would appear to be that part of what I experience in an ordinary case of seeing a chair is myself. To be aware of the chair as "not-me" is to be aware of the chair as standing apart from me. But this would appear to require that in being aware of the chair, I am also aware of that in relation to which the chair stands apart, namely, me. The conclusion is that when seeing a chair, I am really aware of two things: the object perceived (the chair) and the subject having the perception (me). Of course, this is not to say that when seeing a chair I also *see* myself. What I see is the chair. The claim is that in seeing the chair, I am also *aware of* myself. Then, too, none of this should be taken as suggesting that when one sees a chair, the awareness of self is at the forefront of attention. No doubt, in the case before us, that position belongs to the chair, not the self. The point is, however, that the awareness of self is at least part (though, perhaps, a low-profile part) of the total experience. It is, we might say, implicit—implicit in the sense that although it may not be singled out for special notice, it could be identified were one to take a moment for introspective reflection. I might add that on the account I am here trying to put together, what we ordinarily refer to as "self-consciousness" could be understood, at least in part, as an awareness of self that accompanies every instance of ordinary sense perception.

If I am aware of something as being other than me, I am aware of myself as well. Let's now reverse this principle and affirm the contrary as a kind of general psychological or phenomenological principle, as did Kant in that section of the *First Critique* entitled "A Refutation of Idealism": If I am aware of myself, I am also aware of something other than myself. Kant argued that I can pick myself out as a single, continuing thing only if I perceive myself in contrast with something else. Thus, the awareness of self can emerge only in the case where I am aware of something else, something experienced as not-me. If this is right, and if we agree with the speculations recorded in the preceding paragraph, the awareness of self and the awareness of something other than self always go together. Briefly stated, the theory is this: *phenomenologically,* subjects have objects and objects have subjects.

In chapter XI of *The Book of Supreme Truth,* Ruysbroeck relates an experience in which the mystic is totally occupied with a single object (God), which he distinguishes from himself. Using the repertoire of concepts just introduced: God is here experienced as a not-me that stands in contrast to the experiencing subject. The experience has what I shall call "subject-object structure." In chapter XII of the same text, however, Ruysbroeck goes on to describe the succeeding experiential interval as a state of (what he calls) "solitude." This is to say, I think, that in this interval of experience, the mystic does not pick out an object that is distinguished from self. Experientially, the mystic is not in the company of another. Framed in the language of the theory we are using, this is to say that in this moment of experience, nothing is discerned as a not-me, and thus the experience as a whole lacks what we are calling "subject-object structure." But under these conditions, our theory tells us, the experience as a whole is also bereft of a sense of self. And so it is in Ruysbroeck's account as well. Ruysbroeck says that in the union without distinction "uplifted spirits are melted and naughted." As I read this sentence, Ruysbroeck is saying that an awareness of self is not a part of this moment of experience. Let me expand a bit on this suggestion.

In numbered paragraph 27 of his *Treatise on Loving God,* Bernard of Clairvaux speaks of a mystical state he refers to as "the fourth degree of love." It would appear from what he says in this paragraph (and in the following numbered paragraph of the text) that the state he is here discussing is the experience Ruysbroeck labeled "the union without distinction." Part of Bernard's lengthy description of this experience is contained in the following lines:

> When will flesh and blood, this vessel of clay, this earthly dwelling grasp this? When will it experience this kind of love, so that the mind, drunk with divine love and forgetting itself, making itself like a broken vessel, throw itself wholly on God and clinging to God, become one with him in spirit . . . ? I should call him blessed and holy to whom it is given to experience even for a single instant something which is so rare indeed in this life. To lose yourself as though you did not exist and to have no sense of yourself, to be emptied out of yourself and almost annihilated, belongs to heavenly not to human love. (195)

The mind is so "drunk with divine love" that it becomes "one with [God] in spirit." This and other remarks like it in paragraphs 27 and 28 indicate that we are here talking about an experience in which the mystic makes no distinction between self and God. But what is most interesting here, I think, is what is said in this passage about the sense of self. Bernard says that in this state you "lose yourself as though you did not exist." This is to say that you "have no sense of yourself"—you are "emptied out of yourself and almost annihilated." This, I think, is what Ruysbroeck was expressing when he claimed that in the union without distinction the self is "melted and naughted." Phenomenologically, where there is no object, the self is "naughted," does not exist. And whether this is true as a general piece of phenomenological theory, I suspect that it is precisely what Bernard and Ruysbroeck are telling us about union without distinction.

2. When considering the account of Rapture in which Teresa said that the soul of the mystic is felt to depart its normal domain within the body, I paused to ask whether we should think of this as a case in which the soul actually leaves the body or one in which this only *seems* to be what is happening. Teresa pleaded ignorance on the matter: she held that this is a phenomenological fact, whether or not it is also to be regarded as a metaphysical reality. I now want to raise a similar question with respect to the union without

distinction. When it is said that in this state God and the soul of the mystic become one without distinction, how is this claim to be understood as regards its metaphysical implications? The answer we shall get to this question will be very different, indeed, from the one we got in response to our earlier inquiry about the relation between the soul and the body in Rapture.

In the middle of chapter XII of *The Book of Supreme Truth,* Ruysbroeck claims that although it is lifted up into a distinctionless unity, the soul of the mystic does not, in fact, become one with God. He says, "No created essence can become one with God and pass away from its own substance." But, let us ask, why not? How can Ruysbroeck be so sure that in the union without distinction the mystic does not, in fact, become identical with God? The reply given in Ruysbroeck's discussion is as follows: "For so the creature would become God, which is impossible; for the Divine Essence can neither wax nor wane nor can anything be added to It nor taken from It." The idea seems to be that if the soul of the mystic were to become one with God, we should have to allow that something had been added to God and this, Ruysbroeck assures us, is simply "impossible." But, let us persist, why should we think that this is impossible? Perhaps the right conclusion is that since there are occasions when God and the finite spirit become one, it *is* possible to add to the divine essence. That wouldn't do. And the reason why Ruysbroeck describes this as an impossibility reveals something that is both interesting and vitally important as regards the epistemological foundations of Christian mystical theology. I'll elaborate.

According to standard Christian dogmatic theology, God is immutable, that is, incapable of change. It would thus be contrary to the teachings of Church doctrine to suppose that something might be added to, or taken away from the essence of God. This would constitute a change in the divine nature. And herein lies the supposed impossibility that Ruysbroeck refers to. What is being assumed—and, indeed, assumed prior to any consideration of mystical phenomena—is that the doctrines accepted by the Church are true. With varying degrees of explicitness, this point can be found in virtually every important mystical theological treatise in the Christian tradition. It is also emphasized in a great many primary Christian mystical sources, for example, in chapter xxv of Teresa's *Life*.

> I consider it quite certain that the devil will not deceive, and that God will not permit him to deceive, a soul which has no trust whatsoever in itself, and is strengthened in faith and knows full well that for one single article of the Faith it would suffer a thousand deaths. With this love for the Faith, which God immediately infuses into it, and which produces a faith that is living and strong, the soul strives ever to act in conformity with the doctrine of the Church, asking for instruction from this person and from that, and acts as one already strongly established in these truths, so that all the revelations it could imagine, even were it to see the heavens opened, would not cause it to budge an inch from the Church's teachings. (238)

Of course, this is not to say that important religious truths cannot be communicated via the medium of mystical experiences, that is, via the "revelations" that Teresa refers to in this passage. The posture of the orthodox Christian contemplative, however, is that such communications must stand the test of consistency with Church doctrine and, otherwise, are to be regarded as deceptions. In this tradition, in other words, mystical theology is thought of as a kind of subsidiary source of religious knowledge. The articles of standard dogmatics are taken as axiomatic. Under certain very rigid conditions, supplementation from mystical sources may be accepted, but conflicting truth is, to use Ruysbroeck's term "impossible."[6] As further illustration of the sort of reasoning that rests on this same epistemological assumption, consider the following passage from sermon 71 of Bernard's *Sermons on the Canticle of Canticles*. Think of it as juxtaposed with the one just cited from paragraph 27 of the *Treatise on Loving God*.

> The union between God and man is not unity, at least if compared with the unique and sovereign unity of Father and Son. For how can there be unity where there is plurality of natures and difference of substances? The union of God and man is brought about not by

6. I have elaborated this idea in "On Mystic Visions as Sources of Knowledge," in Katz, *Mysticism and Philosophical Analysis*, 214–34.

confusion of natures, but by agreement of wills. Man and God, because they are not one substance or nature, cannot be called "one thing" ("unum" like Father and Son); but they are with strict truth called "one spirit" if they adhere to one another with the glue of love. But this unity is effected not by coherence of essence but by concurrence of wills. God and man, because they exist and are separate with their own wills and substances, abide in one another not blended in substance, but consentaneous in will.[7]

Again, note the argument given in support of the claim that God and the soul do not become one thing. Bernard asks, "How can there be unity where there is plurality of natures and difference of substances?" The answer, of course, is that under *these* conditions, there could not be unity. But let us ask: How can Bernard be so sure that God and the soul of the mystic have different natures and are not the same substance? No answer is given in the text, but I think this is because, from Bernard's point of view, the answer is so obvious as not to need mention. That God and the soul of man have different natures is clearly stated in orthodox doctrine. God is an infinite and perfectly good Being; the soul of man is a finite and imperfect being. They are thus of different natures. That they are also different substances follows directly.

What, then, shall we conclude as regards the metaphysical status of the union without distinction? The answer is clear—it follows immediately from the methodological principle stated in the preceding paragraph. Start with the idea that in union without distinction, the soul becomes "drunk" with love and thus loses track of the distinction between itself and God. This is what Bernard told us in the passage quoted earlier from paragraph 27 of his *Treatise on Loving God*. It is also what Ruysbroeck says in passages scattered throughout his writings—for example, in chapter III of *The Sparkling Stone*, where he claims that it is when the soul is "burnt up in love" that it "feels nothing but unity" with God.[8] Still, although the inebriated soul can make no distinction between itself and God, distinction remains. What we need here is a distinction between appearance and reality. Identity is what *appears* to be the case;

7. Quoted in Butler, *Western Mysticism*, 114.
8. In *John of Ruysbroeck*, 186.

duality is what is the case in fact. This point is fully stated by John of the Cross in book II, chapter V, sections 6–7, of his *Ascent of Mount Carmel*.

> If the window is in any way stained or misty, the sun's ray will be unable to illumine it and transform it into its own light, totally, as it would if it were clean of all these things, and pure. . . . [However if the window] be wholly pure and clean, the ray of sunlight will transform it and illumine it in such wise that it will itself seem to be a ray and will give the same light as the ray. Although in reality the window has a nature distinct from that of the ray itself, however much it may resemble it, yet we may say that the window is a ray of the sun or is light by participation. And the soul is like this window, whereupon is ever beating . . . this Divine light of the Being of God. . . . In thus allowing God to work in it, the soul . . . is at once illumined and transformed in God, and God communicates to it His supernatural Being in such wise that it appears to be God Himself and has all that God Himself has. And this union comes to pass when God grants the soul this supernatural favour, that all the things of God and the soul are one in participant transformation; and the soul seems to be God rather than a soul, and is indeed God by participation; although it is true that its natural being, though thus transformed, is as distinct from the Being of God as it was before, even as the window has likewise a nature distinct from that of the ray, though the ray gives it brightness. (181–82)

The soul "*appears* to be God Himself." But the fact remains that the soul and God are not identical. *Phenomenologically* there is identity; *metaphysically* there is duality. I'll close this part of our discussion with one more passage in which this point is made with particular clarity. It is taken from John Tauler's "First Sermon for the Second Sunday of the Epiphany." He is talking about an instance of Rapture.

> Then the spirit is transported high above all the faculties into a void of immense solitude whereof no mortal can adequately speak. It is *the mysterious darkness* wherein is concealed the limitless Good. To such an extent are we admitted and absorbed into something that is one, simple, divine, and illimitable, that we seem no longer distinguishable from it. I speak not of the reality but of the appearance, of

the impression that is felt. In this unity, the feeling of multiplicity disappears.[9]

The "*appearance*" is one of identity; the "*feeling* of multiplicity disappears." But this is *not* the reality—it is only the "*impression* that is felt."

Given the fact that classical Christian mystics such as Ruysbroeck, Bernard, John of the Cross, and Tauler have frequently paid special attention to the experience we have been calling "the union without distinction," one might suppose that it should be listed along with the Prayer of Quiet, the Prayer of Full Union, and Rapture as a distinct state of union. In fact, however, this way of arranging the mystical typology would obscure a subtle, though persistent, theme in the primary mystical literature, namely, that union without distinction is not a distinct kind of mystical experience but is, instead, an interval in a more comprehensive experience—an interval that, as Bernard suggests in the passage cited earlier from paragraph 27 of his *Treatise on Loving God,* occurs very rarely and then only for an instant. In Ruysbroeck's *The Book of Supreme Truth,* for example, union without distinction is explicitly presented as the climax—call it the "mystical peak"—of the state discussed in chapters XI and XII taken together (probably a case of Rapture). I'll finish this chapter with a brief elaboration of this idea.

Though the following passage from chapter 12 of Blosius's *Book of Spiritual Instruction* is a bit long, I have left it intact because it not only illustrates the point of immediate concern but is virtually packed with an array of the themes we have been studying in this section.

> For when, through love, the soul goes beyond all work of the intellect and all images in the mind, and is rapt above itself (a favor only God can bestow), utterly leaving itself, it flows into God: then is God its peace and fullness. In this peace of mind the soul can rightly sing: *In pace, in idipsum, dormiam et requiescam*—In peace, in the self-same, I will sleep and I will rest.
>
> The loving soul, as I have said, flows out of itself, and completely

9. Quoted in Poulain, *Graces of Interior Prayer,* 272 (pt. II, chap. XVIII, extracts).

swoons away; and, as if brought to nothing, it sinks down into the abyss of divine love, where, dead to itself, it lives in God, knowing nothing, feeling nothing, save only the love that it experiences.

It loses itself in the infinite solitude and darkness of the godhead; but so to lose itself is rather to find itself.

Then, putting off whatever is human and putting on what is divine, it is, as it were, transformed and changed into God, as iron placed in fire receives the form of fire, and is changed into fire. Just as the iron thus glowing with fire does not cease to be iron, so the soul, as it were, deified, does not change its nature and still remain itself.

The soul, therefore, remains itself; but whereas it was cold before, now it burns; whereas it was dark before, now it shines with light; whereas it was hard before, now it has become soft.

The essence of God has so flowed into its essence, that we may say that the soul has, as it were, the same tint or color.

Burnt up with the fire of divine love, and entirely liquified, the soul passes into God, is united with him without any medium, and becomes with him one spirit, even as gold and brass are welded into one mass of metal. (84–85)

It seems clear that we are here dealing with a case of Rapture—or, better, a case of what Saint Thomas would classify as nonviolent ecstasy. The soul is described as flowing "out of itself" and then as flowing into God, as God, in turn, flows into it. This gives us double embrace in a place other than the normal domain of the soul. The soul then enters a state of "solitude" where it "loses itself," becomes "dead to itself," that is, loses track of the distinction between itself and God and thus is "as if, brought to nothing." This is the union without distinction where the sense of self has vanished. The analogy of the iron in the fire is used to convey the message that however it may appear to the soul "burnt up with the fire of divine love," the climax interval does not involve metaphysical identity.[10]

With this material from Blosius handy for purposes of comparison, I want to return for a moment to the lengthy experience description offered by John of the Cross in stanza 1 of *Living Flame*

10. Ruysbroeck draws the same implication out of the iron-fire image. See chap. VIII of *The Book of Supreme Truth*, in *John of Ruysbroeck*, 236–37.

of Love. Recall that in that discussion John described a God-soul encounter which (he said) occurs in the "deepest center" of the soul and in which God absorbs as well as penetrates ("wounds") the "substance of the soul." I used this account in Section 2 of Chapter 1 above when developing the idea that double embrace is a standard feature of the Prayer of Full Union. Now, consider the following passage, which is part of John's account of the encounter just mentioned but which I did not consider in my earlier discussion.

> If it [the soul] attain to the last degree [of love], the love of God will succeed in wounding the soul even in its deepest center—that is, in transforming and enlightening it as regards all the being and power and virtue of the soul, such as it is capable of receiving, until it be brought into such a state that it appears to be God. In this state the soul is like the crystal that is clear and pure; the more degrees of light it receives, the greater concentration of light there is in it, and this enlightenment continues to such a degree that at last it attains a point at which the light is centered in it with such copiousness that it comes to appear to be wholly light, and cannot be distinguished from the light, for it is enlightened to the greatest possible extent and thus appears to be light itself. (41)

According to both Blosius and Saint John, union without distinction is what happens when the soul becomes so deeply absorbed and engulfed in the double embrace that it loses track of the distinction between itself and God. This is what Ruysbroeck and Bernard said too. But what now becomes apparent is that this loss of felt distinction can happen either in a case of Rapture (ecstasy) as described by Blosius or in a case of Full Union as described by John. The upshot would appear to be that union without distinction is not to be thought of as a distinct kind of mystical experience. It is, rather, the climax moment—seldom achieved—of two distinct mystical states, namely, Full Union and Rapture (or ecstasy). This is why I have introduced it here as a variation on Full Union and Rapture rather than as a fourth state simply added to the three basic pictures of mystic union.

[3]
Perceptions of
Spiritual Closeness

In the preceding chapters the three states of infused contemplation were characterized using spatial terms and phrases as uninterpreted primitives. God and the soul of the mystic were described as being "in" or "out" of certain places or domains. God and the soul were characterized as sometimes "close to" or "near" one another and at other times "enwrapping," "penetrating," "saturating," or "embracing" one another. The descriptions obtained using this complex spatial vocabulary have taken the form of a series of verbal pictures—diagrams that could easily be displayed on a piece of paper or on a chalkboard. In the present chapter I want to describe these states again—this time with special emphasis on the perception terms used in Christian mystical literature in discussions of the three states of union. These new descriptions are offered not as alternatives but as supplements to the originals. The union pictures are herein made thicker, more dense. They are also made deeper, more intense.

1. The Doctrine of Spiritual Sensations

As the body has its five exterior senses, with which it perceives the visible and delectable things of this life, and makes experience of them, so the spirit, with its faculties of understanding and will, has

five interior acts corresponding to these senses, which we call
seeing, hearing, smelling, tasting and touching spiritually, with
which it perceives the invisible and delectable things of Almighty
God, and makes *experience* of them; from which springs the experimental knowledge of God, which incomparably exceeds all the
knowledge that proceeds from our reasonings, as the sweetness of
honey is much better known by tasting even a little of it than by
arguing at great length concerning its nature.

This passage is from *Meditations* by the seventeenth-century French
mystic and mystical theologian Venerable Louis du Pont.[1] It contains a general formulation of the thesis I shall be discussing in this
chapter. I shall begin in this first section with a comment concerning the status of this thesis in the literature of the Christian mystical
tradition.

In the second of her letters to Father Rodrigo Alvarez (Relation
VIII), Saint Teresa says, "the soul seems to have other senses within
itself," which, she says, "bear some likeness to the exterior senses
it possesses."[2] Since Teresa made this comment when speaking of
the "lowest" of the mystical states she took to be "supernatural"
(the Prayer of Quiet), in part II, chapter VI, of his well-known and
widely respected treatise on mystical theology *The Graces of Interior
Prayer,* Augustin Poulain concludes that "the saint takes the exercise of the five spiritual senses as a point of departure for her
description of *all* the states of mystic union" (92). This passage
from Teresa together with a wealth of passages from the works of
other primary mystics (some of which I shall review in Section 3 of
this chapter) are then used by Poulain to support a broader contention, namely, that the idea of there being five spiritual sense faculties by which God's presence in the various states of union is
detected is a firm part of the primary Christian mystical tradition.
The thesis advanced in the passage just cited from du Pont's *Meditations* is thus entered as a doctrine in what Poulain refers to as
"descriptive mystical theology." This is to say that although it is
perhaps more general than what most Christian mystics have actu-

1. Quoted in Poulain, *Graces of Interior Prayer,* 101 (pt. II, chap. VI, extracts).
2. Teresa, *Relations,* 402.

ally said, it is, nonetheless, an adequate extrapolation from the primary mystical texts.[3]

Regarding precedence in the theological literature for the doctrine of spiritual sensations, Poulain cites passages from Saints Augustine and Bonaventure that appear to support it in a general way.[4] More impressive on this second point, however, is the discussion in chapter x of Albert Farges's *Mystical Phenomena,* in which are related some of the details of Thomas Aquinas's challenge to Peter Lombard on this topic. Farges says that Lombard "rightly taught that the souls of the mystical saints were endowed with spiritual senses, but he endeavored to restrict these senses to that of touch." Calling on Origen for theological precedent, Thomas insisted on five spiritual senses. Farges says that Thomas might have called on a host of others besides Origen, including not only Augustine and Bonaventure but (among others) Richard of Saint Victor, Saint Gregory, Saint Bernard of Clairvaux, and Albert the Great. In addition to himself, Farges lists a number of other prominent contemporary mystical theologians who have followed Poulain in defending the doctrine of five spiritual faculties.[5] Farges concludes his discussion on this topic by citing, with approval, part of the following passage from the seventeenth-century mystical theologian Jacques Nouet.

"After the opinion of so many saintly and enlightened Fathers, it would be rash to call into question what *all mystic theologians* follow in teaching with regard to the number of the *five spiritual senses.* . . . All the masters of the spiritual life agree on this point, namely, that the most perfect union with God to which the soul can attain in this life consists in this wonderful experience of the interior senses; the main difficulty lies in knowing to which one of the five it properly, in their opinion, belongs. At one time they seem to attribute it to *touch,* which is the lowest of all the exterior and the highest amongst the interior senses. Saint Thomas, in his Opuscule 61, places it as the highest degree of unitive love giving the reason that it achieves the

3. In Section 3 of Chapter 8 I shall discuss in detail Poulain's notion of "descriptive mystical theology."

4. See Poulain, *Graces of Interior Prayer,* 100–101 (pt. II, chap. VI, extracts).

5. Farges, *Mystical Phenomena,* 279–84.

closest union with its object. . . . At another time they seem to give
the preference to taste."[6]

Poulain acknowledges that those who are "uninstructed" in the
Christian mystical literature will find it "disconcerting" to be told
that in the various states of union the mystic perceives the presence
of God via five distinct spiritual sense faculties (98). I think Poulain
here means to be pointing to the fact that some will find it odd
(perhaps even strange) to suppose that God can be detected not
only by a faculty similar to sight (which most would probably
allow) but by spiritual sensations of touch, taste, and smell as well.
Poulain says, however, that this is a "tunnel" one must get through
if one is to understand what he calls the "fundamental character of
the mystic union" (88, 98). Whatever one might think about the
propriety of the doctrine of spiritual sensations, Poulain claims that
in advancing this doctrine he is not "going out after new inven-
tions" but is, instead, "giving the true tradition" (98). On
the strength of the materials reviewed in the two preceding paragraphs, I am inclined to think that Poulain is right about this. For
the remainder of this book, therefore, I shall assume that when a
mystic of the Christian tradition claims to have "seen" God, or to
have "smelled" or "tasted" God in a mystical encounter, it is at
least likely that the mystic means to be affirming that God was
detected in the encounter via actual sensations that are at least
similar (Farges says "analogous") to the bodily perceptions usually
identified with these terms.[7]

2. Some Thoughts on Touch

The doctrine of spiritual sensations has its seat and model in
traditional thinking about the sense faculties of the body. Spiritual
senses are said to "correspond" to bodily sense faculties; each of the
former bears the name of the sense faculty of the body to which it
corresponds. A number of things about the physical senses, however, are not obvious and must be made explicit before the details

6. Quoted in Poulain, *Graces of Interior Prayer*, 101–2 (pt. II, chap. VI, extracts).
7. Farges, *Mystical Phenomena*, 281, 283.

of the doctrine before us can be properly introduced. This is especially true with respect to the sense faculty generally referred to as
"the sense of touch." In this section, therefore, I want to make a
number of introductory remarks about the ordinary physical
senses—focusing, in particular, on just those features of the sense
of touch that will figure importantly in the deliberations to follow.
I should add that in this discussion I shall simply assume there are
five and only five sense faculties of the body. Though this view is
almost universally rejected by contemporary psychobiologists, it is
presupposed in the mystical literature of interest in this chapter. To
challenge it, therefore, would take us too far out of the established
context of our discussion.

Colloquially, the five senses of the body are referred to as (1) the
sense of sight, (2) the sense of hearing, (3) the sense of taste, (4) the
sense of smell, and (5) the sense of touch. And the first thing I want
to note is that in all but one of these cases the perception verb
connected with each of the faculties is either the same as, or directly derived from, the word used to name the faculty itself. So,
for example, it is by virtue of having a sense of *smell* that I can *smell*
things, and it is by virtue of having a sense of *hearing* that I can *hear*
things. The odd case is the fifth. It is not by virtue of having a sense
of *touch* that I can *touch* things. I can touch things because I have
fingers—in fact, I can touch things simply because I have a physical body and not because I have some special sense faculty. This is
evidenced by the fact that I might touch something with my fingers, or with my chin or elbow, even if my sense faculties were
completely inoperative. The verb "to touch" is not a perception
verb as is, for example, "to hear" or "to see." Things having no
sense faculties at all can touch things—as, for example, the bottom
of the boat *touches* the shallow reef in the middle of the lake. The
perception verb that goes with the sense of touch is "feel," not
"touch." It is by virtue of having a sense of *touch* that I can *feel*
things in my physical environment—understanding, of course,
that "feel" is here working as a perception verb and not as an
emotion verb (as in "I feel kindly toward him") or as a cognition
verb (as in "I feel that Empiricism has some serious defects as an
epistemological theory").

It is with the eyes that I see and it is with the ears that I hear.

With respect to the faculties of sight and hearing, we can point to a specific organ of the body that accounts for the faculty in question. Something like this is true as regards the sense of smell and the sense of taste as well. Though here the fine points of technical physiology are somewhat more complex, it is still possible to identify a more or less localized part of the body that connects with each of these last-mentioned faculties. One smells things with the nose (or via receptors located in the nose) and one tastes things with the tongue (or via receptors located on and around the tongue). Although I think it is now a bit anachronistic, sometimes the *palate* is said to be the organ that goes with the sense of taste. Again, however, the odd case is touch. There does not seem to be a specific organ or even a reasonably localized part of the body associated with the sense of touch. As a first thought, one might be inclined to suppose that it is with the skin (or via receptors located in the skin) that one feels things. But this would be to neglect the obvious fact that we often feel things on the *inside* of the body. I feel the food in my mouth. I also feel it going down my throat when I swallow. Very hot foods and liquids are not only felt in the mouth and throat but (clinical studies show) are sometimes felt in the stomach and even in the small intestine. One feels the air in one's lungs on a brisk winter morning. Perhaps, then, we should say that the organ connected with the sense of touch is not only the outside surface of the body (the skin) but the inside surface as well—including the lining of the alimentary canal, the lining of the lungs, and so on. But even this won't do. Children feel their baby teeth wiggle when they push them with their tongues. I can feel tension in my legs after my morning run on the beach. Neither of these sensations is delivered via the skin or some inside lining. Then perhaps we should say that these last-mentioned sensations ought not to be thought of as tactile sensations at all. The trouble with this suggestion is that the scheme with which we are working provides only five sense faculties in all. Where could these last-mentioned sensations be put if excluded from the category of touch?

In a short book published in 1964 entitled *Perception,* Julian Hochberg distinguishes three broad categories of sense faculties, which he refers to as "distance senses," "skin senses," and "deep senses," respectively.[8] Though it would take us too far afield to discuss the details of this typological scheme, suffice it to say that on Hochberg's account, distance senses are sense faculties by which things at some distance from the perceiver can be detected, skin senses are faculties by which are detected only things in contact with the outside surface of the body, and deep senses are those by which one detects states of the body itself, for example, tension in the muscles of one's leg. The point of specific interest here is that when classifying the various sense faculties of the body in accordance with this tri-categorial scheme, Hochberg includes only the sense of sight and the sense of hearing in the category of distance senses (7). The sense of touch, the sense of smell, and the sense of taste are all placed in the category of skin senses. Is this all right? Following is a comment on the adequacy of this arrangement.

I can smell the chicken cooking in the kitchen though I am not, myself, in that part of the house. Shouldn't we then (pace, Hochberg) include the sense of smell in the category of distance senses? Maybe not. Aristotle would say that it is not the chicken but the *odor* of the chicken that constitutes the "proper object" of the perception. Unlike the chicken, the odor of the chicken is not at a distance from my body. But this won't do. When I hear a car pull up in front of my house, it might be said that what I hear is not the car, but the *sound* of the car. The sound, unlike the car, is not at a distance from my body—in fact, it fills the whole room in which I am sitting. Shall we then correct Hochberg's scheme in a different direction and classify the sense of hearing as a skin sense? That would be an obscuration of magnitude. Better, I should think, just to go with our ordinary ways of thinking and allow the sense of smell to count as a distance sense, that is, as a faculty by which we can detect things at a distance from the body.

This last point suggests another that must be made with respect to the sense of touch. I suspect that, like Hochberg, most of us think of this faculty as one that operates only with respect to objects in contact with the body—perhaps after some reflection, allowing inside contact as well as outside contact. I *feel* the surface

8. In its preface, Hochberg describes this book as a "brief introduction" to the study of perception. It is one of a series of texts intended for use in introductory courses in psychology.

of the table only when I *touch* it, and I feel objects in my mouth and throat only when they are in contact with the relevant inside parts. But, again, I am inclined to think that this won't do. I can feel the fire when I am standing at some distance from the hearth. I do not have to touch the flame in order to feel it. Perhaps we should say that it is the *heat* of the fire and not the fire itself that I feel. Heat is an emanation which, in this case, is unlike the thing from which it emanates in that it is not at a distance from the perceiver. But why should we restrict ourselves to this way of talking? The sense of smell and the sense of hearing work by way of emanations too. In these last-mentioned cases, the fact that one perceives something *by way* of nondistant emanations does not mean that one is not perceiving (smelling, hearing) an object at some distance from the body. As above, there is no obscurity in the claim that one feels the *fire* though standing on the other side of the room.

Shall we then classify the sense of touch as a distance sense—meaning that it is a faculty by which we can detect objects at a distance? This would surely cut against our linguistic intuitions, since "touch" suggests contact. But then, as noted above, "touch" is not a perception verb anyway. Maybe the answer is that we should just rename the faculty in question—calling it the "sense of feeling" rather than the "sense of touch." Perhaps we would then have no misgivings about classifying it as a distance sense. Such renaming, however, would obscure an important distinction we shall need in the discussion to come. There appears to be only a restricted range of physical properties that can be detected via the sense of touch (that is, *felt*) when the perceiver is not touching an object having the property in question. Temperature properties such as *hot* and, perhaps, *warm* seem to be the only cases in point. With respect to other physical properties (for example, square, rough, six feet tall), one can detect them via touch *only if* one is in contact with an object so qualified. The point of interest, then, is that the sense of touch is a distance sense or not a distance sense, depending on which quality of the physical object is being considered. Note that the same is not true as regards the paradigms of distance senses. Whatever qualities can be detected via the sense of sight or the sense of hearing can be detected whether or not the perceiver is touching an object bearing those qualities. Perhaps in the end we should think of the sense of touch as a committee of subfaculties rather than as a single capacity. This is suggested as well by something else noted above—that there is no specific organ or even region of the body uniquely associated with the capacity to feel.

3. Perceptions of God

In the Prayer of Quiet, God and the substance of the soul are close but not so close as to preclude their coming closer. By contrast, in Full Union and in the culmination stage of Rapture, God and the soul are in double embrace—though, of course, the embrace takes place in different domains, depending on the case. Now, the doctrine of spiritual sensations tells us that in these encounters, the soul *perceives* God via sense faculties that are "like" the sense faculties of the body. And although we have not yet inquired about the ways or respects in which spiritual sense faculties are supposed to be *like* the sense faculties of the body, let's suppose that at least part of what is meant is that each of the former operates in circumstances analogous to those in which its counterpart bodily sense faculty operates when detecting objects in the environment of the perceiver. Of course, *the perceiver* in the case of bodily sense faculties has a body; and *the environment* consists of objects in certain spatial relations to that body. In the case of spiritual sense faculties, the perceiver is the immaterial soul (soul$^+$) and the environment is the place in which this perceiver encounters God—whether that be in its own domain (soul*) or in the "other world" involved in Rapture. The question I now want to ask is this: Given this setup, which spiritual sense faculties would one antecedently expect to be involved when the soul perceives God in the Prayer of Quiet, the Prayer of Full Union, and Rapture, respectively? Through three subsections, this question will serve as the peg upon which the rest of the discussion in this chapter will be hung. My intent is to develop the details of the claim that the soul has spiritual sensations of God by displaying the relations between this metaphor and the spatial pictures discussed in the first two chapters.

The Prayer of Quiet

In Fourth Mansions, chapter II, of *Interior Castle,* Teresa writes as follows concerning the spiritual sensations that attend the Prayer of Quiet: "The fragrance it [the soul] experiences, we might say, is as if in those interior depths there were a brazier on which were cast sweet perfumes; the light cannot be seen, nor the place where it dwells, but the fragrant smoke and the heat penetrate the entire soul, and very often, as I have said, the effects extend even to the body" (82).[9] Put this together with the following account given by Saint Ambrose. In the context from which this passage is taken, the state under discussion is identified only as "union" but is described in such a way that it appears to be a case that Teresa would classify as the Prayer of Quiet.

> The soul of the just is the bride of the Word. If this soul *burns with desire,* if she *prays without ceasing,* if her whole being goes out towards the Word, then suddenly it seems that she hears His voice *without seeing Him;* that she savors *inwardly* the odor of His Divinity, which thing often comes to those who are strong of faith. Suddenly the soul's *sense of smell* is filled with spiritual grace, and being aware of a sweet breath that tells her of the presence of Him whom she seeks, she says: Behold Him whom I *seek* and whom I *desire.*[10]

In the Prayer of Quiet, God and soul+ are only *close.* If God is then perceived by soul+, he will be perceived as an object still at some distance from the perceiver. Assuming that spiritual sense faculties work on the model of ordinary bodily sense faculties, we should expect that in this state God would be perceived by the spiritual counterparts of what we are calling "distance senses." And so it is. Putting together the two passages just quoted, three sense faculties are mentioned and each is in the expected category. The spiritual sense of smell is emphasized by both Teresa and Ambrose. Teresa says that the soul smells God's "sweet perfumes" and Ambrose speaks of the soul's "sense of smell" being "filled with spiritual grace." In addition, Teresa says that the soul *feels the heat* coming

---

9. See Teresa's *Conceptions of the Love of God,* 383 (chap. IV), for another passage in which is stressed the operation of the spiritual sense of smell in the Prayer of Quiet.

10. Quoted in Poulain, *Graces of Interior Prayer,* 102 (pt. II, chap. VI, extracts).

from the "interior depths"—the "depths" (we can assume) refers to the most interior of the Seventh Mansions. The sense of *touch* thus appears to be operative, though only in the restricted sense appropriate when the object perceived is still at some distance from the perceiver. On the other hand, while Ambrose says nothing about detecting God's presence by sensing heat, he does claim to hear God's voice. The spiritual counterpart of the auditory faculty thus seems to be in play. So far, then, the picture is as might have been expected given the spatial relation between God and soul[+] in the Prayer of Quiet and given, as well, that spiritual sense faculties work in a way analogous to the operations of the bodily sense faculties.

There is one surprise, however. Neither Teresa nor Ambrose claims to *see* God in the Prayer of Quiet. In fact, Ambrose says explicitly that God is not seen and Teresa at least hints of this when she says that the "light cannot be seen, nor the place where it dwells." Elsewhere in her writings Teresa says quite clearly that God is not seen in the Prayer of Quiet.[11] This, I say, is a surprise. The spiritual correlate of what is probably the most informative of the distance senses of the body is not in operation, yet this is precisely the species of union in which one would expect it to play the dominant role. In his discussion of this topic in *The Graces of Interior Prayer*, Poulain claims that apart from exceptional cases, mystics not only do not report seeing God in the Prayer of Quiet but, in fact, do report that they do not see God in this state.[12] Unfortunately, Poulain does little to document this contention.[13] Still, if Teresa and Ambrose can be taken as typical in this regard, it would appear that he is right nonetheless.

Full Union

In the second section of Chapter 1, we looked closely at a theme developed by John of the Cross in stanza 1 of *Living Flame of Love*, namely, that in Full Union, God "wounds" (actually, "burns") the

11. Teresa, *Conceptions of the Love of God*, 384, 385 (chap. IV).

12. Poulain, *Graces of Interior Prayer*, 90–91 (pt. II, chap. VI, paras. 8, 9).

13. Several of the passages Poulain cites in support of this contention say only that in the Prayer of Quiet, God is not seen with bodily eyes and is also not seen imaginatively—see Poulain, *Graces of Interior Prayer*, 99. But this (I am sure) is not to say that God is not seen via the *spiritual* sense of sight.

"substance of the soul" during an embrace that takes place in the soul's "deepest center." Continuing this theme in stanza II of the same text, John speaks of the wound as a "touch"—more precisely as a "substantial touch"—and proceeds to explain how this touch is perceived by the soul. Focusing on the fact that the touch is a burn, in the opening part of the discussion, John says:

> And since God is an infinite fire of love, when therefore He is pleased to touch the soul with some severity, the heat of the soul rises to such a degree that the soul believes that it is being burned with a heat greater than any other in the world. For this reason it speaks of this touch as a burn, for it is experienced where the fire is most intense and most concentrated, and the effect of its heat is greater than that of other fires. And when this Divine fire has trans-formed the substance of the soul into itself, not only is the soul conscious of the burn, but it has itself become one burn of vehement fire. (59)

But as the account continues, John's attention shifts away from the idea that the touch is felt as a burn. He insists, instead, that it is felt as a caress.

> Oh, hand, as generous as thou art powerful and rich, richly and powerfully dost thou give me thy gifts! Oh, soft hand, the softer for this soul, and softly laid upon it, for if thou wert to lean hardly upon it the whole world would perish; for at Thy glance alone the earth shakes and the nations are undone and the mountains crumble to pieces. Once more, then, I say, "O, soft hand!" (66–67)

The soul feels (John says "is conscious of") the heat of God. This is as it was in the Prayer of Quiet. But the point of special interest is that in Full Union, contact has been made and the soul, according-ly, feels the touch as a "soft hand . . . softly laid upon it." Here, for the first time in our discussion, the sense of touch is working not only as a distance sense (detecting heat) but as the spiritual counter-part of a skin sense. Just a few paragraphs after the one just cited, John also says that the soul feels the touch "in the inmost center of the substance of the soul" (62). God is thus felt *within* the substance of the soul and not just as a hand "laid upon it." The sense of spiritual touch thus seems to be in full operation, detecting not only heat but outside as well as inside contact. The following passage adds nothing new to the theme of immediate concern. I cite it here only because it would be a shame to leave stanza II of *Living Flame of Love* without doing so.

> Oh, then, thou delicate touch, Thou Word, Son of God, Who, through the delicateness of Thy Divine Being, dost subtly penetrate the substance of my soul, and touching it wholly and delicately, dost absorb it wholly in Thyself in Divine ways of sweetness which have never been heard of in the land of Chanaan, nor seen in Theman! Oh, delicate touch of the Word, delicate, yea, wondrously delicate to me, which, having overthrown the mountains and broken the stones in Mount Horeb with the shadow of Thy power and strength that went before thee, didst reveal Thyself to the Prophet with the whisper of the gentle air. Oh, gentle air, that art so delicate and gentle! Say, how dost Thou touch the soul so gently and delicately when Thou art so terrible and powerful? Oh, blessed, twice blessed, the soul whom Thou dost touch so gently though Thou art so terrible and so powerful! Tell it out to the world. But nay, tell it not to the world, for the world knows naught of air so gentle, and will not feel Thee because it can neither receive thee nor see thee. (67–68)

We shall have occasion in the next chapter to look at some passages in which John describes the touches felt in Full Union as "kisses," that is, the "kiss of the mouth" asked for by the bride in the Song of Songs.[14]

In chapter x of *The Sparkling Stone,* Jan van Ruysbroeck speaks of a state in which God "dwells within us" and in which we feel what are referred to in the text as "the inward-drawing touch" as well as "the outpouring touch." As the discussion continues it becomes abundantly clear that the setting is one of double embrace, since God is portrayed as flowing "through us and over us" and we (that is, experiencing mystics) are described as "drenched and flooded" with God. Though it is not clear to me what Ruysbroeck means when he says that the touches involved here are

14. See, e.g., John, *Dark Night of the Soul,* 188 (bk. II, chap. XIII).

"inward-drawing" and "outpouring," the rest of the description suggests that the state under discussion is Full Union. Ruysbroeck says that it is a state in which God shows himself to be one who will "dwell in us forever."[15] The following passage picks up the action directly after the reference to "inward-drawing" and "outpouring" touches.

> And therefore, when our feeling shows us that He with all these riches would be ours and dwell in us forever more, then all the powers of the soul open themselves, and especially the desirous power; for all the rivers of the grace of God pour forth, and the more we taste of them, the more we long to taste; and the more we long to taste, the more deeply we press into contact with Him; and the more deeply we press into contact with God, the more the flood of His sweetness flows through us and over us; and the more we are thus drenched and flooded, the better we feel and know that the sweetness of God is incomprehensible and unfathomable. And therefore the prophet says: O TASTE AND SEE THAT THE LORD IS SWEET. But he does not say how sweet He is, for God's sweetness is without measure; and therefore we can neither grasp it nor swallow it. And this is also testified to by the bride of God in the Song of Songs where she says: I SAT DOWN UNDER HIS SHADOW, WITH GREAT DELIGHT, AND HIS FRUIT WAS SWEET TO MY TASTE. (211–12)

In the next chapter I shall develop a theme from the mystical literature in which the idea of tasting God plays a dominant role. At that point I shall provide some additional passages that I think will help to broaden this part of the picture. For the moment, however, I want to make just one observation about this passage from Ruysbroeck.

In Full Union, God embraces and penetrates the soul. In John, though the distance senses continue to operate (God's heat is felt), God's touches are felt both on the outside and on the inside of soul[+]. Though John makes mention of the fact that Full Union involves what he calls a "lively taste of God (which) the soul calls sweet" (a consequence of the operation of what John calls the "palate" of the soul), the emphasis in his various discussions of union is on spiritual touch.[16] Ruysbroeck, too, speaks often of

15. In *John of Ruysbroeck*, 208–10.
16. John, *Living Flame of Love*, 56, 32.

spiritual touches—as do all the so-called bridal mystics we shall be discussing in the next chapter. Still, in the passage just cited from chapter x of *The Sparkling Stone,* though touches are mentioned, taste is introduced as the principal faculty of discernment at precisely the point where Ruysbroeck is stressing the fact that the union embrace tends to *deepen* as it is sustained. An increase in the operation of the sense of taste signals the fact that the soul is *pressing more deeply into contact* with God. This, I want now to suggest, is a subtle but powerful illustration of the idea that spiritual sense faculties mirror the operations of their bodily counterparts. I'll elaborate.

The bodily sense of touch is relatively diversified. By means of its operation we detect objects at a distance as well as objects in contact with both the outside and inside portions of the body. The bodily sense of taste, however, is correspondingly specialized. Paradigmatically, I taste *only* what is *inside* my body, that is, only what is in my mouth. Thus, in the standard case, if I taste something, it is related to my body in the most intimate possible way— it is in contact with an *inside* part. So also (apparently) for the spiritual sensation of taste. The spatial picture that goes with the *taste* of God is, very specifically, God *inside,* that is, God in the most intimate possible contact-relation with me. What we have here, then, is a case where mention of the salient perceptual-like element involved in a given union experience highlights the very particular feature of the spatial picture to which the mystic is calling special attention. The total package is thus one in which the description of the union state in perceptual terms not only supplements the spatial diagram as a whole but marks one of its aspects with a Day-Glo line.

So far I have said nothing about the role played by the spiritual sense of sight in the state of Full Union. Shall we suppose that here the soul is blind, as it was in the Prayer of Quiet? Not so. Sprinkled through the writings of many major mystics are comments to the effect that in Full Union God is detected by the spiritual sense of sight. The following passage from the *Revelations* of Angela of Foligno throws this theme into sharp relief.

At times God comes into the soul without being called; and He instills into her fire, love and sometimes sweetness; and the soul believes this comes from God, and delights therein. But she does not yet know, or see, that He dwells in her. . . . And beyond this the soul receives the gift of seeing God. God says to her "Behold Me!" and the soul sees Him dwelling within her. She sees Him more clearly than one man sees another. For *the eyes of the soul behold a plentitude of which I can not speak: a plentitude which is not bodily but spiritual, of which I can say nothing.* And the soul rejoices in that sight with an ineffable joy; and this is the manifest and certain sign that God dwells in her.[17]

Of course, this passage relates closely to the one from Angela's *Consolations* that I discussed at length in Section 1 of the preceding chapter. There, Angela said that prior to the embrace of Full Union, she saw God with "the eyes of the soul" coming in upon her "in the manner of a sickle." In a footnote appended to that earlier discussion, I suggested that as used in the passages we were studying there, to see something "with the eyes of the soul" is not to see it with the bodily eyes nor to see it in the imagination. I suspect that there, as well as in the passage now before us, Angela is using this phrase to refer to the spiritual sense of sight. Still, as a general remark, spiritual sight gets nothing like the attention given to spiritual touch and to spiritual taste in the literature on Full Union. Poulain agrees. He says that "as a rule" spiritual visual perceptions are absent in Full Union as they are in the Prayer of Quiet.[18]

Rapture

Rapture (as well as nonviolent ecstasy) involves a number of perceptual elements unique to it—most important, the sense of being out of body. But as regards its culmination stage where the mystic is absorbed and saturated by God, the perceptual descriptions of Rapture are in many ways indistinguishable from standard reports of Full Union. Pointing the reader toward the writings of "Blessed Teresa of Jesus, our Mother" (311) for the details, John of the Cross undertakes a brief discussion of the state of Rapture in

17. Quoted in Underhill, *Mysticism*, 282.
18. Poulain, *Graces of Interior Prayer*, 89, 99.

stanzas 13–15 of his *Spiritual Canticle* that illustrates the point. In stanza 13 (sec. 2) the state under discussion is amply identified. It is one in which the soul is "made to issue forth from herself in rapture and ecstasy," that is, one in which the soul seems to herself to be "flying out of her body" (308). As the discussion continues (stanzas 14 and 15) God is portrayed as a "breeze"—an "amorous breeze" (323). Like the "gentle air" mentioned in the passage quoted above from stanza 11 of *Living Flame of Love,* the "amorous breeze" is felt as one feels the breeze on one's face; it is also heard as one hears the "gentle whisper" of the wind. John then launches into an extended discussion of spiritual sound (322–28), which ends with the claim that the "whisper of the amorous breeze" is, indeed, "silent music" and "sounding solitude" because while it "is silent to the senses and natural faculties, it is a most sounding solitude to the spiritual faculties" (331). Along the way there is also mention of seeing and tasting God. My point is that while some of this is new to us (for example, the expansions on spiritual sound) there is really nothing here that could not have been included in an account of Full Union. Nor is this very surprising. After all, in Full Union and in the culmination stage of Rapture, the spatial picture of the relation between God and soul+ are the same. One would expect that the spiritual sense faculties operative in the two cases would be the same as well.

The most interesting part, however, is yet to come. And I think I can best get at it by turning to Angela of Foligno's *Visions and Instructions.* I'll quote two passages; the first is from chapter xxiv and the second is from chapter xxvi.

On one occasion, however, my soul was lifted up and . . . when it was in that darkness, wished to return to itself, and could not, wished to proceed and could not. Then suddenly it was lifted up higher and enlightened, and it saw the unutterable *Power* of God, and it saw the *Will* of God and His *Justice* and *Goodness,* in which I most fully understood all the things about which I had asked [concerning the Fall of man and his Redemption]. . . . And I was so full of charity [*claritatis*] and with such joy did I have understanding of the power and will and justice of God, and not only did I have knowledge of those things about which I had enquired, but I was also satisfied with regard to all things. But this I cannot make known in any words whatsoever; for it is wholly above nature.

Frequently, therefore, do I see God in this way and in this good that
cannot outwardly be related, nor even thought of by the heart. Yea,
I say, in this most certain and enclosed good which I understand
with so much *darkness,* I have all my hope; and in seeing, whatever I
wish to have, I *have all;* whatever I wish to know, I *know all,* and in
it I see all good. . . . [And the soul] delights in an ineffable way in
the All-Good, and . . . because this good is joined with darkness,
the *more it is seen in darkness,* and the more certain it is, and the more
it surpasses all things. . . . Again, when the soul sees the power of
God, and when it sees the wisdom of God, and even when it sees the
will of God, all of which I have seen in other wonderful and ineffable ways, all this is less than this most certain good. For this good
that I see, is whole; but all other things are (so to say) in part. . . .
For in the darkness I see the Holy Trinity, Itself, which I see in such
great darkness, it seemeth to me that I stand and abide in the midst
of It. . . . Again, when I see the good, I do not then, when I am in
it, have any thoughts of the Humanity of Christ, or of the God-
Man, or of anything which hath form; and yet at such a time I see all
things, and see nothing.[19]

The experience under discussion is established in the opening two
sentences as a case of Rapture. Angela says that her soul was "lifted
up" and was, as Teresa would say, "out of itself." When "it wished
to return to itself," it "could not." Her soul was then lifted higher,
and at that point Angela claims to have seen a number of items—in
particular, the *power,* the *will,* the *justice,* and the *goodness* of God.
In the second passage, God's *wisdom* is added to the list of the
divine attributes that Angela presumably saw. In part III, chapter
XVIII, secs. 23–25, of *The Graces of Interior Prayer,* Poulain maintains that Rapture states are usually packed with visual-like perceptions of God and that the things most frequently seen in these cases
are divine attributes such as the ones just mentioned, the Trinity
(as in Angela) and individual members of the Trinity (usually the
Holy Ghost) (249–50). At this point I want to look a bit more
closely at Angela's account. There is a theme here that I think will
repay a more careful review.

We are told that spiritual sense faculties are "like" their counter-

19. Quoted in Poulain, *Graces of Interior Prayer,* 271 (pt. III, chap. XVIII, extracts).

parts among the senses of the body. Accordingly, when we are told, for example, that the soul hears, smells, or tastes God, we are led to think that there must be something attached to God that is "like" what Aristotle called the "proper object" perceived in an ordinary case of hearing, smelling, or tasting—in this case, the *sound* of God, the *odor* of God, or the *flavor* of God. And, indeed, this is just what we are told. What is heard is God's "whisper," what is smelled is God's "sweet perfume," and (using Ruysbroeck's words) the flavor detected when the soul perceives God by the spiritual sense of taste is "sweetness without measure." Of course, with respect to these cases, we are not invited to press for further details. We would no doubt be confronted with the probe-stopper "ineffable" were we to press for particulars concerning God's whisper or odor. Still, the things heard, smelled, and tasted are in the right categories—sounds go with hearing, and odors and flavors go with smelling and tasting, respectively. Thus, with respect to three of the perception types (allegedly) involved in the various states of union, things are in conceptual order. In these cases, the original union pictures have been expanded to include whispers, odors, and so on produced by God. These expansions make room for the idea that God is perceived via faculties that work like ordinary sense faculties of the body. And this, in turn, allows for the construction of bigger union pictures, which include bona fide perceptual elements, just as the doctrine of spiritual sensations declares. Though less obviously so, the case of spiritual touch seems also to be in this category. In its capacity as a distance sense, spiritual tact detects the *heat* of God. When contact is made, spiritual touch then picks up things that appear to be "feels" of God, for example, the *softness* of the hand that delivers the "delicate touch." Thus, here again the basic union pictures have been supplemented in such a way that spiritual perceptions (this time, tactile perceptions) can be hooked into the scheme. When the perceptions are added, the originals then expand to include tactile perceptions on the part of soul$^+$ without threat of conceptual muddle.

What, then, of spiritual sight? In Angela's *Consolations* we were told that it is *God* who is seen. In the Rapture literature, this object is usually more specifically identified as the Trinity or some one person of the Trinity. Already there is a problem of sorts. If I see

something with my eyes, in the typical case what is detected is
some shape and/or color that (as we say) "belongs" to the "something" I see. But that does not appear to be a necessary truth. When
I look at a clear pane of glass while standing with my nose pressed
against it, it is not at all obvious that I detect anything that counts
as a shape or a color, let alone the shape or color of the object I am
seeing. Still, seeing x seems necessarily to involve seeing something of a physical nature that belongs to x—something which
Angela referred to several times as "physical form." And though it
might be hard to provide a perfectly general account of what this
"something" is supposed to be, it would appear that if we are to
retain a parallel between spiritual sight and bodily sight, we shall
here have to introduce an analogue of "bodily form" that can be
spiritually seen, just as we introduced analogues of physical sounds
and physical odors when supplementing the original union pictures so that God could be spiritually heard and spiritually smelled.
This by itself does not seem to be a serious problem, however. I'm
sure that somewhere in the mystical literature there is reference to
something like, for example, "God's spiritual form"—something
that can be detected with the "eyes of the soul" and can also be
characterized with visually oriented property terms such as "beau-
tiful," "exquisite," or "majestic." To be sure, that is not much, but
I think it is all that the union pictures would require in order to
accommodate the idea that God is spiritually seen. It also appears
to be no less than what was added to the originals to make room
for the idea that God is perceived via the spiritual sense of hearing
or the spiritual sense of smell.

In the passage we are here trying to fathom, however, Angela
tells us that what is seen in the state of Rapture is the *power, will,
justice, goodness,* and *wisdom* of God. And the problem here is not
just that because these things are seen via the *spiritual* sense of sight,
they need be only *like* their counterparts in the mundane world
which are perceived with the bodily sense of sight. The problem is,
rather, that their counterparts in the mundane world are the power, will, justice, goodness, and wisdom of human beings, and
while these attributes are no doubt assigned to a human being in a
given case by reference to what is perceived, they are not themselves properties that can be apprehended in simple acts of percep-

tion. The power, goodness, etc., of human beings, in other words, are simply not the *kinds* of things that one *sees*. Thus, at this point we seem to be confronted with the problem that cannot be solved by supplementing the original union pictures with items that are "like" the ones detected when power, will, justice, goodness, and wisdom are visually perceived in the ordinary case. There are no such items. This is because power, will, justice, goodness, and wisdom are not visually perceived in the ordinary case.

At this point, I could imagine someone complaining that the whole idea expressed in the mystical literature in what appears to be visual language has here been misunderstood. "See" is a perception verb, but it also functions as a cognition verb, roughly synonymous with "understand," as in, for example, "I see what you mean." When a mystic such as Angela claims to have seen the Trinity or to have seen God's power, justice, and wisdom in a state of Rapture, what is meant is not that she saw something in a way analogous to ordinary seeing with the eyes, but that she *saw that—understood that*—something is true. In this case (the suggestion goes) what Angela saw was *that* God is a Trinity and, also, *that* God is good, just, and wise. There are at least two reasons, however, for thinking that this way of understanding a text such as Angela's would be incorrect. First, this reading would be out of line with the general message intended in the doctrine of spiritual sensations. The idea there is that spiritual sense faculties are *sense* faculties by which is attained "experimental"—that is, direct *perceptual*—knowledge of God. This point would be lost with respect to the spiritual sense of sight were we now to read "see" in "see God" or "see the Trinity" or "see God's power" as a cognition verb rather than a perception verb. Second, and more important, this way of understanding the matter is all but explicitly excluded in the primary mystical literature. Anticipating confusion on this very point, the seventeenth-century Spanish mystic Alvarez de Paz writes as follows concerning Rapture in book v, part III, chapter xIV, of his *Works:*

In this degree, which is the highest, *eyes are given unto the soul* by which she may see God. . . . God manifests Himself to the soul by an image that represents Him very perfectly. The sensible faculties neither receive it nor give it, it is not composed of forms that are

already in our possession, but it is a new infusion made to the
mind. . . . Thus furnished and strengthened by the highest help, the
mind sees God. It does not accomplish this by *denying* or withdrawing
anything from Him, as when we say: God is not limited or finite.
Neither is it by *affirming* something of Him, attributing it to Him, as
when we say: God is good and wise. But it is by *regarding* the divine
greatness without any admixture of anything else, in the tranquility
of a calm day. Certainly, oh reader, when you see the light with
your bodily eyes, you do not arrive thereat by a comparison of
ideas, as when we say: "Light is not darkness" or "it is a quality."
You simply see light. In the same way the soul, in this degree of
contemplation, affirms nothing, denies nothing, attributes nothing,
avoids nothing, but in complete repose *she sees God.* It will be said:
This is astonishing, or rather unbelievable. For we take it as indispu-
table, that God is not seen here intuitively. If the soul does not see
God, how can we say, nevertheless, that she sees Him; and if she
sees Him, in what sense is it that she does not see Him? I admit that
it is astonishing. The fact, however, is very certain. . . .

In this supernatural manner the soul knows God in the depths of
her being, and *she sees Him,* so to say, more clearly than she sees the
material light with the eyes of the body. She sees God as being One
in three Persons, and she sees how the Father engenders the Son
eternally and without change. She sees that the Holy Spirit proceeds
from the Father and from the Son as from one sole principle; she
sees how these Persons are one sole nature and one sole substance,
and that they are infinitely alike and equal; and how these persons
dwell in the soul. . . . We see all these things and many others in
God, simultaneously, in one glance, just as you, reader, see instan-
taneously a friend's face as a whole, and at the same time, you see
his eyes and cheeks, his mouth and forehead. This sight [of God]
inflames the soul with a very ardent love.[20]

Alvarez says that in Rapture the soul sees God. But, he insists, this
does not mean that one makes some kind of *judgment*—affirming
something, denying something, attributing something to God,
such as that God is good or that God is a Trinity. What we see is
not some truth but the being, itself. The seeing is a simple act of
perception—as when one sees the light or when one sees the face of

20. Quoted in Poulain, *Graces of Interior Prayer,* 282 (pt. III, chap. XVIII, extracts).

a friend. He adds that although this is astonishing, astonishing it will just have to be.[21] Unfortunately, Alvarez does not address the case where what is seen is not God (or the Trinity or some specific member of the Trinity) but God's *power* or God's *wisdom*. I suspect, however, that here as well Alvarez would insist that "see" is a perception verb and is not to be converted into a cognition verb. But if this is right, then I think it must be added that spiritual sight defies the general claim that spiritual sense faculties work in ways that are "like" the operations of their bodily counterparts. While Angela's account of Rapture includes mention of a case of seeing that can be modeled on ordinary visual experience (her seeing of the Trinity), it also includes a range of other seeings that cannot be so modeled—at least in any way that I have so far been able to discover.

I started this section with a question: Given that the spiritual sense faculties work on the model of the bodily sense faculties and given the spatial pictures of the various states of union sketched in Chapter 1, which sense faculties would one antecedently expect to

21. In chaps. VII–XI of *A Literal Commentary on Genesis,* Augustine used the phrase "intellectual vision" to refer to a kind of mental state in which the mystic (visionary) *sees* in the sense of "understands." On Augustine's account, intellectual visions were cognitive events, instances of grasping *truths*. In the later tradition, however, the phrase "intellectual vision" comes to be used differently. Teresa was told by a spiritual adviser that the experience reported in chap. XXVII of *Life* and, again, in Sixth Mansions, chap. VI, of *Interior Castle* was an intellectual vision. As we shall see in detail in Section 3 of Chapter 7, this experience was plainly a *perceptual* experience and not a case of mere understanding. Teresa said that she "saw," that is, "perceived," Christ in physical space, just off her right hand. The object so detected was God "in his *Humanity*," that is, the man Jesus, who has physical form though in this case was not visible to the physical eyes. In modern Christian mystical theological texts, this experience is almost always used as the teaching case when the notion of intellectual vision is introduced. Now, I mention all this because (and alas) the phrase "intellectual vision" is also used in some modern theological texts to cover the visual-like presentations we are now discussing, that is, the perceptions obtained by the spiritual sense of sight in Rapture—see, e.g., Poulain, *Graces of Interior Prayer,* 249ff. And, of course, this is likely to cause confusion, since these last-mentioned perceptions are very different from the one discussed by Teresa. In these cases, the object (allegedly) seen is God in his *Divinity* (a pure spirit, which does not have bodily form), and the object in question does not have location in physical space. Still, for the reasons just given, it seems clear that the "see" that goes with intellectual visions of this latter sort should be understood as a perception verb (as in Teresa) and not as a cognition verb (as in Augustine).

be operative in the Prayer of Quiet, the Prayer of Full Union, and Rapture, respectively? It seems to me that the accounts we have traced for each of these states have placed the operations of spiritual hearing, tasting, smelling, and touching pretty much where we would have guessed, given only the format indicated. The spiritual sense of sight, however, is a maverick. For one thing (as mentioned earlier), since sight is a distance sense, the model of the bodily sense faculties would lead one to expect that it would be operative in the Prayer of Quiet, where God is pictured as being at a distance from soul$^+$. It turns out, however, that in the Prayer of Quiet, soul$^+$ is visually inactive and that it is only in Rapture that this spiritual sense faculty comes fully into play. This last is, itself, a further surprise—again allowing the model to determine expectations. Why should it be that the analogue of a distance sense should be especially busy in a situation where the object perceived is not at a distance but is, instead, smothering and saturating the perceiver? This is just the circumstance in which one would expect the eyes to be closed. Then, of course, there is still the matter of the objects detected—the fact that via spiritual sight one sees such things as the power, will, and goodness of God. Where it is God's "whisper" that is heard and God's "sweet perfume" that is smelled, that could have been expected. But where it is God's *power* or his *will* or his *goodness* that is seen, that must be regarded as yet another of the items for which the model of the bodily senses provides no real preparation.

4. A Closing Observation

In a passage quoted in the opening section of this chapter, Jacques Nouet suggested that while theologians generally agree concerning the number and nature of the spiritual sense faculties, they do not agree as to which of the five is most important. Nouet says that some hold out for the spiritual sense of tact, while others give preference to the spiritual sense of taste. I think we can see why these would be the most promising options. We have noticed that tact is involved in all three states of union, though it is fully operative only in the two higher states, where contact has been made between God and soul$^+$. By way of the sense of touch, God is then detected both on the outside and on the inside. It thus reveals both submersion and penetration, that is, both of the spatial elements required for the double embrace. On the other hand, we have also seen that the spiritual sense of taste plays a very specialized role in the perceptual scheme connected with the states of union. Its function presupposes the most intimate of the positions God assumes in the Prayer of Full Union and Rapture. Thus one can understand why (as Nouet points out) Thomas Aquinas would give the nod to touch and why other theologians would do so as well, as in the following passage from volume I, book III, chapter VI, of the *Treatise on the Love of God* by the seventeenth-century Jesuit theologian Father Jean-Joseph Surin: "For the spiritual senses, tact is the most delicate, although of the corporeal senses it is the most gross. This *experience* of God gives a perception of Him which is more exquisite and which approaches Him more nearly than any other thing can do; and even the Blessed, who see God, find the fullness of their felicity in that they *touch Him and Possess Him.*"[22] Still, one can see, too, why some would opt for taste as the principal sense faculty of the spiritual life. In his *Commentaries on the Psalms* (Ps. 33) even Aquinas (as tact man) says: "In bodily things we first see and then we taste; but in spiritual things, taste comes before sight. Unless he taste, none knoweth. And this is why it is said: O taste; and then: see."[23]

22. Quoted in Poulain, *Graces of Interior Prayer,* 106 (pt. II, chap. VI, extracts).
23. Quoted in Poulain, *Graces of Interior Prayer,* 100 (pt. II, chap. VI, extracts).

[4]
God as Lover
and Mother

In this chapter I shall first present and then discuss two meta-phors that, though widely used by Christian mystics when dis-cussing the various states of union, do not fit well with standard Christian ways of thinking about God. The first centers on the idea that God is a bridegroom who takes the soul of the mystic as his bride in sexual embrace—the so-called "bridal metaphor." The second invites us to think of God as a mother who suckles the soul of the mystic at her breast. Since this second image has not been given a name in the secondary literature, I shall refer to it with one of my own—the "nursery metaphor." My discussion of these two metaphors will bring to a close that portion of the present essay devoted to the gathering of data concerning the Christian mystical notion of union with God. It is offered both as a summary and as an expansion of the materials already in hand.

1. My Soul the Bride

The Song of Songs is a short love poem in which the principal figure is a young woman who speaks tenderly, indeed, passion-ately, of her absent lover while anxiously awaiting his return. It is hard to believe that the author of the poem intended to convey anything other than the feelings and tender longings therein expressed. And since it does not contain anything that appears on the surface to have specifically religious significance, it is also hard to imagine why this piece should have been included in the Christian Bible. The history of the matter provides no very satisfying explanation. The Song was included in the Jewish canon by the Synod of Jamnia (c. A.D. 100). Such texts were more or less automatically retained as canon literature when the Christian movement took form. But, as I say, this is not very satisfying; one wonders why a love poem, however touching, should have been chosen for inclusion among the sacred books of the Jewish religion. The answer is, apparently, that this poem was seen as a vehicle by which might be expressed the special relationship between God (the Bridegroom) and the Jewish Nation (the Bride). In the hands of succeeding generations of Christians, the relationship in question was between Christ (the Bridegroom) and the Church collective (the Bride). In this last-mentioned context, three themes in particular seem to have been of special interest: (1) as the absent king in the Song is the acknowledged head of his lover's household, so Christ is the acknowledged head of the Church collective; (2) as the absent king in the Song is the object of respect, honor, and, above all, adoration, so Christ is the object of such attitudes and emotions for those in the Church; and (3) as the Bride of the Song anxiously awaits the return of her lover with faith that he will not forsake her, so the Church collective awaits Christ's return to earth with complete assurance but with deep and passionate longing. That these were the messages officially found in the text is readily apparent in the King James Version of the Bible, where each of the eight chapters making up the text is supplemented with a heading explaining the religious significance of the verses to follow. It is interesting to note that these headings were not part of the original; nor were they felt to be necessary by those who put together the Jewish or the original Christian canon. It would appear that it was only when the Bible was to be translated into a vulgar tongue that need was felt to guard against the surface (call it the "vulgar") meaning of the text.

If one were to judge solely on the basis of the primary literature of the Christian mystical tradition, one would suppose that the Song of Songs is, by far, the most important book contained in either the Old or New Testament. Bernard of Clairvaux wrote a lengthy and detailed commentary on the text consisting of eighty-one sermons in all. Two of the most provocative poems written by John of the Cross are staged as literary imitations of the biblical text: his commentaries on these poems are generally counted as two of his four major works on mystical theology.[1] And these are but two cases. In fact, it is hard to find a mystic of stature in the Christian mystical tradition who has failed to utilize the text in one way or another—either by commenting on its meaning or, at least, by employing its rich and abundant imagery. On this last point, in this literature the terms "Bridegroom" and "Spouse" function almost universally as names—actually nicknames—of God. In most cases, no explanation is offered. It is simply assumed that the reader will make the appropriate associations.

In the context of the Christian mystical literature, however, there are two differences between the way in which the imagery of the Song is developed and the way it is officially interpreted by the Church. First, while Christ (or God) is still pictured as the Bridegroom whose return is anxiously awaited by the Bride, the individual soul of the mystic takes the place of the Church collective as the female figure in the picture. And second, in the hands of the mystics, the sensual imagery evident in the book itself is exploited much more openly than it is in the official interpretation. Though the erotic "kiss of the mouth" asked for by the Bride is still regarded as an image, it is clear in the primary mystical literature that it is not a *mere* figure—it becomes a metaphor worked so closely that at times it is hard to remember that it is not intended in a straightforward, literal way. I'll elaborate these two themes a bit further.

According to Dean Inge, in appendix D of his well-known work *Christian Mysticism,* the notion of the spiritual marriage between God and the individual soul made its entrance into Western mystical thought from the Greek mystery cults by way of the Alexandrian Jews and the Gnostics (369–72). It appears in Origen's commentaries on the Song and can be found, as well, in the writings of Augustine, Tertullian, Hilary, and a number of other early

1. I refer here to John's *Spiritual Canticle* and its sequel, *Living Flame of Love.*

Christian thinkers. In his very instructive text *Western Mysticism,* Dom Cuthbert Butler adds that the idea of the consecrated virgin considered as the "spouse of Christ" was a very early Christian concept found, for example, in Cyprian and is still very much a part of standard Christian thought. Butler also points out that the first to give expression to the features of the mystical experience in categories also applicable to human love was Plotinus but that it is largely due to the influence of Bernard of Clairvaux that the specific imagery of the Song came to be widely employed by Christian mystics (110). Looking, then, at Bernard's sermons on the Song with special attention, we find that Bernard, when explicitly commenting on the matter, usually identifies the figure of the Bride in accordance with the official Church interpretation—she is the Church collective. In the same texts, however, when the bridal imagery is actually put to work, the Bride seems clearly to be the individual soul of the mystic. It was the latter idea that connected importantly with the earlier traditions just mentioned and that also survived in the subsequent mystical literature. In the writings of Ruysbroeck, Suso, Tauler, Blosius, Teresa, John of the Cross, and a host of other post-Bernardian mystics, the Bride of the Song is unmistakably the soul of the individual mystic—called by John the "Bride-Soul"[2] and almost always referred to in mystical texts using the feminine pronoun "she." Here even the pretense that "she" stands for the Church collective has entirely disappeared.

It is said that Saint Jerome once advised a friend that for the good of his daughter, he ought to forbid her to look upon her own nakedness and ought also to encourage her to master Chronicles and Kings before turning to the study of the Song of Songs. Otherwise, he said, she might fail to observe that the love given expression in the Canticle is spiritual love—love between God and his Church—and not the sensuous love of the sexual embrace between lovers. A warning of this sort was issued by Saint Bernard as well. In sermon 61 of his *Sermons on the Canticle of Canticles,* he says, "Take heed that you bring chaste ears to this discourse of love; and when you think of these two lovers, remember always that not a man and a woman are to be thought of, but the Word of

---

2. See, for example, John, *Spiritual Canticle,* 358 (stanzas xx and xxi).

God and a soul."[3] Yet in Bernard's own writings on the Song, the passionate flavor of the original often breaks through as it does, for example, in this passage from sermon 31: "And then the soul knows that the Lord is at hand, when it feels itself consumed in that fire, and it says, with the prophet: 'from above hath He sent fire into my bones' and again: 'My heart was hot within me, and while I was musing the fire burned forth.'"[4] And as the mystical tradition of the West developed, the language of passionate love came more and more to be used. To take but a single case, the works of Henry Suso are filled with outcries such as this one from chapter 3 of *The Soul's Love Book:* "What, my Beloved, you realization of all my desires, what, my beloved Lord, should I say to you while I am struck dumb with love? My heart is full of loving thoughts, if only my tongue could express them! What I experience is bottomless; what I love is endless; and therefore, what I want to say is wordless. You are my King, you are my Lord, you are my Love, you are my joy, you are my hour of gladness."[5] Then again, paging through just one of the chapters in Suso's *Little Book of Eternal Wisdom,* one finds:

> The Servant Speaks: Ah, gentle Lord, my heart pines, my spirit yearns, my whole soul longs to hear you tell me of your love. Speak, then, my only chosen Consoler, one little word to the soul of your lowly handmaiden whose heart is wakeful while she sleeps in your shadow.

> Answer of Eternal Wisdom: Hearken, my daughter, and see; incline your ears toward me, convert yourself thoroughly as to forget yourself and all creatures. . . . If a man were to remain in a blazing furnace until the last day just in order to get one glimpse of me, he would not have deserved to look at my clear eyes, my gentle mouth, my rose-tinted cheeks, and my person so comely and perfect in every respect. . . .

> The Servant responds: Ah, tender, lovely flower of the field, you are my heart's only treasure. These truths are familiar to the enam-

3. Quoted in Butler, *Western Mysticism,* 97.
4. Quoted in Butler, *Western Mysticism,* 103.
5. In Suso, *The Exemplar,* 344.

ored soul of anyone who has ever experienced your love in a spiritual embrace. . . . Alas, what a sad prodigy, that anyone could
look at you with the eyes of his heart and not feel himself melting
with love! Ah, what bliss to be invited to your nuptials![6]

The following passage from book vi, chapter xiv, of Jacques
Nouet's *Conduct of the Man of Prayer* needs little in the way of
interpretation. Nouet is describing the moment in which God and
the soul are embraced in what he calls "unitive love," that is (I
think), the state of Full Union.

> God, who was formerly in the soul of the just *as a hidden treasure,* by
> way of sanctifying grace, now presents Himself to her as *a Treasure
> that is found.* He enlightens her, He *touches* her, He *embraces* her, He
> *penetrates* her, He flows into her faculties, *He gives Himself to her,* He
> *fills her* with the fullness of His Being. The soul, in return, ravished
> by His charms and by the spectacle of His beauty, *holds Him, em-
> braces Him, clasps Him* closely, and, all on fire with love, she flows,
> she plunges, she buries and loses herself deliciously in God with
> sentiments of inconceivable joy.[7]

Meister Eckhart once said: "'Woman' is the most noble word one
can apply to the soul, more noble than 'virgin.'"[8]

Why should it be that mystics of the Christian tradition regularly model the mystical encounter on the image of carnal love
and desire? Dean Inge suggests an answer. He says that the "highest" and "lowest" emotions in man lie very close together and thus
are easily confused. He says that one must be constantly on guard
against the "occasional revenges" of the lower nature against the
higher.[9] The bridal imagery is thus dismissed by him as a "morbid
emotionalism that disfigures the writings of many mystics."[10] It is
a "mischief" introduced into the literature by Origen[11] which has
been sustained by the misdirection of the lower emotions. Much

6. In Suso, *The Exemplar,* 28–31.
7. Quoted in Poulain, *Graces of Interior Prayer,* 111 (pt. II, chap. vi, extracts).
8. Quoted in Zaehner, *Mysticism,* 151.
9. Inge, *Christian Mysticism,* 372.
10. Inge, *Studies of the English Mystics,* 74.
11. Inge, *Christian Mysticism,* 370.

this same verdict, though in a slightly more sophisticated form, is issued by Walter Stace in his text *Mysticism and Philosophy*. Following the early-twentieth-century psychologist J. H. Leuba, Stace suggests that the sexual imagery utilized in the mystical literature is probably best explained as resulting from sexual frustrations on the part of mystics, many of whom were celibate priests and nuns. What Stace calls the "hyperemotionalism" thereby displayed is, as he says, "an unpalatable characteristic" of the Christian mystical literature, "tending to show lack of balance, good judgement and critical ability." Stace generously adds, however, that this hyperemotionalism "is no more objectionable than the unwashed and dirty habits notoriously indulged in by some medieval saints" (53–54).

Whatever might be one's own view concerning the morality of the matter, these comments by Inge and Stace seem to me to underscore at least one point of interest. Though Christian morality has run both hot and cold as regards the status of human sex appetites, the underlying tendency has been to think of them as symptomatic of humankind's low and fallen nature. Perhaps extreme, though not so far removed as to be unrecognizable, is the view of Jacob Boehme, who held not only that the sexual appetite is evidence of man's depraved and degenerate condition but that all animals are "ashamed" of their genitals and of their method of reproduction; this is why they hide themselves from others when engaging in sexual intercourse.[12] Given this general disposition of the cultural attitude, it would seem surprising that the mystics, who were themselves subject to the same tradition and who, for the most part, regarded themselves as strict followers of orthodox opinion, would choose the bridal metaphor as a means of expression in the present context. The mystical encounter is thought by them to be the highest and finest experience one can have short of the beatific vision of God that will come in the next life. Didn't they, themselves, feel some discrepancy here? Wouldn't they be inclined to ask themselves the question put by Paul Elmer More in his text *Christian Mysticism?* "Is it wise, is it delicate, so to mingle the divine and the human loves in a metaphor? Is it really quite

12. Passages from Boehme's writings on this topic are nicely collected in Hartmann, *Personal Christianity*, 195–203.

decent to deck the Uranian Aphrodite in the seductive garments of her Pandemian sister?" (53)

2. My Soul the Nursling

The following passage is from chapter 31 of Saint Teresa's *Way of Perfection*.

> Pay great attention to the following comparison, which *the Lord suggested to me when I was in this state of prayer, and which* seems to me very appropriate. The soul is like an infant still at its mother's breast: such is the mother's care for it that she gives it its milk without its having to ask for it so much as by moving its lips. That is what happens here. The will simply loves, and no effort needs to be made by the understanding, for it is the Lord's pleasure that, without exercising its thought, the soul should realize that it is in His company, and should merely drink the milk which His Majesty puts into its mouth and enjoy its sweetness. (205–6)

We are here being asked to think of the soul as an infant nursing at the breast of its mother. Teresa is obviously partial to the "comparison"—she says that it was suggested to her by God himself. God *himself* . . . but, of course, that's the catch. Though the fatherhood of God is a familiar idea to those steeped in Christian imagery, how often does the *motherhood* of God play a role in traditional Christian thinking? There are a number of mothers in standard pageantry—Mother Mary, Mother Church, Mother Superior. But how about *Mother Christ* or, more pointedly, *Mother Jesus?* Consider the following two passages from chapter 58 and chapter 60, respectively, of Julian of Norwich's *Revelations of Divine Love:*

> In our mother Christ we grow and develop; and in his mercy he reforms and restores us; through his passion, death, and resurrection he has united us to our being. So does our Mother work in mercy for all his children who respond to him and obey him. (166)

> The human mother may put her child tenderly to her breast, but our tender Mother Jesus simply leads us into his blessed breast through

his open side, and there gives us a glimpse of the Godhead and
heavenly joy—the inner certainty of eternal bliss. (170)

One can't help but respect Teresa's claim that the nursery metaphor (as I am calling it) came to her from an outside source. Like
the bridal metaphor, it is not a customary Christian image. In fact,
in this case, the image stands in sharp contrast to standard ways of
thinking about God. Note the gender jangle in the last two quoted
passages, which results from Julian's assignment of a mother role
to a male figure. *Mother* Jesus leads the infant soul to *his* blessed
breast: the *mother* works in mercy for *his* children: In our *mother* we
grow and develop; in *his* mercy *he* reforms and restores us. The
same jangle is only slightly less apparent in the passage with which
we started from Teresa's *Way of Perfection. His* Majesty is the one
whose milk flows into the mouth of the soul.

Speaking to God of those enjoying the Prayer of Full Union, in
part II, chapter VII, of his *Instructions in the Ascetic Life,* Venerable
Blosius says this: "What see they, what hear they, *what do they
perceive by way of the sense of smell, taste and otherwise?* No tongue
can express it. The tender *embraces,* the delicate kisses that a mother
gives to her dear child or the bridegroom to his beloved bride, are
but the feeble image and shadow of those that Thou bestowest
upon the chaste soul that loves thee."[13] In this passage, the nursery
metaphor is juxtaposed with the bridal metaphor in such a way as
to suggest that the two are, as it were, pictorially equivalent as
regards their facility to provide an image of the mystical moment.
Such juxtaposition is common in the mystical literature more generally. For example, stanza XXVII of John's *Spiritual Canticle* reads
as follows:

> There he gave me His breast;
> There He taught me a science most delectable;
> And I gave myself to him indeed, reserving nothing;
> There I promised him to be his bride. (407)

In the introduction to the detailed commentary on this stanza, John
of the Cross identifies the setting as one in which God and the soul

13. Quoted in Poulain, *Graces of Interior Prayer,* 110 (pt. II, chap. VI, extracts).

are in "interior union" (Full Union) and in which God addresses the soul in a "communication of love." He continues:

> And even so He (God) is here employed in cherishing and caressing the soul, as is the mother in serving and caressing her child, and nursing it at her breast; wherein the soul knows the truth of the saying of Isaiah, where he says: "To the breast of God you shall be brought and upon His knees shall you be caressed.
>
> What, then, will the feelings of the soul be here among such sovereign favours? How it will melt with love! How thankful will it be when it sees this breast of God opened to it with such wide and sovereign love! Conscious of being set among so many delights, it surrenders itself to Him wholly and gives Him also the breasts of its own will and love, for it feels it passing in its soul, in the same way as the Bride felt it in the Songs, where she speaks with her Spouse after this manner: "I to my Beloved and His turning is toward me. Come, my Beloved, let us go forth into the field, let us lodge together in the villages; let us get up early in the morning to the vineyards and see if the vineyard has flourished and if the flowers are bringing forth fruit; if the pomegranates have flourished."

Here the nursery metaphor appears to be the primary model of the union state. But as the passage unfolds, this first representation is clarified by use of the bridal image. The latter is thus used to sharpen and reenforce the former. Of course, at this point we are only one step away (if at all) from the case in which the two metaphors are mixed together into a single picture. This is what happens in the following passage from chapter IV of Teresa's *Conceptions of the Love of God*.

> But when this most wealthy Spouse desires to enrich and comfort the Bride still more, He draws her so closely to Him that she is like one who swoons from excess of pleasure and joy and seems suspended in those Divine arms and drawn near to that sacred side and to those Divine breasts. Sustained by that Divine milk with which her Spouse continually nourishes her and growing in grace so that she may be enabled to receive His comforts, she can do nothing but rejoice. . . . With what to compare this [the soul] knows not, save to the caress of a mother who so dearly loves her child and feeds and caresses it. (384–85)

The soul—here amply identified as a female figure—feeds at the breast of her "wealthy Spouse." Note, again, the gender jangle created when the Spouse of the Bride (obviously a male figure) is then identified as the one at whose *breasts* she is suckled. But the final image is even more deeply bizarre than this. The nurse is not only a male, he is also the husband, that is, the *lover,* of the child who feeds at his breasts.

3. Metaphorical Overlap

Three curiosities emerge from the preceding two sections. First, given the low status traditionally assigned to human sexuality, it is strange to find the bridal metaphor used at all as a model for the union embrace. Second, that the soul should be portrayed as a child cared for and nurtured by a divine parent fits well with standard imagery of the Christian tradition, but that the parent in question should be a mother, rather than a father, must surely be regarded as a pictorial divergence not easily reconciled with the imagery encouraged by ordinary Christian training. That the bridal metaphor and the nursery metaphor should be treated by the mystics who employ them as virtually interchangeable, I offer as the third in my list of curiosities. Though there are no doubt similarities between the sex act and the act of feeding at the breast, these are very different kinds of encounters presupposing very different kinds of relationship between the principals involved. I turn now to the task of rendering this list of curiosities a little less curious. I'll start by simply listing five theses, all of which were established in earlier chapters of this book.

1. In Full Union and in the culmination stage of Rapture, God and the soul are in mutual embrace. The soul is submerged and penetrated by God (my soul the sponge).

2. With respect to the states of union generally, a wide variety of spiritual sensations are involved, but in Full Union and in the culmination stage of Rapture, the emphasis is on the spiritual sensations of touch and taste. As regards the spiritual sensation of touch, God is felt both on the outside and on the inside. We might call this the "epistemic corollary" of the idea that in the two "highest" states of union God both enwraps and penetrates the substance of the soul.

3. Union states generally are regarded as "supernatural"—meaning by this that they are imposed or, as is said, "infused" by God and are not to be thought of as achievements on the part of the experiencing mystic. This point was emphasized in connection with our discussion of the Prayer of Quiet in the first section of Chapter 1. And though I did not take pains to underline it in our discussions of the other two states of union, these, too, are regarded as "supernatural" in this sense. With respect to Rapture, for example, Teresa says she was raised into the air. Teresa did not herself fly—she was *raised,* as by an eagle. The same is true of Marina Escobar. She did not *get herself* to the vault above the heavens. She was *carried* there by a host of angels. This same point comes out in Teresa's various discussions of the "irresistibility" of both Rapture and Full Union.

4. All three of the states of union are accompanied by positive emotional reactions on the part of the experiencing mystic. "Bliss" is the term that most readily comes to mind with respect to the Prayer of Quiet, Full Union, and nonviolent ecstasy such as is reported by Saint Francis de Sales. In Rapture (violent ecstasy), however, the positive emotions involved are not bliss and peace but excitement, passion, and involvement with another.

5. Full Union and Rapture sometimes reach a mystical peak where involvement with God becomes so intimate that the experiencing mystic loses track of the distinction between self and God. This is what Ruysbroeck refers to as "the union without distinction."

In the sexual embrace, the bride is typically covered by her mate. She is then enwrapped by him and submerged beneath him. He penetrates her as well—he saturates her with his issue. Her sensations are various. She smells his breath and hears his breathing and sweet whispers. But the love act is most importantly associated with its massive tactile element. She feels her mate in contact with the outside of her body. She also feels him on the inside. Third, and dealing for the moment with the commonplace image of the sexual encounter, the female is the receiver of the action. The male initiates and sustains the act—her action is reaction. Of course, this is only the commonplace image—a caricature. But the caricature is what is important: the image is here being employed for purposes of emphasis. As for the emotional tone of the sexual encounter, that can vary. Sometimes it is bliss. More frequently, the mood is one of excitement and passion. In either case, however, involvement with another can become so intense and the relationship so close as to result in a loss of the distinction between oneself and one's partner. This last-mentioned phenomenon is not usual but characterizes rare moments of sexual love at its best. Martin Buber makes note of this in part 3, section 6, of *I and Thou*.

> Those human beings may serve as a metaphor who in the passion of erotic fulfillment are so carried away by the miracle of the embrace that all knowledge of I and You drowns in the feeling of a unity that neither exists nor can exist. What the ecstatic calls unification is the rapturous dynamic of the relationship; not a unity that has come into being at this moment in world time, fusing I and You, but the dynamics of the relationship itself which can stand before the two carriers of this relationship, although they confront each other immovably, and cover the eyes of the enraptured. What we find here is a marginal exorbitance of the act of relation: the relationship itself in its vital unity is felt so vehemently that its members pale in the process: its life predominates so much that the I and the You between whom it is established are forgotten. This is one of the phenomena that we find on the margins where actuality becomes blurred. (135)

Buber's words could easily have been written by Ruysbroeck or Bernard. At the mystical peak, identity between God and (in their words) the "inebriated soul" is "felt so vehemently" that it "blurs" the final reality, which is, of course, duality.

At the moment of feeding, the child is wrapped in its mother's arms and pressed closely to her body. It is submerged in its mother's embrace. The child takes the breast into its mouth. It is thus penetrated both by the mother and by her milk. As for the sensations involved, they are various (for example, the child hears her soft words delivered in tender tones), but outside and inside tactile sensations are probably the ones that dominate. Here, too (and for the first time), sensations of taste come into play. The outward and inward touches are accompanied by the sweet taste of the milk. Third, while the child can ask for (cry for) and anticipate the feeding, the child is fed by the mother. She initiates the action and it lasts only as long as she chooses to stay. But, and alas, there is one way in which this last thesis fails. The child must suck and swallow; it is thus not entirely a passive receiver in the encounter. Interestingly, Teresa herself took note of this discrepancy and corrected the nursery image accordingly. In the paragraph following the one quoted above from chapter 31 of *The Way of Perfection,* she said that in Full Union (as opposed to the Prayer of Quiet) the Lord "places" the milk directly into the stomach of the child. No action on the child's part is thus required. As for emotional tone, "bliss" would appear to cover it. And what about the loss of the sense of distinction? Well, maybe that is just too hard to say.

Considered individually, the bridal metaphor and the nursery metaphor each function as presentational devices whereby the mystic can give expression and direct attention to a rather wide range of the salient features of the several states of union. Already, I think, this removes at least some of the mystery as to why these metaphors should be favored by those whose writings we are studying. When considered within the context of the Christian tradition generally, these metaphors seem strained and awkward. But when considered within the narrower context of the specific literature in which they occur, they appear more as working components than as unannounced intruders. Further, not only does each of these metaphors carry a message of importance both to and from the Christian mystical community, the message they carry is at least in part the same. It is important to see that there is what might be called metaphorical or pictorial "overlap" here. It is because of this overlap that Blosius could intelligibly stand these two metaphors side by side, suggesting that they are interchangeable images. It explains, too, how John could use one of them (the bridal metaphor) to clarify a point he was at the time making with the other. Surely, it was this overlap that Teresa was utilizing when she mingled the figure of the Spouse from the bridal metaphor with the figure of the Mother from the nursery metaphor and emerged with the exquisite image of the Lover-Mother presented in chapter IV of *The Conceptions of Divine Love.* Of course, this is not to suggest that the bridal metaphor and the nursery metaphor are in fact pictorially equivalent. For one thing, the bridal image is more versatile than the nursery image as regards

its ability to convey variations of emotional tone. Bliss goes with
both, but passion and excitement go only with the former. In the
next section I shall explore a feature of the nursery metaphor that
renders it the more versatile of the two on another count. Still, it is
in a way surprising to discover how much detail concerning the
various states of union is carried by each of these metaphors individually as well as how parallel they are as regards the message
they deliver. When looked at from this perspective, their juxtaposition in the mystical literature is not nearly as enigmatic as it
might at first have appeared.

4. Spiritual Nourishment

In the preceding section I focused on themes developed in the
mystical literature on union that are conveyed with equal facility
by both the bridal metaphor and the nursery metaphor. In explicat-
ing these two images, I thus stressed what I referred to above as
the metaphorical "overlap" between the two. Now, however, I
want to call attention to a way in which the nursery metaphor is
used in the mystical literature that has no counterpart in the case of
the bridal metaphor. The nursery metaphor is richer in content
than has so far been suggested. I want to identify the residue before
bringing this discussion to a close.

I'll start by looking again—this time more closely—at the passage I quoted at the beginning of the second section of this chapter
from chapter 31 of Teresa's *Way of Perfection*. So as to have it before
us, here is most of it again.

> The soul is like an infant still at its mother's breast: such is the
> mother's care for it that she gives it its milk without its having to
> ask for it so much as by moving its lips. That is what happens here
> . . . for it is the Lord's pleasure that . . . the soul should realize that
> it is in His company, and should merely drink the milk which His
> Majesty puts into its mouth and enjoy its sweetness.

God is a mother. But, as the metaphor is developed in this passage,
the emphasis is *not* on the idea that the mother enwraps and penetrates the child. Teresa seems to be entirely occupied with the

thought that the soul is the passive receiver of a certain benefit we are here encouraged to classify as a kind of *nourishment*. Now, for purposes of contrast, consider the following passage which Poulain attributes to The Blessed Curé d'Ars in the extract section of part II, chapter VI, of *The Graces of Interior Prayer:* "The inner life is a bath of love into which the soul plunges. She is, as it were, drowned in love. God holds the inner man as a mother holds her infant's head between her hands, to cover it with *kisses and caresses*" (112). Again, God is a mother. But this time the mother is exclusively an embracer, a kisser, a caresser—the one in whose arms the child is "bathed" and "drowned." There is no hint of the idea that the mother is one who provides some kind of nourishment. What we have here, I think, are two quite distinct *developments* of the nursery metaphor. That they are distinct is, perhaps, not immediately obvious. Let me see if I can make this point a little clearer.

As the Bride of God, soul⁺ is the recipient of a definite benefit. She is embraced and loved by her tender and attentive lover. But note, the same goes in the other direction. As the Bridegroom of soul⁺, God is also the receiver of a definite benefit. He, too, is embraced and loved by his submissive and adoring Bride. God benefits too!? Of course. In stanzas XXX–XXXV of *Spiritual Canticle,* John of the Cross says that the "Bride-Soul" is "wounded" and "captivated"—that is, made "prisoner"—by God's love. The soul gives thanks to God for the gift she receives. But, John says, God too is "wounded" and "captivated"—that is, made "prisoner"—by the love received from the soul. Appropriately enough, God also gives thanks to the soul for the gift he receives (434–36). What John has noticed, I think, is that the mutual embrace of union is, indeed, *mutual* embrace and that the bridal metaphor carries the pictorial implication of *equal* partners sharing *equally* the benefits of the love embrace. The equality of the benefits is stressed in the passages just mentioned. That the image of the Bride is intended to picture the soul as God's equal in the embrace is framed quite explicitly in stanza XXVIII as follows: "For the property of love is to make the lover equal to the object loved. Wherefore, since its love is now perfect, the soul is called Bride of the Son of God, which signifies equality with Him" (411). Not surprisingly, John covers

the seemingly inappropriate overtones of this analysis by insisting
that it is God who is ultimately responsible for the fact that the soul
is his equal. He says that it is via his actions that she has come to
"merit being placed on an equality with Him even as a queen by
His side" (425–26). Still, insofar as she is his Bride, she is his equal.
Bride and Bridegroom are equal partners engaged in a symmetrical
exchange of delights.

When I stressed the metaphorical overlap between the bridal
metaphor and the nursery metaphor in the preceding section, one
of the items mentioned was that both images convey the idea of
mutual embrace. I should now like to add that insofar as the nursery embrace involves physical contact between the principals, the
nursery metaphor, like the bridal metaphor, carries the message of
a symmetrical exchange between equals—the exchange of love in
the form of touches, caresses, and kisses. But, of course, the nursery metaphor has more to it than that. In fact, what seems clearly
to be its dominant message has not yet been scratched and appears
to have nothing to do with a symmetrical exchange between
equals. The mother is not just the child's embracer, she is also its
feeder—that is, more broadly, its *nurturer,* or, in a word, its *sustainer*. In this respect, the child is not an equal of the mother nor
does it give a gift to the mother that correlates with the one received. Here the nursery image is developed in such a way as to
exceed its metaphorical "overlap" with the bridal image. God as
Mother-Embracer is a pictorial near-equivalent of God as Bridegroom of the soul. It is thus in this development that the nursery
metaphor can be used as a virtual alternative to the bridal metaphor
as it is in the passage quoted in section 2 of this chapter from
Blosius. But God as Mother-Sustainer is another figure altogether—one who cannot be identified with the Bridegroom. She is an
asymmetrical giver in relationship with an utterly dependent partner. This is the nursery metaphor as it is developed in the passage
from Teresa's *Way of Perfection* quoted at the beginning of both this
and the preceding sections. Of course, God portrayed as *both*
Mother-Embracer *and* Mother-Sustainer also appears. When this
happens the nursery metaphor does double duty. Mother is then
the Embracer (that is, the near-equivalent of the Bridegroom) as
well as the Sustainer: The soul of the mystic is then the receiver of

two distinct gifts—one from the Embracer, which it symmet-
rically returns, and a second from the Sustainer, which it can only
gratefully enjoy. Note that this is how the "wealthy Spouse" from
chapter IV of Teresa's *Conceptions of Divine Love* came to be fitted
out with the breasts used to feed his infant Bride. Teresa first
identified the Bridegroom with Mother-Embracer—an easy meta-
morphosis either way. But once he was established as her Mother,
Teresa then felt free to call on him to "nourish" and "feed" as well
as to "comfort" and "caress" his adoring Bride.[14]

It might at first seem peculiar that Teresa introduced the nursery
metaphor in chapter 31 of *The Way of Perfection,* where the discussion was specifically devoted to explaining the features of the
Prayer of Quiet. After all, the Prayer of Quiet is the one union
state in which God and the soul of the mystic are *not* in mutual
embrace and thus are not in a relation similar to the one involved
when the mother and child are nestled together in a moment of
feeding. If we attend to the distinction made in the last paragraph
between God as Mother-Embracer and God as Mother-Sustainer,
however, it seems to me that this apparent incongruity all but
completely disappears. In the passage under discussion, God is
portrayed in the figure of Mother-Sustainer: and in the Prayer of
Quiet—as in all three of the states of union—the soul of the mystic
is, presumably, the asymmetrical receiver of God's nurturing activity. Thus, the image works—the message fits—even though the
Prayer of Quiet does not involve the double embrace of Full Union
and Rapture. To be sure, God as Mother-Embracer may still be in
the shadows of Teresa's picture. Regardless of how it is specifically
developed, I suspect that neither Mother-Embracer nor Mother-
Sustainer is ever completely absent when the nursery metaphor is
used. But the point remains that Teresa has channeled the metaphor in such a way as to at least reduce the possibility of pictorial
confusion. Although God as Mother-Embracer may still be in the
background, it is God as Mother-Sustainer who is pushed to center
stage when the discussion concerns the Prayer of Quiet.

Before leaving this topic I want to comment very briefly on the

14. The relevant passage from Teresa's *Conceptions of the Love of God* is quoted
at the end of Section 2 above.

way in which the bridal metaphor and the nursery metaphor are worked together in the following very subtle passage from part III, chapter XXXIII, of the *Considerations Regarding the Exercise of Prayer* by the eighteenth-century mystical theologian Father Pierre Joseph Picot de Cloriviere. As in the passage just considered from Teresa, the subject under discussion (as will be obvious) is the Prayer of Quiet.

> When the soul presents herself at prayer, even if she should come to it with the design of occupying herself with some special subject, she at once finds herself, without knowing how, *recollected* within herself *with a sweet feeling of the presence* of Our Lord. This feeling, it is true, is not very distinct; but the *peace* of the sweetness that accompanies it convinces the soul that He whom she loves is *near*, that He *comes Himself* to give her proofs of His love, and that she should then think of nothing else than of the happiness that is offered her. [The soul is then] an infant half asleep upon its mother's knees, which, pressed against her breast, with scarcely any movement of the lips . . . receives the milk that flows gently into its mouth and becomes its sustenance. Saint Teresa and Saint Francis of Sales make use of this comparison. . . . Such is the soul's disposition in the prayer of quiet, feeling, although in a confused manner, that the celestial Bridegroom designs in a manner to *take her in His arms*. She dares aspire to a yet closer union, or, rather, it is the Bridegroom Himself who suggests this desire to her heart. . . . She then does nothing, she can do nothing else than rejoice in the blessing that she possesses.[15]

As in Teresa, the figure of the Mother is here developed as the Sustainer rather than the Embracer. But unlike the description given by Teresa, God as Embracer (in the form of the Bridegroom) is also at center stage even though the state under discussion is the Prayer of Quiet. Note how this is done. The nursery metaphor (suitably channeled) is fully deployed: the soul is portrayed as nursing at the breast of the Mother. But the bridal metaphor is utilized only in truncated form: the Bridegroom does not embrace, he only *designs* to embrace the adoring soul. Thus both God as Sustainer and God as Embracer are articulated elements of

15. Quoted in Poulain, *Graces of Interior Prayer,* 78 (pt. II, chap. V, extracts).

the picture even though the state under discussion is the Prayer of Quiet. The thing to see, however, is that the Embracer can be present without causing pictorial confusion only because he appears in the role of one whose usual function is yet to be performed in a future state, that is, in the state of Full Union to which the would-be Bride-Soul aspires. Perhaps interesting to see is that the whole thing could have been framed using only the double imagery of the nursery metaphor: in the Prayer of Quiet, God as Mother-Sustainer feeds the soul with a spoon while *designing* to embrace it someday at her breast. This image, too, puts both God the Sustainer and God the Embracer (in diminished form) at center stage. But, of course, this image lacks integrity: it would hardly count as more than a mere cartoon. It also lacks the delicately balanced moment in de Cloriviere's image when the Bridegroom fully "designs," while the retiring soul only "dares aspire to," the lover's embrace someday to be realized in Full Union.

5. A Closing Comment on God as Lover and Mother

Concerning the bridal metaphor, Paul Elmer More asked whether it is "decent" to suggest that union with God can be modeled as a sexual embrace. Although I don't know the answer to this question, I suspect that the bridal metaphor and the nursery metaphor are used in the classical mystical literature because they work, and it is not at all clear that, given the nature of the experiences under discussion, images any less vivid or any less complex would work anywhere near as well. This is true, I submit, in spite of the fact that both metaphors conflict in important ways with culturally determined expectations concerning the images by which God can be properly portrayed. Still, I would like to think that there may also be another reason why these two images are used. Our Greek heritage tells us that the intellect is a remarkable gift—the "highest" of our natural capacities. It seems to me, however, that no less remarkable is our ability to feel and to become passionately involved with another. Though these two capacities are very different, neither is less wondrous or more mundane than the other. As regards the writings of the Christian mystics, perhaps part of the intended message—and, if not, then surely one that can at least be gleaned—concerns the dignity and beauty of the passionate and sensuous elements of human life. What better vehicle of instruction than this: that the mystical encounter between God and the soul should be modeled on the two occasions in human experience where these very elements are most eloquently and yet most delicately displayed?

Walter Stace on "Union with God"

In section 11 of a book published in 1932 entitled *Christian Mysticism,* Paul Elmer More advanced the following thesis concerning the similarities and differences between mystical traditions of various cultures.

> There is thus a ground of psychological experience, potential in all men, actually realized in a few, common to all mystics of all lands and times and accountable for the similarity of their reports. But upon that common basis we need not be surprised to see them also erecting various superstructures in accordance with their particular tenets of philosophy or religion. At bottom, their actual experiences, at the highest point at least, will be amazingly alike, but their theories in regard to what has happened to them may be radically different. (93)

With respect to the "psychological experience" mentioned in the opening sentence of this passage, More maintains that its "phenomenal content" consists of being "swallowed up, for the most part only momentarily, in an abysmal sense of absolute unity" (89). It is, he says, "the ecstasy of unconscious oblivion," which is "utterly without content and therefore indescribable, incommunicable (and) ineffable" (93–94). This experience, More says, has been common to all mystics of "all lands and times." It has served as what he calls the "common basis" of all mystical traditions. More then goes on to claim, however, that although mystics from various cultures and from different religious backgrounds all agree concerning the nature of this "ultimate mystical state" (94), this experience, he says, "is variously interpreted in accordance with the particular religious beliefs of the time and place" (86). On this last point, More elaborates so:

> To Plotinus it will seem that in the mystic ascent the soul has retrod the path on which the universe, by a kind of mechanical necessity, descended from unity to multiplicity, and at the last loses herself in blissful reunion with the absolute source of all. A Çankara will explain the state of liberation not as a return to what has been left, but as a sudden awakening whereby the soul learns that she has never been what she has seemed to be nor cared for what has seemed to attract her, has always been that which she now knows herself to be, the infinite Reality detached from all finite illusions. To the Christian mystic on the contrary, the ecstasy of unconscious oblivion will become in memory a reunion with an infinite, loving and creative deity, operated by no power of the soul herself but by the infusion of divine grace. (93)

More concludes: "In this way we can explain the agreement of the mystics on certain fundamental facts together with their disagreement in detail of creed and practice" (86). Though all three—Neoplatonist, Vedantist, and Christian—begin with the same experience, "each of them, looking back upon the void after his return to consciousness, will use it to assert the truth of his peculiar philosophy or religion" (94).

More's theory concerning the source of the similarities and differences between mystical traditions of all lands and times has been developed in the contemporary literature on comparative mysticism by Walter Stace and has been defended in several papers by Ninian Smart as well. Both Stace and Smart introduce this theory by contrasting it with a thesis advanced in R. C. Zaehner's *Mysticism, Sacred and Profane,* namely, that there is a specifically *theistic* mystical phenomenon that is described by Christian mystics as the experience of "union with God." According to Stace and Smart, there is no specifically theistic mystical experience. The relevant underlying phenomenon is what Stace refers to as the "introvertive" mystical state. This is what Smart (following Zaehner) calls the "monistic" mystical experience; it is what More describes in one of the passages just cited as "the abysmal sense of absolute unity." Of course, there is nothing inherently *theistic* about this phenomenon. Stace and Smart maintain that it is described by Christian mystics as the experience of "union with God" only because they come to it antecedently committed to a theistic world picture and thus *interpret* the phenomenon as an experience of encounter with the Christian God. What is specifically theistic, therefore, is the way in which the experience is understood and thus described. This tells us nothing about what More calls the "phenomenal content" indigenous to the experience itself.

As a first step into my analysis of Christian mystical experiences of union I want to review this theory in some detail. Since the theory is now principally associated with Stace, I shall use the relevant parts of his various writings as my principal sources. The focus will thus be on chapter 2 of Stace's *Mysticism and Philosophy* (1960) and on the materials contained in the general introduction to his reader *The Teachings of the Mystics* (1960). My task in this chapter will be to explicate these materials as carefully as I can. I shall save critical comments for the next chapter.

1. The Introvertive Mystical State

The following passage is quoted by Stace from the Mandukya Upanishad. The author of the text has just distinguished three kinds of consciousness: waking consciousness, dreaming, and dreamless sleep.

> The Fourth, say the wise . . . is not knowledge of the senses, nor is it relative knowledge, nor yet inferential knowledge. Beyond the senses, beyond the understanding, beyond expression, is the Fourth. It is the pure unitary consciousness wherein awareness of the world and of multiplicity is completely obliterated. It is ineffable peace. It is the Supreme Good. It is One without a second. It is the Self.[1]

1. Stace, *Mysticism and Philosophy*, 88.

What is referred to in this passage as "the Fourth" is a state of consciousness that Stace calls "the introvertive mystical experience" or, sometimes, just "mystical consciousness." I want now to review what Stace has to say about the phenomenological features of this state.

In the normal case, the state of consciousness that goes with everyday waking life consists of sense images, thoughts, feelings, desires, emotions, volitions, and the like. Stace refers to this as "the sensory-intellectual consciousness." And, Stace tells us, the first thing to notice about mystical consciousness is that it is not like sensory-intellectual consciousness. Mystical consciousness involves no experiential elements of any of the kinds just mentioned. The Fourth is "not knowledge of the senses," it is "beyond the senses [and] beyond the understanding" as well. This point receives considerable attention in both of Stace's texts. In *Teachings of the Mystics* the point is framed as follows:

> Now the mystical consciousness is quite different from this [i.e., our ordinary sensory-intellectual consciousness]. It is not merely that it involves different kinds of sensations, thoughts or feelings. We are told that some insects or animals can perceive ultra-violet color and infrared color; and that some animals can hear sounds which are inaudible to us; even that some creatures may have a sixth sense quite different from any of our five senses. These are all, no doubt, kinds of sensations different from any we have. But they are still sensations. And the mystical consciousness is destitute of any sensations at all. Nor does it contain any concepts or thoughts. It is not sensory-intellectual consciousness at all. Accordingly, it cannot be described or analyzed in terms of any elements of the sensory-intellectual consciousness with which it is wholly incommensurable. (12–13)

It follows (Stace seems to think) that mystical consciousness is not consciousness of the world. To be aware of the world is to be aware of a multiplicity of objects (trees, thumbtacks, and the like) via sensations and thought. Since sensation and thought are herein excluded, it cannot be consciousness of the world. It follows further (Stace continues), that mystical consciousness is ineffable. As it is said in the passage quoted above from the Mandukya Upanishad, the Fourth is "beyond expression." Stace says that natural languages are "products" of the sensory-intellectual consciousness and can express only its elements or some combination of its elements.[2] Thus natural languages cannot be used to describe mystical consciousness. They are simply not set up to do the job.

If mystical consciousness is not consciousness of the world, what can be said about its experiential content? Stace's own theory is that what is experienced in mystical consciousness is something he calls "the Self."[3] Of course, it is not the self understood as a collection of sense perceptions, thoughts, pains, and so on, as in Hume. It is the self "stripped of all psychological content." Stace says, "It is the pure unity of the manifold of consciousness from which the manifold itself has been obliterated."[4] Stace points out, however, that this account of the matter is not to be taken as an unadorned report of what is directly given. That it is "the Self" that is experienced is a conclusion reached by inference. And though we are assured in the text that the inference in question is both "natural and justifiable," it must still be recognized for what it is.[5] Thus, this doesn't answer the question we are asking. Disregarding the speculative conclusion (however well justified), we want to know what it is that is directly and immediately experienced in the introvertive state.

There are numerous passages in both of Stace's texts in which it is claimed that the introvertive mystical experience is an awareness of "pure unity," "undifferentiated unity," "oneness," or "the One." The mind is emptied of sensations, thoughts, feelings, etc., and what is left is a simple awareness of unity. Still, in the end, this, too, is rejected by Stace as an answer to the question we are pursuing. I'll take time here to review the reasoning by which these answers are dismissed.

As quoted by Stace, Plotinus writes as follows in *Enneads* VI, IX, and XI:

No doubt we should not speak of seeing, but, instead of seen and seer, speak boldly of simple unity. For in this seeing we neither distinguish nor are there two. The man . . . is merged with the

2. Stace, *Teachings of the Mystics*, 13.
3. Stace, *Mysticism and Philosophy*, 161 and 178.
4. Stace, *Mysticism and Philosophy*, 86.
5. Stace, *Mysticism and Philosophy*, 125.

Supreme, one with it. Only in separation is there duality. This is why the vision baffles the telling; for how can a man bring back tidings of the Supreme as detached when he has seen it as one with himself. . . . Beholder is one with the beheld. . . . he is become unity, having no diversity either in relation to himself or anything else. . . . reason is in abeyance and intellection and even the very self, caught away, God-possessed, in perfect stillness, all the being is calmed. . . .

This is the life of the gods, and of god-like and blessed men— liberation from the alien that besets us here, a life of taking no pleasure in the things of earth—a flight of the alone to the alone.[6]

Stace says that this passage contains a "perfect specimen description" of the introvertive mystical state. Explicit, for example, is the claim that the experience is ineffable (it "baffles the telling") and that it is beyond the scope of the intellect or reason. A third theme is evident as well—the experience involves what Stace calls "a religious sense of the holy or the divine." All these are listed in *Mysticism and Philosophy* as identifying features of mystical consciousness (131–32). At the very center of this passage, however, is yet another thesis—one of special interest in the present discussion. Plotinus says that within the experience no distinctions are made between items of experiential content, but "what is mainly emphasized," Stace maintains, "is the transcendence of the duality of subject and object, the distinction between the individual self and the One" (105). The experience lacks what I referred to in Section 3 of Chapter 2 as "subject-object structure." No object distinct from self is given. Thus, the sense of self as an object distinct from other things completely disappears. Stace makes note of the fact that in the literature of Islamic mysticism, a special term is used to label this phenomenon. It is called *fana,* which means "passing away" (115). This is precisely the idea encountered in Section 3 of Chapter 2 in the discussion of the union without distinction. Experientially, the self "passes away" or "melts." In the words of Blosius, the soul here "loses itself" and is, as it were, "brought to nothing." And now I think we can see why Stace ultimately rejects the claim that in the introvertive mystical experience one is aware *of* undifferenti-

6. Quoted in Stace, *Mysticism and Philosophy,* 104.

ated unity or aware *of* the One. This form of words suggests that there is an object or condition called "unity" or "oneness" that is apprehended in the experience. In turn, this implies that a distinction is to be made between the object or condition apprehended and the experiencing subject. Thus, this way of talking does not reveal the phenomenological facts. It suggests the presence of subject-object structure, which, in this case, simply isn't there.[7]

I think we now have an answer to the question we are asking. In mystical consciousness, *nothing* is given. There is no "what" that is directly experienced. Phenomenologically, the introvertive mystical state is not an awareness *of* the Self or an awareness *of* the One. According to the author of the Mandukya Upanishad, it *is* the Self: Stace says that it *is* the One.[8] And although these last-mentioned formulas may well be short of literal meaning, their positive form serves to underscore the negative point of central concern. Stace insists that the introvertive mystical experience is *of* nothing at all.[9]

Is this intelligible? Surprisingly, one of the theses argued at length in *Mysticism and Philosophy* is that it is *not*. Although it cannot be doubted that the introvertive mystical experience (as just described) actually occurs, Stace claims that it is inherently "paradoxical." On his account, the paradox rests in the fact "that although it is completely negative, a mere absence, yet it is also a positive experience; and although it is a consciousness, it is a consciousness which is not a consciousness of any particular existence" (92–93). This, Stace tells us, is the same as saying that the introvertive mystical experience is "both something and nothing" (86).

I'm not sure how seriously Stace meant this last claim to be taken. On the above account, the introvertive mystical state is not portrayed as being both something and nothing. The claim is, only, that it is something which is *of* nothing or, better, that it is something (an experience) which is *not of* anything. By itself, this does not seem paradoxical—no more so than does a canvas upon which nothing is painted or a stage that is empty though the

---

7. See Stace, *Teachings of the Mystics*, 15.
8. Stace, *Teachings of the Mystics*, 15.
9. Stace, *Mysticism and Philosophy*, 86, 162, 256. See also Stace, *Teachings of the Mystics*, 22.

footlights are on. Still, there is probably a point to be gleaned from Stace's insistence that mystical consciousness is paradoxical. On Stace's account, the introvertive mystical state is at least unusual in the extreme. It appears to be a state of consciousness that lacks intentionality. It is an experience; but (apparently) it is a state of consciousness devoid of anything that might even marginally be counted as experiential content.[10]

2. Experience versus Interpretation

I shall be turning presently to a study of Stace's view concerning the use of the phrase "union with God" in classical Christian mystical texts. Before getting to the substantive part of the discussion, however, I need to make clear (or as clear as I can) a distinction working at the very center of Stace's thinking on this topic, namely, the distinction between what he calls "experience and interpretation." I shall do this now.

Consider pictures 1 and 2.[11] Suppose that someone (say a child) were to describe the content of picture 1 using the following caption (C):

C: A man walking on State Street

The child says: "This is a picture of a man walking on State Street." We ask: "How do you know it is, specifically, *State Street*." The child responds: "The man in the picture is the Tin Man walking on the Yellow Brick Road just after the Wizard of Oz named it 'State Street.'" That would be a creative reply. The child has constructed a story to go along with the picture. And, important to see, it is in the story and not in the picture that the

---

10. It is often claimed that Edmund Husserl and Franz Brentano held the view that all experiences are "intentional" and thus that no experience could be of nothing at all. Assuming that this was their position, I have yet to discover a reason for thinking that they were right. And since the mystical literature is virtually loaded with passages that at least appear to imply that such experiences actually occur, I am inclined to think that if this was their position they were probably wrong.

11. The pictures were sketched by Kurt Smith of the Claremont Graduate School (Philosophy). I am grateful to him for the assist and also indebted to him for preparing the index to this volume.

[1]   [2]

street is identified as *State* Street. Now, contrast this case with another. This time the child uses C to describe the content of picture 2 instead of picture 1. Again we ask: "How do you know it is *State* Street." The child replies: "It says so—right there on the street sign." That it is, specifically, *State* Street is one of the things explicitly pictured. It is, we might say, one of the pictured facts.

As it relates to the content of picture 1, I shall call C an "expanded" description. By contrast, as it relates to the content of picture 2, C is not expanded. This is to say that with respect to picture 1, but not with respect to picture 2, C includes mention of an item not pictured in the picture. It should be clear that the question of whether C is or is not an expanded description of the content of a given picture cannot be determined by isolated inspection of C. It depends on the content of the picture being considered. C is or is not an expanded description, depending on whether one is considering the content of picture 1 or the content of picture 2.

Statements of the form "This is a picture of *x*" may or may not commit the speaker to the actual existence of *x*. For example, if I were to use C when describing the content of picture 2, I might be saying that there is (or was) a real man who walked on a real street named "State" and that this picture bears a special relation to him, the street, and the walking event, namely, the one marked by the term "of." This would be the most plausible understanding of my statement if, for example, I uttered it in court while testifying under oath and submitting picture 2 as part of my testimony regarding what I saw on the night of the murder. On the other hand, one could imagine circumstances in which I might say of picture 2 that it is of a man walking on State Street and in which my statement would carry no implications about the constitution of the real world apart from the picture itself. This would be the preferred reading if, for example, I were describing picture 2 in front of an art class to which I was giving instruction in the fine points of drawing. Here, one might suppose, the question of whether there is (or was) a real man on a real street or a real walking event depicted by the picture would not arise. My claim that it is of a man walking on State Street would be most plausibly interpreted not as a claim about the world apart from the picture but as a claim about the contours of the figures making up the picture, that is, about the picture facts, or the facts as pictured.

Two more labels: In the case where a description of the form "This is a picture of x" carries the implication that x exists (or existed) in the real world apart from the picture, I shall refer to it as an "extended" description of the content of the picture. In the case where a statement of the form "This is a picture of x" is used to describe only the picture content and is not intended to carry any implication about the existence of anything in the real world apart from the picture, I shall refer to the description in question as "not extended." The idea here is that in the first case, the picture description, as it were, reaches out—extends—to the real world and affirms a correspondence relation between it and the picture. In the second case, the existential reach carried by the language of the extended description is inoperative. It has been (to use Husserl's term) "bracketed," that is, fenced off or suspended.

Whether a given picture description is extended or not extended in a particular case is not always clear. In some cases, explicit verbal context will settle the matter as, for example, when I hold up a canvas, saying, "This is a picture of King Arthur," adding, "Of course, we know that King Arthur did not really exist." Here, the addendum makes clear that the picture description is not extended. It effectively cancels (brackets) the existential implication that might otherwise be thought to attend. In cases where no verbal directions are given about how a given picture description is to be taken, however, the issue will turn on more subtle factors. Sometimes it is easy—as, for example, when I open a lecture to a room full of educated adults with the words "This is a picture of Paul Bunyan riding his blue ox Babe" (pointing to the canvas on the easel in front of the room). Here, background knowledge on the part of the listener is presupposed by the speaker and vice versa. That the picture description is not extended is assumed by both as a matter of common understanding. But, of course, sometimes it is not easy at all—as, for example, when a child opens his performance at show-and-tell with the comment "This is a picture of Paul Bunyan riding his blue ox Babe." Is this description extended or not extended? We may not be able to tell, apart from a probe of the child's beliefs concerning Paul Bunyan and his intentions in the circumstances at hand. One more point on this: the believing child and the knowing adult might both agree that a given painting is a picture of Paul Bunyan riding his blue ox Babe. However, an utterance to this effect might well be an extended description in the first case and not extended in the second. The words by themselves will not tell us. The issue here turns on the intentions of the speaker.

Given the distinctions developed in the last several paragraphs, four categories of picture descriptions can be identified:

1. *Expanded and Extended.* Example: Caption (C) attached to picture 1 by a child who believes (and means to be communicating) that the Tin Man is (or was) real, that he really did walk on the Yellow Brick Road after the Wizard of Oz re-named it "State Street," and that the picture is *of* those real objects and that real event.
2. *Expanded and Not Extended.* Example: C attached to picture 1 by one who is simply inventing the Tin Man story for his own amusement and/or the amusement of another. Both the speaker and the listener know (and knows that the other knows) that the Tin Man and other such characters do not and never did exist.
3. *Not Expanded and Extended.* Example: C attached to pic-

ture 2 as picture 2 is submitted as part of sworn testimony regarding what I saw on the night of the murder.

4. *Not Expanded and Not Extended.* Example: C attached to picture 2 when one is instructing a class in the techniques of drawing.

I should add that I do not here mean to be suggesting that a given picture description can always be sorted into one of these four kinds. Both pictures and intentions can be hopelessly obscure. Still, we can imagine relatively clear instances of each category. That is enough to ensure that the criteria determining the categories are, at least, intelligible.

In *The Teachings of the Mystics,* Stace writes as follows concerning the distinction between experience and interpretation:

> On a dark night out of doors one may see something glimmering white. One person may think it is a ghost. A second person may take it for a sheet hung out on a clothesline. A third may suppose that it is a white-painted rock. Here we have a single experience with three different interpretations. The experience is genuine, but the interpretations may be either true or false. If we are to understand anything at all about mysticism, it is essential that we should make a similar distinction between a mystical experience and the interpretations that may be put on it either by mystics themselves or by nonmystics. For instance, the same mystical experience may be interpreted by a Christian in terms of Christian beliefs and by a Buddhist in terms of Buddhist beliefs. (10)

Consistent with Stace's intentions, I think we can model the example herein given using the procedure followed in our discussion of pictures 1 and 2. First, draw (imagine) a picture—a dark landscape with a blob of glimmering white in the middle distance. Next, entertain a caption (C'):

C': A sheet hung out on a clothesline

Now consider the case in which someone uses C' to describe the content of the picture. He says, "This is a picture of a sheet hung out on a clothesline." The description in question would then count as an *expanded* description of the picture content. That it is, specifically, a *sheet* (etc.) is not something one could just read off the picture. Of course, at this point we could introduce a second picture—for example, a photograph taken in my backyard on washday. As used to describe the content of this second picture, C' might not be expanded. As a general remark, it is clear that at least part of what Stace has in mind when referring to the three judgments mentioned in the passage just quoted as "interpretations" is that each makes use of a content description that is expanded relative to the content of the experience supposed. In this regard, C' used to describe the content the "single experience" mentioned in the quoted passage would be an interpretation. The unexpanded— and in this regard uninterpreted—content description of that experience would be

C": Something glimmering white

Although the passages in which Stace explains the distinction between experience and interpretation are dominated by discussions of the distinction between experience descriptions that are expanded versus those that are not expanded, Stace also uses the term "interpretation" to refer to experience descriptions that are *extended,* that is, to those which describe the content of experience in such a way as to imply that the experience correlates with something in the real world apart from experience. Thus, in the case before us, if C" were used to describe the content of the "single experience" Stace talks about in the passage quoted above, though not expanded, the resulting experience description would still count as an "interpretation" if in offering the description the speaker intended to be affirming the existence of something out there in the real world independent of the experience that is glimmering white.

For Stace, an experience description counts as an interpretation if the description is expanded (relative to the content of the experience described) and/or if the description is extended. Referring to the four categories of picture descriptions itemized above, the experience description counterparts of categories 1–3 are categories of interpretations. What Stace usually refers to in his texts as "uninterpreted descriptions," or, more often, "mere descriptive reports" are experience descriptions that are not expanded and not extended, that is, the counterparts of the picture descriptions in category 4.

In *Mysticism and Philosophy*, Stace defines the term "interpretation" so: "I use the word 'interpretation' to mean anything which the conceptual intellect adds to the experience for the purposes of understanding it, whether what is added is only classificatory concepts, or a logical inference, or an explanatory hypothesis" (37). Stace then allows that on this understanding of the term, there may be no such thing as a pure, uninterpreted experience—such experiences, he tells us, may even be "psychologically impossible" (31). Stace says, too, that interpretations may vary as regards the *amount* of intellectual addition involved. "Low-level" interpretations are those in which intellectual addition is slight. These contrast with "high-level" interpretations, where intellectual addition is relatively abundant. Stace illustrates this distinction so: "If a man says, 'I see a red colour', this is a low-level interpretation, since it involves nothing except simple classificatory concepts. But a physicist's wave theory of colours is a very high-level interpretation" (37). Using the concepts introduced above, Stace seems here to be saying that experience descriptions are always to some extent *expanded* and the amount of expansion may vary from one case to another. This means that we will never find a pure instance of either category 3 or category 4 and that instances of categories 1 and 2 can be ranked with respect to the amount of expansion involved. Note that much this same thing might be said of picture descriptions as well. In the case of the child who uses C when describing the content of picture 2, we might have asked, "How do you know it is a *man* or a *street*—in fact, how do you know that any of the patterns in the frame marked 'picture 2' are *of* anything at all?" One must learn to "read" pictures—a talent requiring exercise of one's conceptual capacities. Thus, even had I provided full-featured photographs instead of freehand drawings as materials for our discussion, the child who applied C to picture 2 would have displayed at least *some* creative conceptual ability.

Does this make a difference as regards Stace's distinction between experience and interpretation? Interestingly, in *Mysticism and*

Philosophy, Stace says that it does not. Working with the case of an American visitor in London who tried to shake hands with what he took to be a policeman in the entrance of Madame Tussaud's wax-works museum before realizing that the policeman in question was a wax figure, Stace says this:

There were two successive interpretations, although it may be true that at no time was the experience free of interpretation and even that a pure experience is psychologically impossible. No doubt the original something seen at the entrance was immediately recognized as a material object, as having some sort of colour, and as having the general shape of a human being. And since this involved the application of classificatory concepts to the sensations, there was from the first some degree of interpretation. (Still) it seems a safe position to say that there is an intelligible distinction between experience and interpretation, even if it be true that we can never come upon a quite uninterpreted experience. (31–32)

The "intelligible distinction" that remains after it is admitted that there are no pure (uninterpreted) experiences is presumably illustrated in the case of the American visitor to Madame Tussaud's. It is the distinction between (1) the visual awareness in which the object seen was, as Stace says, "immediately recognized as a material object, as having some sort of colour, and as having the general shape of a human being"; and (2) the two cognitions that emerged therefrom. Stace adds that "however rough" it may be, this distinction "is used every day in our practical living, and we could hardly get on without it." He continues:

A witness in a law court is instructed to give evidence only of what he actually observes, avoiding inferences and interpretations. This instruction is essential and works well enough, notwithstanding that if the witness says he observed the defendant at the scene of the crime, some philosopher might try to insist, like Mill, that all the witness actually saw was a coloured surface, and that to call this "the defendant" would be to indulge in an inference. (32)

The point seems to be that the "rough," "every day" distinction between experience and interpretation is the one upon which Stace means to be focusing attention. Although I think Stace would agree that the more finely honed epistemological distinction between sensing a colored patch (a so-called sense datum) and what Stace calls the "immediate recognition of a material object" may be relevant and important in some philosophical contexts, Stace seems clearly to be identifying it here only in order to assure the reader that it will have no direct bearing on the discussion to follow. Allowing that philosophers have been right in insisting that some kind of *judgment* (inference, intellectual addition) is involved when a perceiver sees something and immediately *recognizes* it to be a physical object having a certain shape and color, Stace seems clearly to be including this element on the *experience* side of the dichotomy between experience and interpretation. (I shall have more to say on this topic in Section 4 of Chapter 7.)

3. "Union with God"

Grant, first of all, that in the typical case (for example, chapter XI of Ruysbroeck's *Book of Supreme Truth*) when a Christian mystic claims to have experienced union with God, he means to be describing an encounter (or kind of encounter) in the real world between two distinct beings: the soul of the mystic and a being whom he believes to be, I would suppose, the almighty, omniscient, and perfectly good person who created the universe. The language, in other words, carries existential import—the experience description in part affirms the existence of an almighty, omniscient, and perfectly good person who created the universe. If this is right, then to claim that on a given occasion one experienced union with God is to offer an experience description that is (to use our new way of talking) *extended.* For Stace, this is enough to ensure that the description in question is an "interpretation" and not a "mere descriptive report." He writes in *Mysticism and Philosophy:* "If a mystic says that he experiences a 'mystical union with the Creator of the universe', this is a high-level interpretation since it includes far more intellectual addition than a mere descriptive report. It includes an assumption about the origin of the world and a belief in the existence of a personal God" (37). This is the first

argument Stace offers for the claim that "union with God" is always used in the Christian mystical literature as a "theological
interpretation" of the underlying mystical experience.

So far, there is nothing very surprising about Stace's position
concerning the use of "union with God" in the Christian mystical
literature. But the heart of the theory is yet to come. According to
Stace, the phenomenon referred to when the Christian mystic
claims to have experienced union with God is the introvertive
mystical state. The experience, itself, is thus devoid of experiential
content—including subject-object structure. But the mystic's *description* of the experience is packed with content. It conveys a
highly complex story about a meeting being two distinct beings—
one of which is an omnipotent, omniscient, and perfectly good
person who created the universe. The upshot is that when the
mystic claims to have experienced union with God, she is offering
a description of her experience that is not only extended but is also
vastly *expanded*. We can identify at least two (nested) elements in
the expansion: (1) the experience is described as being *of another,*
that is, it is described as having subject-object structure, and (2) the
Other in question is understood to possess all the identifying attributes of the Christian God. I turn now to a review of Stace's
argument for this position. What we need to know, of course, is
why Stace thinks that it is, specifically, the introvertive mystical
state that the Christian mystic is so describing.

In the writings of what Stace characterizes as the more "intellectual" Christian mystics, such as Meister Eckhart and Jan van Ruysbroeck, explicit mention is made of the introvertive mystical experience. As we have seen, Ruysbroeck says that in the union
without distinction, the spirit is (in his words) "undifferentiated
and without distinction and feels nothing but unity." Similar passages can be found in the writings of Eckhart. Also, both Ruysbroeck and Eckhart emphasize the lack of sensual imagery in the
mystical state—recall that Ruysbroeck spoke of "the abysmal absence of image." It is thus clear, Stace thinks, that what is being
referred to in these cases as the experience of "union" is, in fact, the
introvertive state. He claims that the texts leave little room for
doubt on the matter (94–100).

Stace admits that Eckhart and Ruysbroeck are unusual cases in that most Christian mystics do not make explicit mention of the introvertive state. He adds, however, that even in the more usual cases, it is reasonable to suppose that it is the experience of un-differentiated unity that underlies the various discussions of union. Two kinds of clues give it away. First, going back to the passage quoted earlier from chapter xii of *The Book of Supreme Truth*, Ruysbroeck characterized the mystical state as a "wayless abyss," a state of "solitude and ignorance that is fathomless." Stace says that not just Ruysbroeck but Christian mystics generally make abun-dant use of such negative metaphors (call them "emptiness meta-phors") when describing the mystical experience. Other such met-aphors include "darkness," "silence," "nakedness," "nudity," "barren," "desert," and, of course, "emptiness" itself. The claim is that negative figures such as these express lack of experiential con-tent and thus, Stace says, "point to the fact" that what is experi-enced in mystical consciousness is the void of undifferentiated uni-ty.[12] Second, Stace claims that we can see in the writings of most Christian mystics a definite "drift toward monism."[13] From what they say in their texts, Stace insists, it is clear that if left to their own spontaneous inclinations, most Christian mystics would af-firm metaphysical identity between themselves and God. But, of course, Christian mystics, for the most part, do not affirm meta-physical identity between themselves and God. Stace says this is because the mystics in question are "pressured" into interpreting their experiences in terms of the dualistic metaphysical picture explicit in Church doctrine. They are so pressured, he says, by the "threat of possible punishment for heresy" from "theologians and the ecclesiastical authorities."[14] With what he calls "a certain mea-sure of amusement," Stace notes on this last point that "Catholic mystics frequently make what seem to be unguarded statements which imply complete pantheistic identity, and then hastily add a qualifying clause, as if they had suddenly remembered their ecclesiastical superiors."[15] Stace does not identify any of the "un-

12. Stace, *Mysticism and Philosophy*, 100.
13. Stace, *Mysticism and Philosophy*, 232.
14. See, e.g., Stace, *Mysticism and Philosophy*, 113–14, 219–20, and esp. 232–34.
15. Stace, *Mysticism and Philosophy*, 114.

guarded statements" referred to in this passage.[16] This is unfortunate because without them it is hard to evaluate the claim here
being made. Stace's view seems to be that despite the (alleged)
hastily added qualifying clauses that project an orthodox dualistic
metaphysical posture, there is enough in the (unidentified) "unguarded statements" to permit the conclusion that the experience
being reported is the introvertive state. I, for one, am not convinced. I would have preferred to have had the opportunity to
examine the passages Stace here has in mind for myself. (In Supplementary Study 3 I shall address the question of whether it is
plausible to suppose that if left to their own spontaneous inclinations most Christian mystics would affirm metaphysical identity
between God and the soul.)

Are there no Christian mystics who report having experiences of
union with God but whose writings not only lack explicit mention
of the undifferentiated unity but do not abound with emptiness
metaphors and do not contain "unguarded statements" symptomatic of "the drift toward monism"? Stace treats Saint Teresa as a
case of this sort. His position is that even here it is reasonable to
suppose that the underlying mystical experience is of the introvertive sort and thus that "union with God" is a theological expansion. Stace offers a kind of argument from coherence in support of
this contention. I'll review it now.[17]

Start with the fact that all Christian mystics use the phrase
"union with God" when reporting their mystical experiences.
Given this as a datum, Stace holds that it is "natural to suppose that
they all mean the same thing by it unless given positive evidence to
the contrary." Stace continues:

> If one can imagine Eckhart and St. Teresa meeting across the cen-
> turies and comparing notes, it would surely be very surprising to

16. On pages 224–25 of *Mysticism and Philosophy*, Stace provides some passages
from Eckhart's Sermons that carry monistic import. However, these can hardly be
taken as examples of the statements here in question. Statements such as Eckhart's
are not "frequently" to be found in the writings of Catholic mystics. Also, they are
not attended with "qualifying clauses" that in any way suggest that Eckhart was
concerned with the reactions of his "ecclesiastical superiors."

17. Following is a summary of the argument offered by Stace, *Mysticism and
Philosophy*, 101–4.

find that in speaking of "union with God" they meant quite different experiences and were in fact talking at cross-purposes. And if
there were any such radically different kinds of experience among
Christian mystics which by some misunderstanding had been indiscriminately labeled "union with God", it is extraordinary that this
fact was never discovered by the Christian mystics themselves. Yet
there is no mention of it anywhere in the literature. It is quite
evident that they all suppose that there is some one supremely great
experience which they refer to as "union with God", and which
they all believe themselves to share with one another—although
perhaps in different degrees. (101)

It is thus reasonable to suppose that all Christian mystics use
"union with God" to refer to the same "supremely great experience." And since we already know that in some cases (for example,
Ruysbroeck and Eckhart) this phrase is used to refer to the introvertive mystical state, we can conclude that the same is true in all
cases—for example, Saint Teresa.

Even if one were to accept the conclusion just reached, it might
seem surprising that Teresa regularly had introvertive mystical
experiences and yet that there should be no explicit mention or
even indirect evidence of this fact in any of her many writings.
Keep in mind that we are here dealing with what Stace describes as
a "supremely great experience," and Teresa is generally credited in
the Christian mystical community with being an informant who
had extraordinary facility for discriminating and communicating
the details of her various religious experiences. Stace's explanation
of this peculiar hiatus is that in addition to being a highly emotional and somewhat unstable person, Teresa was "a women of ex-
tremely simple Christian piety with no interest in theory, or ab-
stract thinking, or philosophical distinctions and analyses, and no
capacity for them" (103). Thus, Teresa, he says, "did not have a
sufficiently analytical mind to distinguish between experience and
interpretation."[18] Stace summarizes his position regarding the use

18. Stace, *Teachings of the Mystics*, 24. Negative remarks about Teresa's intellectual and emotional qualities can be found throughout Stace's writings on mysticism. See, for example, Stace, *Mysticism and Philosophy*, 26, 66, 68, 80.

of "union with God" in the writings of Saint Teresa, and in the Christian mystical literature more generally, as follows:

> "Union with God" is not an uninterpreted description of any human being's experience. It is a theistic interpretation of the undifferentiated unity. St. Teresa's uninterpreted experience is the same as Eckhart's, but she is incapable of distinguishing between experience and interpretation so that when she experiences the divisionless oneness of the mystical consciousness she jumps at once to its conventional interpretation in terms of Christian beliefs. She is after all no different in this respect from J. S. Mill's example of the plain man who senses "a colored surface of a certain shape" and forthwith says, "I see my brother."[19]

Unfortunately, Stace's closing example suggests that he has here abandoned the "rough" and "every day" distinction between experience and interpretation with which he began his inquiry. His point seems here to depend on the philosophical distinction between sensing a colored surface (a sense datum) and perceiving a material object—a distinction explicitly put aside in his earlier discussion. I think that this is best regarded as a slip on Stace's part: one that we can easily fix for ourselves. Let the context be one in which the "plain man" is testifying in court about what he saw on the night of the murder. Under cross-examination he admits that although what he saw in the garden he "immediately recognized" to be a material object having the general shape and color of a human being, it was only later that he came to realize that it must have been his brother. He explains: "After all, who beside myself and my brother had a key to the garden gate?" Given this as background, "I saw my brother" would then have to be counted as an *interpretation* of his visual experience on two separate counts—it would be both an extended description and an expanded description. In summary form, this is what Stace is claiming about the relation between the introvertive mystical state considered as a datum and the standard Christian mystical description of that datum formulated in the phrase "union with God."

19. Stace, *Mysticism and Philosophy*, 104.

[6]

Walter Stace and the
Data on Union

I move now to consider the merits of the theory reviewed in the preceding chapter. My deliberations on this topic will be brief.

1. The Prima Facie Case against Stace

On the surface it would appear that the position Stace develops concerning the use of "union with God" in the Christian mystical literature is plainly wrong. At least two broad desiderata suggest this verdict:

1. Recall that in the Prayer of Quiet, God and the soul of the mystic are said to be *close,* while in Full Union and in the culmination stage of Rapture these same two objects are pictured as being in *mutual embrace.* But in a world containing less than two, there could be no instance of closeness nor could there be anything that would count as a case of embrace. The same is true of the other descriptions persistently offered of union phenomena. God *enwraps* and *penetrates* the soul; the soul is *submerged in* and *saturated by* God; God and the soul are *mingled.* Again, the language is radically dualistic. Nothing enwraps unless something *else* is enwrapped. And even in the case where one might be said to enwrap oneself (for example, I fold my right hand into my left), the description makes sense only if it is understood that that which enwraps (my

left hand) is other than that which is enwrapped (my right hand). Similar remarks apply in cases of penetration, submersion, saturation, and mingling.

Now, Stace maintains that the dualistic phrase "union with God" occurs in the Christian mystical literature as an interpretation (that is, as what I have called "expanded description") of the introvertive state. His view is that this phrase tells us nothing about the phenomenological content of the experience itself. He says that Christian mystics describe their experiences in this way because doctrine requires that God be portrayed as a being distinct from the experiencing mystic. What, then, shall we say about the more detailed descriptions of union just mentioned? Though Stace says nothing about them, it is clear that on his theory these descriptions, too, must be regarded as interpretations—I'll call them "elaborative expansions"—of the introvertive state. Each carries precisely the same dualistic implications that lead Stace to classify the generic phrase "union with God" as a theological interpretation. It seems to me, however, that this way of understanding these more detailed descriptions would be hard to square with Stace's general theory. Two points in particular would seem to me to be awkward in the extreme.

First, allow that when describing the Prayer of Quiet, Full Union, and Rapture, Christian mystics are providing expanded descriptions of the introvertive state. We thus have three elaborative expansions of a single underlying phenomenon. On Stace's theory, however, differences in interpretation of the introvertive state are explained by differences in theological belief on the part of those offering the various interpretations. So how shall we explain the fact that we here have *three* interpretations instead of only one? Those who offer these three descriptions presumably share a common set of theological beliefs. In fact, the very same mystic sometimes offers one of these (alleged) elaborative expansions and sometimes another. Differences between these various descriptions thus do not appear to reflect differences in theological belief. It would seem much more reasonable to suppose that they reflect differences in the content of the experiences being reported in each case. But, of course, this last suggestion would not be consistent with the claim that they are all interpretations of the same mystical state. This problem is intensified by the fact that on Stace's theory, the mystical state in question is experientially vacant and thus has no content that could admit of possible variations.

Second, Stace tells us that Christian mystics describe the introvertive experience using the dualistic expression "union with God" because they are pressured by ecclesiastical authorities to preserve an orthodox posture regarding the metaphysics of the mystical encounter. Shall we then say the same about the three more detailed dualistic descriptions we are now considering? But this would make no sense at all. While standard Christian doctrine requires that God and the created soul be regarded as distinct beings (a message amply conveyed by just the generic description "union with God"), it is *not* an item of orthodox faith that God is sometimes close to the soul in its own domain (the Prayer of Quiet) and at other times enwraps and penetrates the soul either in its own domain (Full Union) or in what Teresa referred to as "another world" (Rapture). So why do Christian mystics insist on these further dualistic elaborations? "Menaces and Pressures" of "ecclesiastical authorities" can hardly be the answer. A far more likely hypothesis is that these descriptions have their seat in experiential items that Stace's theory is simply not taking into account.

2. According to Stace, the introvertive mystical experience is not only devoid of ordinary sense perceptions, it is vacant of anything even remotely similar to such contents of consciousness. Recall that this was the point emphasized in the passage from *The Teachings of the Mystics* cited near the beginning of Section 1 of Chapter 5. There Stace allowed that certain insects and animals may have sensations unlike those enjoyed by human beings—for example, sensations by which infrared color is detected. He then maintained that although different from ours, these phenomena would still have to count as sensations. He insisted that mystical consciousness is devoid of *anything* that could be included in this general category. In this respect (as well as others), Stace said that mystical consciousness is "wholly incommensurable" with ordinary "sensory-intellectual consciousness."

How, then, shall we greet the fact that mystics from the Christian tradition repeatedly insist that although experiences of union are devoid of ordinary bodily sensations,[1] they are amply supplied with experiential elements explicitly said to be *like* bodily sensations—the (so-called) "spiritual sensations"? Perhaps the answer is that this, too, must be understood as an interpretive element in the mystical discourse. It is a further interpretive ingredient in the three elaborative expansions just discussed. It seems to me, however, that this reply would have two deficiencies. First, it would make liars of mystics such as Alvarez, who emphasize the fact that spiritual sensations are items of immediate experience.[2] And second, it is not clear how we would then explain the (alleged) fact that mystics interpret the introvertive mystical state in these terms. Pressure from ecclesiastical authorities? Hardly. Where in the catechism does it say that God is sometimes felt as a burn or is heard as the whisper of a gentle breeze? Does the Church have a position regarding the flavor of God? . . . and how about the *smell!* Prima facie, it would seem that the only plausible way of dealing with the materials discussed in Chapter 3 of this book would be to suppose that union experiences have sensory-like elements of a kind that Stace explicitly excludes from the introvertive mystical state. Whatever may be the final verdict concerning their phenomenological features, it would at least appear that union experiences are not *wholly* incommensurable with ordinary sensory-intellectual consciousness.

2. Stace's Argument Revisited

Nothing said in the section just completed shows that Stace is wrong concerning the interpretive status of "union with God" in the Christian mystical literature. The problems raised may have answers. Stace's theory may be correct even if they have no answers. Still, given that the theory is clearly at odds with two of the more pervasive themes evident in the primary mystical literature, a

1. This is not quite right. Recall that on Teresa's account, ordinary sense faculties are dysfunctional but they are still operative in the prelude stage of Rapture. Teresa says that with respect to Rapture, bodily sense faculties fail altogether only at the "highest point." See Section 3 of Chapter 1 above.
2. See the long passage quoted from Alvarez in the subsection "Rapture," in Section 3 of Chapter 3 above.

closer look at the reasons Stace gives in support of the theory is surely in order. I proceed now to a review of what I take to be Stace's major supporting argument—the one characterized above in Section 3 of Chapter 5 as "a kind of argument from coherence." So that we may have the argument before us, I'll frame it again— this time in schematic form.

1. As used in the Christian mystical literature, the phrase "[experience of] union with God" always carries the same meaning.
2. ∴ As used in the Christian mystical literature, the phrase "[experience of] union with God" always refers to the same type of experience.
3. In some cases, Christian mystics use "[experience of] union with God" to refer to the introvertive mystical state.
4. ∴ In all cases, Christian mystics use "[experience of] union with God" to refer to the introvertive mystical state.

Clarification: In Stace's text, the bracketed material is not included—Stace says, for example, that Christian mystics use "union with God" (rather than "*experience of* union with God") to refer to the introvertive state.[3] This is not right. By Stace's own insistence, Christian mystics use the phrase "union with God" to refer not to an *experience,* but to an *encounter* in the real world between two distinct beings. Of course, we could say that as used in the Christian mystical literature, "union with God" is used as a kind of caption—that is, not to *refer to* but to *describe the content of* a mystical experience.[4] But in the present context, this would be an obscuration. Stace could not allow that Christian mystics use "union with God" to *describe the content of* (rather than to refer to) the introvertive state. On his account, the introvertive state has no content to describe. Hence, in what is to follow I shall assume that Stace's argument is as it would be formulated were we to remove the brackets and thus were to include the bracketed material in all four lines.

3. See, e.g., Stace, *Mysticism and Philosophy,* 101.
4. See the discussion in Section 2 of Chapter 5 above.

I discover that on a given occasion, Jones uses the term "ache" to refer to a painful throbbing sensation in his head. Assuming that Jones uses "ache" with constant meaning, I conclude that Jones always uses "ache" to refer to a throbbing sensation in his head. But, of course, I am wrong. Though on a given occasion Jones uses "ache" to refer to a throbbing sensation in his head, on other occasions he uses this term to refer to throbbing sensations in his knee. On still other occasions Jones uses this term when calling attention to dull steady pains in his back. Shall we then conclude that in these various circumstances Jones uses "ache" with different meanings? Of course not. Jones uses "ache" with constant meaning, that is, he uses it to refer to members of the same type of experience. The reasoning above failed because I misidentified the relevant experience type. The inference suffered from a defect that might be called "undergeneralization." "Ache" is a genus term. The relevant genus is broader than I originally thought it to be.

Looking again at the four-step argument of present concern, I think it is clear that it works only if supplemented with a very specific proviso concerning the constitutive-breadth of the type of experience mentioned in step 2, namely, that the type in question does not include subtypes of which the introvertive mystical experience is only one. If it did, then Stace's argument would suffer from the fallacy of undergeneralization, as did the reasoning sketched at the beginning of the preceding paragraph. Thus, for Stace, the supposition must be that "[experience of] union with God" is the name of a one-species genus. And, indeed, this supposition is not only needed, it is fully explicit in Stace's text. Recall that in a passage from *Mysticism and Philosophy* that I quoted at length in Section 3 of Chapter 5 above, Stace said, "It is quite evident that [Christian mystics] all suppose that there is some one supremely great experience which they refer to as 'union with God', and which they all believe themselves to share with one another—although perhaps in different degrees."[5] Further, not only did Stace make explicit mention of the (alleged) fact his argu-

5. I think that Stace here means to be allowing "different degrees" of "the one supremely great experience" in exactly the same sense as I might have allowed different degrees of intensity when concluding that Jones always uses "ache" to refer to throbbing sensations in his head.

ment requires, in the same passage he explained what it is that makes this supposed fact "quite evident." It is another (alleged) fact—this time a negative fact—namely, that there "is no mention . . . anywhere in the [Christian mystical] literature" of there being "radically different kinds of experiences among Christian mystics which by some misunderstanding had been indiscriminately labeled 'union with God.'" Thus, the argument for Stace's general position on "union with God" requires a supposition that is explicitly supplied. And the final appeal is to a negative item presumably established by a survey of the data—that there is no evidence to support the contention that through some "misunderstanding," "radically different" types of experiences have been "indiscriminately" referred to as experiences of "union."

The problem, of course, is only thinly screened in spite of the veil of bombast and tinsel. The issue here is not whether *radically* different kinds of experiences, through some *misunderstanding,* have been *indiscriminately* referred to with the same phrase. The question, instead, is whether Christian mystics use "[experience of] union with God" when characterizing a group of different, though related mystical phenomena. And when the question is put in this way, it is simply false to say that there is nothing in the Christian mystical literature that would lead one to think that this is so. As we saw in the first two chapters of this book, tradition has it that there are *three* species within the genus of union experiences. That these are distinct states is often a point of emphasis—for example, the distinction between Full Union and Rapture is the central topic under discussion in chapter xx of Teresa's *Life.* But, of course, this is not to say that "[experience of] union with God" is used differently by different mystics or that it has a variety of meanings. This phrase is a *genus designator* like "ache." As such, it applies equally to members of a variety of species within the genus. One can only suppose that Stace failed to do his homework on this topic. If the final appeal is to what is said or not said in Christian mystical texts, the right conclusion is that there is no "*one* supremely great experience" that Christian mystics classify as *the* experience of union.

Shall we then conclude that the four-step argument with which we have been dealing in this section suffers from the fallacy of undergeneralization? In Section 3 of Chapter 2, I called attention to the fact that the state that Ruysbroeck referred to as "the union without distinction" and that Stace equates with the introvertive mystical experience is probably not to be counted as a separate species of union. I suggested that it is best regarded as the mystical peak (not always reached) of two distinct union states, namely, Full Union and Rapture. I argued that this suggestion is amply supported by discussions in primary mystical texts, for example, Ruysbroeck's *Book of Supreme Truth* (chapters xi and xii), John of the Cross's *Living Flame of Love* (stanza ii), and Blosius's *Book of Spiritual Instruction* (chapter 12). I should add that this is not to deny that Christian mystics often make special mention of this climax interval—as do Ruysbroeck, John of the Cross, Bernard of Clairvaux, Tauler, and others. It is also not to discount the fact that the distinctionless mystical moment is often referred to as "union"—as in Ruysbroeck. Still, I think that, strictly speaking, the answer to the question just posed should be no. Not only is the introvertive mystical experience not the *only* mystical phenomenon included in the class of union experiences, it is misleading to say that it is even *one* among the various states that constitute the extension of this class. Let me add that I do not want to attach too much emphasis to this last (somewhat fussy) point of mystical typology. Still, it does add force to a theme that I think has been steadily accumulating in this chapter—that the theory advanced in *Mysticism and Philosophy* concerning the use of "union with God" in the Christian mystical literature makes precious little contact with what is actually said in the datum discourse on this topic.

Though it conflicts with what Christian mystics tell us about the details of their union experiences and though it has been given nothing in the way of effective support, I shall not conclude that Stace's analysis of "union with God" is false. I think better to say that it is *evidentially bankrupt*. By this I mean that unless more can be said in Stace's behalf than what is actually given in *Mysticism and Philosophy*, it would be *irrational* to suppose that this analysis is correct.

[7]

On the Possibility of
Theistic Experience

Let us say that a given experience counts as a *theistic experience* just in case the experience in question is, *phenomenologically,* of God. In this chapter I shall address the question of whether theistic experience is possible. And on this topic I shall structure my deliberations around a complex argument developed by William Forgie in a paper published in 1984 entitled "Theistic Experience and the Doctrine of Unanimity." The argument in question is intended to show that theistic experience is not possible, that the idea of someone having such an experience is incoherent. Although for Forgie theistic experience descriptions have no special connection with the introvertive mystical state, his paper contains the best defense I have encountered for the claim that these descriptions are what Stace would call "interpretations" rather than "mere descriptive reports." My treatment of Forgie's argument is offered as a prologue to the discussion in the next chapter, where I shall argue (among other things) that the several states of union are, in fact, theistic experiences.

1. Dreams of God

Consider the following report from an unidentified informant cited by William James in the third chapter of *The Varieties of Religious Experience.*

I was in perfect health: we were on our sixth day of tramping, and in good training. . . . I felt neither fatigue, hunger, nor thirst, and my state of mind was equally healthy. . . . I can best describe the condition in which I was by calling it a state of equilibrium. When all at once I experienced a feeling of being raised above myself, I felt the presence of God—I tell of the thing just as I was conscious of it—as if his goodness and his power were penetrating me altogether. The throb of emotion was so violent that I could barely tell the boys to pass on and not wait for me. I then sat down on a stone, unable to stand any longer, and my eyes overflowed with tears. (67)

Since I shall have a good deal to say about this passage during the course of the present chapter, it will be convenient to have a name by which to refer to the reporter. I'll name him "Tramper." Subsequent to the remarks already quoted he says, "The state of ecstasy may have lasted four or five minutes, although it seemed at the time to last much longer." And after some discussion of his reaction to the experience, Tramper ends the report with the following comments:

I think it well to add that in this ecstasy of mine God had neither form, color, odor, nor taste; moreover that the feeling of his presence was accompanied by no determinate localization. It was rather as if my personality had been transformed by the presence of a *spiritual spirit*. But the more I seek words to express this intimate intercourse, the more I feel the impossibility of describing the thing by any of our usual images. At bottom the expression most apt to render what I felt was this: God was present, though invisible; he fell under no one of my senses, yet my consciousness perceived him. (68)

In this passage, the reporter seems clearly to be saying that the experience he is reporting was one in which he perceived himself to be in the presence of another, a "not-me"—someone whose goodness and power penetrated him completely. Further, Tramper says that the not-me in question was *God*—adding that this is to "tell of the thing just as I was conscious of it." On the most natural reading of the passage it would appear that Tramper is reporting an experience that was phenomenologically of God. In other words, it looks as if Tramper had a *theistic* experience. At this point, I want to make three observations about this case.

First, were we to describe the experience reported by James's informant as one in which the subject was aware of God, we would not be committing ourselves to the existence of some being referred to as "God." In fact, Tramper himself might describe his experience in this way and then go on to deny the existence of such a being. This would be to acknowledge that the experience was a hallucination. Though this is not usual in cases of this sort, there would be no conceptual difficulty in such an admission. The situation here is as it was when dealing with picture descriptions in Section 2 of Chapter 5. I might describe one of the pictures in my collection as being of Paul Bunyan riding his blue ox Babe without thereby committing myself to the existence of Bunyan or to the existence of his blue ox Babe.

Second, let us suppose that Tramper was a Christian believer. Let us suppose, further, that he was a committed Christian prior to his experience. Under these conditions one might suppose that the specific content of Tramper's religious experience had been caused or conditioned by his prior theological belief. Had he not believed in the existence of the Christian God, he would not have had a theistic experience. Let me add that it will not matter for our purposes whether any of this is true—that is, whether Tramper was a Christian or whether it is reasonable to think that theistic belief could play a role in determining the content of a religious experience. My point is that even were we to grant these items for the sake of discussion, this would in no way mitigate the possibility that Tramper's experience was, phenomenologically, of God and thus that his claim to have perceived God was a purely descriptive report and not a Stacean interpretation. Prior to dreaming about Paul Bunyan, my son believed that Bunyan's ox was blue. As a consequence, my son dreamed of Bunyan riding on a *blue* ox. But that the ox in the dream was experienced as *blue* is part of the phenomenological description of the dream. It is not an item my son incorporated into the description of the dream after waking as a consequence of his belief that Bunyan's ox was blue.

Third, Tramper tells us that God was present and that he felt God's goodness and power penetrating him. *Question:* How did he know, that is, by what marks did he determine, that the individual who was present and whose goodness and power were penetrating him, was, specifically, God? Perhaps it was someone else—say, Gabriel or Saint Peter. It might even have been Satan penetrating him with a special kind of evil that only seems to be goodness. I could well imagine a case in which these kinds of questions would have answers. For example, suppose that Tramper had had an experience involving a visual image of a large and stately looking man, wearing a long white robe, sitting on a throne surrounded by angels. In this case, were we to ask the question posed above, he might cite the items visually detected as reasons for thinking that the individual he perceived was God. We might then try to evaluate those reasons in an effort to decide whether his identification of the individual was justified. But in the case before us the reporter tells us that no such visual or other sensory data were involved. So now, let us ask again: How did he know it was God? I think that this question may have no answer. I also think that if, in fact, the case we are considering is one in which this question has no answer, this would in no way affect the claim that Tramper's perception was, specifically, of God. I'll elaborate.

Suppose I report a dream in which I was riding a carousel and the president of the United States was riding the horse beside me. By what marks did I determine that there was a person riding beside me; or, given that I experienced a person riding beside me, by what marks did I determine that the person in question was the president of the United States? We can imagine a case in which this question would have an answer; for example, suppose that in the dream I turned to see George Bush, who then was introduced to me as the president by a Secret Service agent standing by his side. But, we could also imagine a contrary case. Suppose that in the dream I was so nervous about my frolic with the president that I could not bring myself to look at him. I had no visual image of a person bearing certain presidential features. In fact, I had no visual image of a person at all. Let's add that the dream contained no other giveaway items, such as a Secret Service agent who told me that someone was riding beside me and that the person in question was the president. In this case, that I was aware of a person and that the person in question was the president was an immediate datum of the dream. In the dream, there were no special marks by which I determined the existence or identity of an object beside me. In

relating the experience I do not need to be able to itemize identifying features in order to be justified in claiming that the experience
was, phenomenologically, of the president.

So, too, with respect to the experience related by Tramper. He
might well have experienced himself in the presence of God without being aware of any marks or features by which God can be
distinguished from other individuals. That he experienced God
(and not, for example, Gabriel or Saint Peter) might have been an
immediate datum of the experience. Of course, were the reporter
to go on to claim that the experience was veridical—that is, that
God was, in fact, present—we might *then* insist that he specify
criteria by which the identification was made. But, so long as we
are considering just the phenomenological content of the experience (and are not interested in its epistemological status) we can be
content with what we have. Given our purposes, his report can be
treated as a fully complete and accurate account even if the informant could not explain *how* he knew that he was perceiving God.
In this case, it might be that there simply was no *how* about it.

The remarks I have just made concerning Tramper's religious
experience were taken (with some changes) from a response I made
at a colloquium held at Oberlin College in April 1965 to a paper
delivered by Ninian Smart entitled "Mysticism," later published
under the title "Interpretation and Mystical Experience."[1] In that
paper Smart contended, against R. C. Zaehner, that Christian experiences of union are "monistic" (what Stace called "introvertive") mystical experiences theologically interpreted. In essential
respects, then, Smart's position on this topic was the same as the
one defended by Stace. In my response to Smart, the remarks
made above about Tramper's experience were intended to show
there is no reason to deny that a mystic could have a *phenomenologically* theistic experience, that is, an experience (1) phenomenologically of-another (dualistic); and (2) in which the Other in question
is given or experienced as God. The point I was trying thereby to
establish was this: the issue between Smart (Stace) and Zaehner
does not turn on a conceptual question; there is no reason in princi-

---

1. Smart's original paper and my response to it are printed in Capitan and
Merrill, *Art, Mind, and Religion.*

ple why a typology for mystical experience might not include a theistic category with members. The question is, rather, whether it is reasonable to think that experiences of this type *in fact* occur, or occur often enough to warrant a separate category in a mystical typology. Though I did not try to answer that question in my response to Smart, I did suggest one case from the Christian mystical literature on union that seemed to me to be an especially promising candidate for inclusion in this class, namely, the experience described in chapter xi of Ruysbroeck's *Book of Supreme Truth*.[2]

2. Forgie on the Impossibility of Theistic Experience

I turn now to Forgie's argument for the claim that theistic experience is not possible. I'll start by reviewing his argument. My review will be organized into three subsections.

1. Tim Tibbetts and Tom Tibbetts are identical twins—not just in the biological sense but in the sense that they are visually indistinguishable. On a given occasion, I look over the fence in my backyard (the Tibbetts twins live next door) and I see a person whom I confidently judge to be Tim, rather than Tom. How did I do it? Forgie says that in any given perceptual circumstance, I enter the situation with a collection of beliefs related to that situation. So, for example, let us suppose that in this case I happened to know that Tom was out of town and I also believed it highly unlikely that anyone other than his twin brother would look exactly like Tim. Thus, given the phenomenological content of the visual experience and drawing on this backlog of previously held beliefs, I came up with the judgment that the person I was seeing was Tim. Forgie refers to the collection of beliefs herein utilized as the "epistemic base" of the judgment. And as part of the general thesis developed in part 1 of his essay, Forgie claims that any judgment

2. I discuss this experience in Chapter 2, Section 3, and will say some more about it in the first section of the next chapter. I should add that in my response to Smart, I did not use Tramper's experience as an illustrating case. Instead, I used an experience described in another of the reports included in chap. 3 of James, *Varieties of Religious Experience*. I make this change now because in a variety of ways Tramper's experience is a better choice for my purposes. This change, however, has not altered any of the points made in my original paper nor will it affect any of the points Forgie will make in the section to follow.

made by a perceiver concerning the identity of an individual perceived will rest, in part, on the epistemic base of the judgment in
question. No identity judgment could be based exclusively on the
phenomenological content of a sensory experience. Forgie says:

> Sense experiences are not phenomenologically of individuals, but at
> best only of things that appear in certain ways. A visual experience,
> for example, is at best phenomenologically of something that looks
> a certain way. And auditory and tactile experiences are at best phe-
> nomenologically of things that sound and feel certain ways. But
> numerically distinct individuals can look the same, or sound or feel
> the same. What is necessarily unique to a particular individual does
> not include how it looks or sounds or feels. (17)

Now, let's think about Tramper's claim that in his experience he
perceived God. Let's hypothesize that in this case, the choice of the
term "perceive" was intended to convey the idea that the experience was analogous to an ordinary sense (for example, visual)
perception. We speculate, too, that in this report, the term "God"
was used as the proper name of a particular individual. On this
understanding, the case is parallel to the one just considered in
which I claimed to see Tim Tibbetts. Forgie maintains that under
these conditions, we could not suppose that Tramper had provided
a purely phenomenological description of his experience. In order
to suppose this, we should have to assume that one and only one
individual is capable of appearing in just the way the individual
appeared in Tramper's experience. Forgie thinks that it is implausible to suppose that one and only one individual could appear in
some particular way. With respect to the sort of case we are here
considering, therefore, Forgie says this:

> Given any experience which is alleged to be phenomenologically of
> God, it seems intuitively that there is a possible world in which the
> causal laws pertaining to the relations between possible objects of
> "perception" and the "perceivers" of those objects are such that
> some individual, not identical to God, is capable of appearing in just
> the way displayed in the experience in question. If so, then nothing
> in the content of the experience will render it phenomenologically
> of God as opposed to another possible individual. (18)

Where religious experience is understood on the model of ordinary sense experience and where "God" is taken as a proper name, Forgie concludes that an experience that is phenomenologically of God is not possible.

2. Again working with Tramper's report, let's change our analysis and suppose that when he claimed to have perceived God, the term "God" was being used, not as the proper name of some individual, but as shorthand for a definite description. Since Tramper was Swiss and was thus speaking in the context of a Christian culture, we might plausibly suppose the description in question would be this: "The all-powerful, all-knowing, all-good creator of heaven and earth." Given this understanding of the case, we might agree that no religious experience is phenomenologically of God, where "God" is understood as the name of some particular individual, but we might still insist that Tramper's perception was of God in that it was, phenomenologically, of an all-powerful, all-knowing, all-good person who created heaven and earth. Forgie argues that no perception analogous to that of an ordinary sense perception could be phenomenologically of an individual having any one, let alone all, of the properties just itemized. As we noted above in our discussion of Angela of Foligno's (alleged) Rapture perceptions of God's *power, wisdom, and goodness*,[3] no one of these properties is of a sort which can be seen or otherwise observed via an ordinary sense perception. At best, one can observe only *manifestations* of such properties—for example, exhibitions of power, expressions of knowledge, displays of morally good behavior. Forgie argues that to observe someone manifesting a property is to observe that person *causing* something to happen or producing some state of affairs. Forgie maintains that a causal relation between some act of an agent and some (alleged) manifestation of one of his properties is not phenomenologically presentable. In fact Forgie insists that insofar as a causal relation involves something more than mere sequence, causal relations cannot be directly observed by means of an ordinary sense experience. Of course, this last puts an end to the idea that one might have an experience that is, phenomenologically, of the creator of heaven and earth. Even if

3. See the subsection "Rapture" in Section 3 of Chapter 3.

one were to perceive some individual actually bringing heaven and earth into existence, the claim to have had such a perception could not be justified by reference to its phenomenological content alone.[4]

The conclusion is this: whether we think of "God" as a proper name or as an abbreviation for "the all-powerful, all-knowing, all-good creator of the universe," no perception understood as analogous to an ordinary sense perception could be, phenomenologically, of God.

3. There is still another option. Suppose we drop the idea that the sort of perception involved in Tramper's case is analogous to an ordinary sense perception. In my reply to Smart, I suggested, in effect, that we use a dream rather than an ordinary sense perception as a model when thinking of Tramper's experience. Given this model we could think of the experience as having been phenomenologically and specifically of God even though it involved no ordinary visual, auditory, tactile, or other sense experiences. In part 2 of his paper, Forgie critiques this effort on my part to establish the possibility of theistic experience. Having reviewed my argument in the first few paragraphs of the text, Forgie formats the rest of his discussion of this topic as follows:

Let us say, following what appears to be Pike's usage, that some aspect φ is an immediate datum of N's experience just in case (1) the experience has φ; and (2) N knows (or, perhaps, can know) that the experience has φ without determining that fact from features or marks. We will also say that one is employing "Pike's stratagem" if he attempts to reject questions of the form "How did you know, by what marks or features did you determine, that that experience has aspect φ?" by replying "Its having φ was simply an immediate datum of the experience". Now Pike's defense of the possibility of theistic experience depends on his making intelligible how something can be an "immediate datum" of an experience. Only in this way will he be able to explain how Pike's stratagem can legitimately be used by James' reporter. Pike thinks he can do this by citing the example of dreams. I will suggest, however, that although Pike's

4. The argument given in this paragraph is a digest of Forgie, "Theistic Experience," 19–21.

stratagem does seem to work for dreams, the dream model fails to make intelligible how something can be an immediate datum of a non-dream experience. If this is correct, then Pike's defense of theistic experience fails: he will not have shown how James' reporter can use Pike's stratagem to overcome skeptical doubts about the object of his experience. (24)

I'll expand from here.

Suppose I dream that I have a veridical visual experience of Tim Tibbetts. In my dream (as in real life) Tim has an identical twin brother, Tom. Question 1: In my dream, how did I know (by what marks did I determine) that the object of the visual perception was Tim rather than Tom? Question 2: In my dream how did I know (by what marks did I determine) that the visual perception I was having of Tim was veridical? Forgie acknowledges that there may well be cases in which neither of these questions has an answer. That the visual experience was a perception of Tim and not Tom may well have been an immediate datum of the dream. This would be true if, for example, in my dream nobody told me it was Tim and I did not think to myself "Tom is out of town so that must be Tim." So also for the dream fact that the perception was veridical. In the dream I did not consult other witnesses, check to see whether my visual perception cohered with other sensory data of the dream, and so on. In my dream, the visual perception was *veridical* and was *of Tim*. Each of these features of the visual experience was an immediate datum of the dream.

Now let's switch to a case of a waking-life visual experience. Again, I have a visual experience that I take to be a veridical perception of Tim Tibbetts. I ask the same two questions posed above about the dream: (1) how do I know that the visual perception is of Tim rather than Tom? and (2) how do I know that the visual perception is veridical? Suppose we try "Pike's stratagem" here. I answer (1) that the visual perception is of Tim rather than Tom is an immediate datum of the experience, and (2) that the visual perception is veridical rather than hallucinatory is also an immediate datum of the experience. Forgie argues that each of these answers would be absurd. With respect to the first, the visual experience of Tim and the visual experience of Tom will not be distinguishable by reference to some experiential datum. In Forgie's words, "Any 'datum' of the one experience is going to be a datum of the other" (26). And as regards the second answer, the question of whether a visual experience is or is not veridical is not one that can be answered by reference to some part of the content of the experience itself. The issue here concerns the causal connections between the experience and the world outside of experience. Forgie says:

> Indeed, for any datum one might think could be added to an experience in order to assure its veridicality—from the inside, so to speak—it would still seem open to inquire whether that augmented experience was itself veridical, i.e., whether it bore the appropriate causal relations to that of which it is presumably a perception. Pike's stratagem, applied to claims of veridicality, would amount to a novel defense of "self-authenticating" experiences. (26)

Why should it be that Pike's stratagem can be used legitimately when answering questions about the content of dreams but cannot be used without generating absurdity when answering precisely the same questions about ordinary waking-life visual experiences? Forgie thinks he has the answer.

First, observe that in the typical case, the content of a dream is not exhausted by what Forgie refers to as "the content of the perceptual experiences occurring in that dream." "In dreams certain things are not learned, let alone learned from the content of the perceptual experiences occurring in the dream. They are just understood, 'given' if we like. They are known *in* the dream without being known *from* something (e.g., some perceptual experiences) in the dream. Such things might naturally be called 'immediate data' of the dream" (26). Thus, for example, with respect to my dream about the president, Forgie says that it may have contained a few auditory and visual experiences that (by hypothesis) did not inform me that the president was riding beside me. But the important point is that it also contained another item that was not a perceptual (for example, visual or auditory) ingredient. Forgie describes this further ingredient as "Pike's awareness that he was riding next to the President." This, he says, was just "given, some-

thing understood, an immediate datum of the dream" (26–27).
The same holds for the dream about Tim Tibbetts. In the dream, I
know that it is Tim rather than Tom, and I also know that the
visual perception is veridical. Forgie says that "these items of
awareness may be just understood. They may be known in my
dream without being known or determined from anything in that
dream" (27). In the case of a dream, therefore, we can usually
distinguish two kinds of contents, which Forgie refers to as "phenomenological" and "non-phenomenological," respectively. The
first consists of the perceptual (for example, visual or auditory)
experiences that occur in the dream. The second is comprised of
the nonperceptual materials just identified—in Forgie's words,
"those things that are simply understood" (27).

Turning now to an ordinary waking-life experience, such as my
visual perception of Tim Tibbetts, Forgie says this: "If something
is part of the content of a visual experience, . . . it will have to be
part of its phenomenological content, for that is all the content
there is. There is nothing analogous here to those things which in
dreams are simply understood or given" (27). And, on Forgie's
view, this difference between dream experiences and ordinary
waking-life perceptual experiences accounts for the fact that Pike's
stratagem can be used legitimately when answering questions
about the content of the former but cannot be used when answering similar questions about the latter. His claim is that the plau-
sibility—indeed, the intelligibility—of using Pike's stratagem
when discussing the content of dreams depends on the fact that
dreams have nonphenomenological content. Its use in the case of
an ordinary waking-life visual experience where there is no such
content (for example, my visual perception of Tim Tibbetts) thus
makes no sense at all.

We are now ready for Forgie's conclusion concerning Tramper's
experience. Forgie says that we can treat it in either of two ways:
(1) we can think of it as parallel to ordinary waking-life visual
experiences having phenomenological content only (as we did in
the first two subsections above); or (2) we can employ the dream
model (as I did in my response to Smart) and conceive of it as
having both phenomenological and nonphenomenological content. In the first case, to claim that an experience of this sort is, for

example, of God and that this is an immediate datum of the experience is, Forgie thinks, non-sense. This would be to suppose that the experience has nonphenomenological content, which, on the first alternative, is (by hypothesis) precluded. In the second case, though it may be true that a given experience is of God and that this is an immediate datum of the experience, this tells us something about its nonphenomenological content only. Thus, in neither case can one claim that such an experience is *phenomenologically* of God. Since "theistic experience" has been defined as an experience that is *phenomenologically* of God, my defense of the possibility of theistic experience fails. Forgie's conclusion thus stands as it was formulated at the end of the second subsection above.

Looking back over this argument, it is clear that it rests importantly on the distinction Forgie makes between what he calls the "phenomenological content" and the "non-phenomenological content" of dream experiences. Without this distinction Forgie could not allow that Tramper's experience can be modeled on the case of a dream without also admitting that it is a bona fide theistic experience. But on the surface, at least, this distinction is poorly drawn. What exactly is "non-phenomenological content"? Indeed, if something counts as *content* of a dream (that is, part of what is dreamed), that fact alone would appear to require that we include it as part of the *phenomenological* material of the total dream experience. Forgie, himself, encourages this reply when he speaks of the (alleged) non-phenomenological element of my dream as "Pike's *awareness* that he was riding next to the President" (26), going on to refer to the materials classified as non-phenomenological in the dream about Tim Tibbetts as, again, "items of *awareness*" (27). What follows in the next paragraph is offered as a way of understanding Forgie's distinction, which relieves at least some of the tension on this point.

In my dream about the president, I held a certain number of *beliefs* about objects and persons in the dream environment. That there was a person riding beside me and, more specifically, that the person in question was the president were things I believed in the dream. They must, then, be listed among the contents of the dream along with the perceptual (sensory) experiences also included.[5] Thus, in my dream I was conscious of two kinds of things: (1) objects and events, for example, the wooden horses, children laughing; and (2) facts, propositions, or at least something describable only in propositional language, namely, *that* there was a person riding beside me and *that* the person in question was the president. The items in the first list were *perceived;* the items in the second list were *believed,* or, in Forgie's words, "simply understood." As in the interval of waking-life experience in which I perceived Tim Tibbetts in the yard next door, two mental modes were thus functional in the dream—I perceived things and I believed things. As in the waking-life interval, the first provided the "phenomenological content" of the dream and the second provided its "non-phenomenological content." Forgie's final position, then, is that if we model Tramper's experience on the dream case, his alleged "perception" of God will have to be classified as a *belief that* God was present. He was aware of God only in the sense that he was aware *that* (believed that) God was present. This cannot be counted as a theistic experience.

3. Teresa's Intellectual Vision of Christ

In what is to follow I shall not protest Forgie's analysis of my dream about the president. Though in my reply to Smart I chose to work with the case of a dream in order to ensure that the awareness under discussion would be one whose content description would have to be read as a purely phenomenological account, I think I must admit that there is nothing about the way I characterized my dream about the president that is not accommodated on Forgie's quite ingenious analysis. This being so, I now want to develop a richer and more stable analogue to Tramper's (alleged) perception of God—one that I think will allow deeper penetration into the case. The analogue in question is a vision reported by Saint Teresa in chapter xxvii of her autobiography and again in *Interior Castle* (Sixth Mansions, chapter viii). Teresa tells us that this vision was of considerable moment in her spiritual life. It is one that is reg-

5. This way of putting the matter is tentatively suggested by Forgie in note 22.

ularly used in the Christian mystical theological literature as the
illustrating case of a type of mystical apprehension called "intellectual vision." Following the lead of one of her advisers (Peter Alcantara), Teresa herself classifies the vision in this way.[6] In the
discussion of this experience in *Interior Castle*, however, she adds
that she does not know why it should be called an "intellectual"
vision (197).[7]

Following is part of Teresa's report taken from chapter XXVII of
her *Life*.

> I was at prayer on a festival of the glorious Saint Peter when I saw
> Christ at my side—or, to put it better, I was conscious of Him, for
> neither with the eyes of the body nor with those of the soul did I see
> anything. I thought He was quite close to me and I saw that it was
> He Who, as I thought, was speaking to me. Being completely igno-
> rant that visions of this kind could occur, I was at first very much
> afraid, and did nothing but weep, though, as soon as He addressed a
> single word to me to reassure me, I became quiet again, as I had
> been before, and was quite happy and free from fear. All the time
> Jesus Christ seemed to be beside me, but as this was not an imagi-
> nary vision, I could not discern in what form: what I felt very clearly
> was that all the time He was at my right hand, and a witness of
> everything that I was doing, and that, whenever I became slightly
> recollected or was not greatly distracted, I could not help but be
> aware of His nearness to me.
>
> Sorely troubled, I went at once to my confessor, to tell him about
> it. He asked me in what form I had seen Him. I told him that I had
> not seem Him at all. Then he asked me how I knew it was Christ. I
> told him that I did not know how, but that I could not help realizing
> that He was beside me, and that I saw and felt this clearly. (249)

At the beginning of chapter XXVIII of her *Life*, Teresa adds that this
vision remained with her for "some days." Here she says that she

---

6. Teresa, *Life*, 249.
7. In note 21 of Chapter 3 I provided some data concerning ways in which the
phrase "intellectual vision" has been used in the history of Christian mystical
theology. With reference to the material therein given as well as to that which will
be given in the next three paragraphs, I suspect that Augustine, too, would have
trouble understanding why Peter Alcantara classified Teresa's vision of Christ as
an "intellectual" vision.

"clearly perceived" that Christ was a "witness" to everything she did during this time. I proceed now to the details of Teresa's account of this experience.

Teresa says that she saw Christ, but, she adds, she saw him "neither with the eyes of the body nor with those of the soul." As noted above in Section 1 of Chapter 1, this is Teresa's way of saying that the awareness she had of the object detected did not consist of ordinary visual imagery gained via the eyes, nor did it consist of imaginative visual imagery such as is involved when one sees something in the imagination. In this passage, Teresa puts this by saying that the vision was not "imaginary"—meaning, I think, that it involved no visual images. Why, then, say that this is a case of "seeing"? Teresa herself obviously sensed the incongruity. Directly after claiming that she *saw* Christ, she corrects her description, claiming that it would be better to say that she was "conscious" of him. As the passage continues, Teresa employs a number of other ways of expressing the point—saying that she "felt" him and was "aware of" him—but in the closing sentence she says again that she "saw" him, and two paragraphs later, when discussing visions of this general sort, Teresa says that in these cases "the soul distinctly *sees* that Jesus Christ, the Son of the Virgin, is present" (250). Though for obvious reasons Teresa seems reluctant to employ the term "see" in this context, for reasons that are perhaps not so obvious she seems equally reluctant to abandon her initial use of this specific perception verb.

Can we get a little clearer about the kind of seeing involved in this case? At the close of the paragraph that includes the quotation given above, Teresa provides an analogy designed to clarify the point. The same analogy is developed more fully in the last paragraph of her first letter to Rodrigo Alvarez. The following passage is taken from this last-mentioned source.

As for the vision about which you, my father, wish to know something, it is of this kind: She [the soul] sees nothing either outwardly or inwardly, for the vision is not imaginary; but without seeing anything, she understands what it is, and where it is, more clearly than if she saw it, only nothing in particular presents itself to her. She is like a person who feels that another is close beside her; but

because she is in the dark she sees him not, yet is certain that he is
there present. Still, this comparison is not exact; for he who is in the
dark, in some way or other, through hearing a noise or having seen
that person before, knows he is there, or knew it before; but here
there is nothing of the kind, for without a word, inward or outward, the soul clearly perceives who it is, where he is, and occasion-
ally what he means. Why, or how, she perceives it, she knoweth
not; but so it is; and while it lasts, she cannot help being aware of it.[8]

Again Teresa insists that in the type of vision here under discussion, one sees nothing "outwardly" (with the eyes of the body) or
"inwardly" (in the imagination); the vision is not "imaginary." But
Teresa also provides something positive to work with. She says
that it is like the case where one feels that another is present in the
dark. Is this to say that she *thinks* or is *convinced* that someone is
there? Although this seems to be part of the message, there is
clearly more to it than that. Teresa says that in the ordinary case,
one might know that someone is there in the dark on the basis of
auditory clues (one hears the other speak or move) or on the basis
of previous knowledge gained when the lights were on. One *infers*
that the other is there—one thus knows it on the basis of *evidence*.
But this case, Teresa tells us, is different. Here one directly "feels"
the presence of the other—no inference of the sort just mentioned
is involved. In the last part of the passage quoted, Teresa says that
one "clearly perceives" who it is and where he is, adding that one
"cannot help being aware" of his presence. The point seems to be
not only that one is convinced that someone is there, but that the
ground of this conviction is a kind of *perception* at least akin to a
definite sensation. I suspect that this is why Teresa was reluctant to
abandon the perception verb "see" when reporting the vision. "*See*
Christ beside me" as opposed to "am *conscious of* Christ beside me"
carries the clear implication that the experience in question was
perceptual. Also, since sight is a distance sense (in the sense spec-
ified in Section 2 of Chapter 3 above), "see Christ beside me,"
unlike "feel Christ beside me," carries only the suggestion that
Christ was perceived to be *near*, not touched.

A few pages before citing Tramper's report in lecture 3 of *The*

8. Teresa, *Relations*, 400–401.

Varieties of Religious Experience, William James comments as follows on the sort of experience we are here discussing: "It often happens that an hallucination is imperfectly developed: the person affected will feel a 'presence' in the room, definitely localized, facing in one particular way, real in the most emphatic sense of the word, often coming suddenly, and as suddenly gone; and yet neither seen, heard, touched, or cognized in any of the usual 'sensible' ways" (58). Following his usual procedure in this text, James then provides a number of firsthand testimonials to illustrate the point. What follows is part of one of those cited in this case. It is from a letter to James written by someone whom he describes as "an intimate friend of mine, one of the keenest intellects I know."

> After I got into bed and blown out the candle, I lay awake awhile thinking on the previous night's experience, when suddenly I *felt* something come into the room and stay close to the bed. It remained only a minute or two. I did not recognize it by any ordinary sense, and yet there was a horribly unpleasant "sensation" connected with it. It stirred something more at the roots of my being than any ordinary perception. The feeling had something of the quality of a very large tearing vital pain spreading chiefly over the chest, but within the organism—and yet the feeling was not *pain* so much as *abhorrence.* At all events, something was present with me, and I knew its presence far more surely than I have ever known the presence of any fleshy living creature. I was conscious of its departure as of its coming: an almost instantaneously swift going through the door, and the "horrible sensation" disappeared. . . .
>
> On two other occasions in my life I have had precisely the same "horrible sensation". Once it lasted for a full quarter of an hour. In all three instances the certainty that there in outward space there stood *something* was indescribably *stronger* than the ordinary certainty of companionship when we are in the close presence of ordinary living people. The something seemed close to me, and intensely more real than any ordinary perception. Although I felt it to be like unto myself, so to speak, or finite, small, and distressful, as it were, I didn't recognize it as any individual being or person. (58–60)

In the course of the discussion following these passages, James cites a number of other firsthand reports describing experiences of a similar sort. In some cases (as in the one just cited) the object detected is assigned properties such as "small, finite and distressful" and is also given location in space (for example, "close to the bed") but is not identified as a specific person or individual. In other cases, the object detected is not only characterized and/or located but is also specifically identified—for example, as a friend whom the informant was able to call by name (61, 62). In all cases, though the presence of the object is said to have been "felt" rather than seen or otherwise perceived via ordinary sensory channels, the "feeling" involved is invariably characterized in such a way as to encourage the idea that it was a perceptual experience rather than just a thought or conviction. As in Teresa, the objects so detected were perceived to be near but were not touched. James adds that this sort of phenomenon is a "well-marked natural kind of fact" that is not at all uncommon (60). My own suspicion is that most normal people (especially children) could readily identify an experience of their own that could be added to James's collection.

Returning to Teresa's intellectual vision of Christ, let's ask a question: Given that she was directly aware of someone (or something) there on her right hand, how did she know that the object in question was the specific individual whom she identified as "Jesus Christ, the Son of the Virgin"? Recall that this was the question raised by Teresa's confessor to which she replied, "I did not know how [I knew it], but . . . I could not help realizing that He was beside me, and . . . I saw and felt this clearly." In the account of this vision related in *Interior Castle,* Sixth Mansions, chapter VIII, Teresa says that her confessor asked her, "If you see nothing, how do you know it is our Lord?" He then asked her to tell him what Christ's face looked like. But, of course, Teresa did not see his face—in fact, she did not *see* anything at all if to "see" is visually to apprehend physical form or color. A little after the passage quoted above from her *Life,* Teresa says that her confessor also asked her who it was who told her it was Christ. On her account, she replied that Christ himself told her but that she knew who it was even before he did so. That it was, specifically, Christ thus appears to have been what I called above an "immediate datum" of Teresa's vision. Teresa knew it was Christ, but, she says, she did not know *how* she knew it. As in the case of my dream about the president, no visual or auditory clues were involved. Here again there appears to have been no *how* about it.

Using Forgie's label, we are here confronting another instance of "Pike's stratagem" used in answer to an inquiry about the content of experience. And, of course, the question of interest is how this case is to be analyzed. Consistent with his earlier remarks on this topic, I think Forgie would have to say that if Teresa's answer to her confessor is to be regarded as intelligible, we shall have to think of Teresa's vision experience on the model of a dream, thus allowing that it had both phenomenological and non-phenomenological content. On the Feast of Saint Peter, Teresa had a number of perceptions; for example, she saw the church steeple, she felt the rosary in her hand, and she heard the choir singing. In addition to these perceptions, however, Teresa also *believed that* Christ was standing beside her. This is not something Teresa came to believe via the perceptions. As Forgie put it earlier, it was something that was "simply understood" in the vision. As in my dream about the president, the latter constituted the non-phenomenological content of the total vision experience. On Forgie's account, Teresa's use of Pike's stratagem must be taken as signaling the presence of this belief element.

I said above that I can find no fault with Forgie's analysis of my dream about the president. It seems clear to me, however, that Teresa's intellectual vision of Christ is such as to preclude the possibility of a similar analysis. For purposes of discussion, let's suppose that as a result of having the vision, Teresa *believed* that Christ was there beside her. Still, in her report of the vision, Teresa says very clearly that she *perceived* Christ. In fact, the very special nature of the perception is clearly one of the topics at the very center of her concern. This is especially evident in the several places in her writings where Teresa compares her awareness of Christ with the awareness one might have of someone present in the dark. Thus, whether or not Teresa actually believed that Christ was there beside her, to summarily *reduce* her awareness of Christ to such a belief would be to disregard her all but fully explicit disclaimer to the contrary. Of course, this leaves open the question of whether Teresa's answer to her confessor can be given some other, still intelligible, interpretation. I shall delay my response to

this further question until the end of the next section. I move now
to develop the concept that will play the central role in the answer I
shall give.

4. Perceptual Identification

Forgie claims that no ordinary sense experience could be phenomenologically and specifically of some particular individual.
This is true, he tells us, because, phenomenologically, sense experiences are exclusively of things that appear in certain ways; and for
any given way of appearing, it is always possible that there is more
than one individual that appears in that way. I think that Forgie's
reasoning on this point contains an important, though subtle, mistake. Before trying to identify the mistake, however, I shall develop Forgie's argument in a bit more detail.

Extrapolating from remarks he makes on pages 17 and 18 of his
paper Forgie apparently thinks that the following principle is true.

> For any individual (A) that appears in a certain way (S), there exists
> a possible world (W) in which the circumstances that obtain and the
> causal laws pertaining to the relations between perceivers and the
> objects they perceive are such that in W, not only does A appear in
> way S, but some individual (B), not identical to A, appears in way S
> as well.

Following Forgie, let's call the actual world "Alpha." In the Tibbetts example we suppose that in Alpha, circumstances and causal
laws pertaining to the relations between perceivers and the objects
they perceive are such that Tim Tibbetts (A) and Tom Tibbetts (B)
visually appear in the same way (S) even though Tim and Tom are
not identical. But if, in Alpha, Tim Tibbetts and Tom Tibbetts
both appear in way S, then, in Alpha, the visual perception of Tim
and the visual perception of Tom will have the same visual content
and will thus be what Forgie describes as "phenomenologically
indistinguishable." With this much in mind, I think we can see why
it should be that in Alpha no visual perception could be phenomenologically and specifically of Tim Tibbetts. This is so because, in

Alpha, visual perceptions produced by looking at Tim and visual perceptions produced by looking at Tom are phenomenologically indistinguishable and thus are neither phenomenologically and specifically of Tim nor phenomenologically and specifically of Tom. This point paves the way for a bigger conclusion—that in *no* possible world could a visual perception (P) be, phenomenologically and specifically, of Tim Tibbetts. To be such, the perceiver would have to be able to tell on the basis of its content alone that P was occurring in some world other than Alpha—in particular, some world not containing a look-alike (for example, Tom) who was causing P. Forgie rightly supposes that this last-mentioned item is not something one could determine solely on the basis of the data constituting the experiential content of P.[9] The argument can be generalized to cover all types of perceptions—auditory, tactile, and, we can presume, nonsensory perceptions, such as Teresa's intellectual vision and Tramper's religious experience. It can also be generalized to cover all individuals, whether they be Tim Tibbetts, Jesus Christ, or, indeed, God.

Now, the first thing to notice about this argument is that if it is sound, it will show that no visual perception could be, phenomenologically, of a tiger or of a tree or of any other individual identified only by a generic description. *Thesis:* No perception could be, phenomenologically, of a tiger. *Argument:* For any individual (A) that appears in a tigerlike manner (S), there exists a possible world (Beta) in which the circumstances that obtain and the causal laws pertaining to the relations between perceivers and the things they perceive are such that in Beta, there exists a cleverly disguised hologram (B) that appears in a tigerlike manner (S), and tigers are not identical to holograms of tigers. Thus in Beta, visual perceptions of tigers and visual perceptions of holograms of tigers are, Forgie would say, "phenomenologically indistinguishable." And according to the pattern of the argument traced above, it follows from this that no visual perception could be, phenomenologically, of a tiger. In order for there to be such a perception, it would have to be such that one could tell, on the basis of its phenomenological content alone, that it was not occurring in

9. This argument is taken directly from Forgie, "Theistic Experience," n. 6.

Beta—which (Forgie tells us) is impossible. With a little imagination, I suspect one could construct an argument of similar structure showing that no sense perception could be, phenomenologically, of a physical object. All one would need to suppose is that there is a possible world in which perceptions caused by physical objects are phenomenologically indistinguishable from perceptions caused by, for example, a play of light in empty space brought about by some gleeful Cartesian spirit.

Is this an acceptable conclusion? I suspect that in fact Forgie would say that it is (14). And what this shows, I think, is that Forgie's resistance to the idea that a sense perception could be, phenomenologically, of a specific individual does not stem from anything having uniquely to do with perceptions of specific individuals. I suspect that at the root of his misgivings is a view that Forgie has brought with him to the discussion concerning what is to count as *phenomenological content* when dealing with perceptions of objects generally—whether the perceptions be of specific individuals, such as Tim Tibbetts, or of generic individuals, such as a tiger or a physical object. I'll try now to identify the view in question.

For the moment, restrict attention to cases of veridical sense perceptions of an object. For Forgie, to perceive something veridically is to be affected in a certain way. What one perceives (phenomenologically) is the product of a causal chain that begins with the object perceived (for example, Tim Tibbetts or a tiger), proceeds through the physiological mechanisms connected with the operation of sensory faculties, and ends with a datum. Since the process is governed by the "causal laws pertaining to the relations between perceivers and the objects they perceive," we are encouraged to think of the datum as a kind of mechanically produced appearance—the last in a complex series of law-abiding happenings. As for the datum, Forgie says that it consists of "looks," "sounds," "feels," etc. (17), obviously excluding the element of consciousness expressed when I say, "It's Tim Tibbetts" or "It's a tiger." Of course, were this last-mentioned item to be so included, then the datum involved when I perceive Tim Tibbetts would not be the same as the datum involved when I perceive Tom Tibbetts. My visual perception of Tim and my visual perception of Tom would then *not* be phenomenologically indistinguishable. *Question:* Why is the "identification element" of consciousness (as I shall call it) not included in the datum? I suspect it is because Forgie is thinking of the datum as the immediate product of a complex, causally regulated, physical mechanism, while at the same time thinking of identification as a specifically mental act—a cognitive *reaction* to the physically produced datum. The final picture thus places the act of identification at a point *after* the object has been perceived and thus after the phenomenological content of the sense perception has been established.

Now let's switch to nonveridical sense perceptions, such as a visual hallucination or a perception I might have in a dream. Of course, Forgie cannot treat these perceptions in quite the same way, since in these cases the causal sequence starts from some object or condition other than the putative object perceived. But Forgie's picture of the nonveridical perception and its phenomenological content is still the same. Here the phenomenological content consists of just those looks, feels, and the like that *would* have resulted by way of the *normal* causal route *had* the perception been veridical.[10] Using the veridical case as a paradigm, Forgie thus isolates the phenomenological content of sense perceptions generally. The phenomenological content of a sense perception consists of just those data that, in the veridical case, are caused by the object via the normal sensory mechanisms and, in the nonveridical case, would have been so caused had the perception been veridical. In neither case does the phenomenological content of a sense perception include the perceiver's awareness of the identity of the object perceived.

I move now to my critique of this argument.

Return to Stace's case of the three men who, as Stace put it, "see something glimmering white" and then proceed to judge that the "something" in question is, respectively, a ghost, a sheet hung out on a clothesline, and a white-painted rock.[11] Here, the visual perception is, phenomenologically, of something glimmering white,

---

10. This account is not explicit in Forgie's text. It is, however, strongly suggested by the remarks made on p. 14.

11. See Section 2 of Chapter 5 above.

which, we can suppose, is then greeted with a kind of interior question: "What is that?" Identification of the object on the part of the perceiver is not included in the act of perception. That it is not so included is precisely what prompts the perceiver first to wonder and then to make a *judgment* about what it is that is being perceived. One can think of a myriad of such cases. If I am concentrating on an intellectual problem, the visual perceptions I have while staring out of the window may contain little more than colored patterns as data. I do not register the tree in the front yard or the car in the driveway. The experiential elements making up my perceptions are thus readily distinguishable from any recognition of the tree or the car that might follow subsequent to the perception. "Oh, yes, come to think about it, I did see the car in the driveway just a few minutes ago." So too when I survey a room full of people looking for a friend or the president. "That looks like him over there. . . . Yes (looking more closely), I think it is." From a phenomenological point of view, these kinds of cases show that perceiving an object and identifying an object are often distinct events. They also sustain the idea that identification is a kind of cognitive reaction to the datum perceived. They thus lend commonsense credence to Stace's distinction between experience and interpretation and to Forgie's insistence that the phenomenological content of sense experience be limited in such a way as to exclude the identification element of consciousness.

Still, while there appear to be cases that clearly illustrate the need for a phenomenological distinction between perception and identification, there also appear to be cases in which, as clearly, no such distinction can be made. I enter my kitchen on a sunny morning after a good night's sleep and head for the coffee maker. There it is—right there on the counter, as always. Experientially, this case is very different from one in which I perceive something glimmering white, wonder what it is, and then go on to identify it (rightly or wrongly) as a sheet hung out on a clothesline. In this second case there is no discernible distinction between seeing an object and the act of recognizing the object in question to be a coffee maker. From a phenomenological point of view, "it's a coffee maker" expresses an item as directly given in the second case as the one expressed in the first case by "it's something glimmering white."

Of course, this is the point where my understanding of the concept of *phenomenological content* begins to contrast with Forgie's. I proceed now to the details of my thinking about this contrast.

Suppose I were asked to *justify* my claim that the object I see in the kitchen is a coffee maker. No doubt I would list some of the features of the object I perceive, for example, its shape, its color, its size, and so on. That I see an object having a certain shape, color, and size would then be offered as a reason for thinking that the object I see is a coffee maker. Shall we then conclude that what is "given" is a colored shape having a certain size from which I then *infer* that it is a coffee maker? On this account we could then explain why it is that my awareness of the object's phenomenal qualities is assigned a certain epistemic priority over my awareness of its being a coffee maker. Filling in details, the story is this. What I *see* (immediately) are the coffee maker's phenomenal properties— I register "looks" that in the world as we know it are normally produced in some lawlike way by a coffee maker out there in space. Still, we know that there is a possible world (W) in which objects other than coffee makers produce "looks" that are "phenomenologically indistinguishable" from the one I am getting. We might suppose, for example, that in W, holograms of coffee makers produce "looks" like this on a regular basis. We might even suppose that in W, I would register a "look" like this even if the object producing that "look" were a tiger. In fact, in W, I might register a "look" like this even if there were nothing out there in space producing the "look" in question. Of course, given only the content of my present perception, I cannot be sure that it (the perception) is not occurring in W. So the conclusion is (1) that the coffee maker is something I only *believe* to exist, (2) that the belief in question is *derived* from immediate perception by way of an *inference,* and (3) that although my judgment concerning the coffee maker is based on immediate perception, it also reflects a complex set of fallible convictions and expectations acquired via experience with things having just this sort of "look." This is what explains the fact that my awareness of the coffee maker has second-class status when the issue concerns epistemic reliability.

Now, while the theory just sketched may have ample warrant when considered as a piece of *epistemology,* it seems to me clear that it cannot be taken as an accurate description of *phenomenological fact*. From a phenomenological point of view, my awareness of the coffee maker is not the product of an inference or a judgment based on perception. It is not a cognitive reaction to a perceptual event distinct from the alleged reaction. Of course, this is not to deny that the coffee maker has a "look" and that its look is registered in the perception. Phenomenologically, however, its look is not something from which my awareness of the coffee maker is *derived*. Experientially, my apprehension of its phenomenal qualities and my awareness of the coffee maker are aspects of a single mental act. Stated with the kind of deliberate naïveté appropriate when describing phenomenological facts, the act in question is, simply, the act of *seeing* a *coffee maker*. But if this is right, then although there may be epistemological reasons for restricting the content of perception to looks, feels, etc., and thus for striking a distinction, in principle, between *perceiving* an object and *recognizing* the object in question to be of some particular kind ("it's a coffee maker" or "it's a tiger"), this distinction cannot be justified on phenomenological grounds. Since this point constitutes the nub of what I take to be the mistake at the center of Forgie's thinking on this matter, I'll frame it again after making a distinction I hope will throw it into sharp relief.

Allow that the "given" in perception is that which is, as we say, directly or immediately presented. Allow, further, that the "discernible given" is that which would be discerned in an act of reflection as having been "given" in some specific perception. The discernible given stands in contrast to that which would be perceived in an act of reflection as having been *derived* by way of judgment. Now, the distinction I here want to mark is between the discernible given and what might be called the "theoretical given." The theoretical given is that which is taken or treated as the "given" in a *theory* designed to *explain* the fact that we are generally more confident about the "looks" and "feels" of the objects we perceive than we are about their status as coffee makers or tigers. Depending on the case, the theoretical given may or may not be an instance of the discernible given. In the case of the coffee maker—though *not* in Stace's case of seeing something glimmering white—my claim is that the identification element in consciousness (expressed by "it's a coffee maker") should be included as part of the *discernible* even though it might not be a candidate for inclusion in the *theoretical* given. Further, it seems to me clear that the discernible given is the only "given" of any interest to the phenomenologist: the theoretical given is an *epistemological,* not a *phenomenological,* category. The implication is that Forgie's account of what should be included in the *phenomenological* content of perception is mistaken. I suspect it turns on failure to distinguish between two quite distinct enterprises—both of which have philosophical interest—namely, epistemological explanation and phenomenological description. Forgie has, in effect, imported an epistemological concept to work at the very center of what is described in his text as a phenomenological account.

The two points following are intended to help clarify the criticism just offered of Forgie's position regarding the phenomenological content of sense perception.

1. "It's a coffee maker," like "it's glimmering white," is typically used by a speaker to affirm the existence of something in the external world and thus, in the typical case, would have to be counted as what I referred to in Section 2 of Chapter 5 above as an "*extended* description" and not a purely descriptive report. In my discussion of the case entertained above, however, I have focused entirely on the fact that "it's a coffee maker" expresses a *presentational* element of consciousness—part of the discernible given. I have said nothing about the *further* fact that in the case envisioned it would *also* express a *belief* concerning the contents of the external world independent of experience. Of course in the present context, this further fact is of no particular interest. Still, as a hedge against misunderstanding, perhaps a second (less complicated) illustrating case would be helpful. Consider, then, a visual perception described by the perceiver as having been "of a coffee maker" but known by the perceiver at the time of perception to be nonveridical. I am sure Forgie would allow the possibility of such a perception. And with respect to a perception answering this description, I think we could safely suppose that the perceiver's report of the experience as having been *of a coffee maker* would be expressive of nothing other than phenomenological content.

2. Return for a moment to Stace's discussion of the distinction

between experience and interpretation in chapter 1 (section 5) of
Mysticism and Philosophy. Recall that in the case of the American
visitor in London who tried to shake hands with a waxwork policeman in the entrance of Madame Tussaud's, Stace allowed that
"the original something" seen by the visitor was "immediately
recognized as a material object, as having some sort of colour, and
as having the general shape of a human being" (31–32). And although Stace acknowledged that the act of *recognizing* a material
object having a certain set of qualities involves "the application of
classificatory concepts to the sensations" and thus involves "some
degree of interpretation," he insisted that for purposes of his discussion these interpretative elements could be included on the experience side of the distinction between experience and interpretation. Using the vocabulary introduced above, I suspect that Stace
was here exhibiting at least some understanding of the fact that his
attention should be focused on the *discernible* given to the exclusion of the *theoretical* given. Keep in mind that at this point in
Mysticism and Philosophy he was preparing a tool for use in his
investigation of the *phenomenological* features of mystical experience. This being so, the distinction of interest between what is
perceived and what is believed about what is perceived was not the
technical distinction Stace identified in this passage as the one utilized by philosophers such as J. S. Mill. It was, rather, the distinction readily made by the common man via an act of reflection and,
as Stace put it, "used every day in practical life." In other words,
the distinction Stace wanted was a phenomenological and *not* an
epistemological distinction. In effect, Stace seems here to have
anticipated the point I am now urging against Forgie, namely, that
the standard *epistemological* concept of the sense datum has no obvious role to play in discussions concerning the *phenomenology* of
sense perception.

   In the preceding discussion, I have contended that a rather wide
variety of ordinary visual perceptions include what I have called an
"identification element" as part of their phenomenological content.
Before ending this discussion, however, I also want to suggest that
the same can probably be said of at least some nonvisual perceptions
as well. Although it is impossible to say for sure, I suspect that
my old dog, Kelsey, is as immediately aware that it is *mine* as he

is of the scent he detects on my boots. In a less speculative vein, consider the child who is awakened from a nightmare by the sound of his mother's voice at his bedside: "There, there, my child, it's all right now." Experientially, "it's mother" does not express the product of an *inference* from the sound. That it is, specifically, *mother's voice* intruding into fretful consciousness is as much a part of what is given in the perception as is the tone and timber of the sound itself. So also for the gentle touches of the lover's embrace. In whatever way the epistemologist might analyze the case, "'What is that?' followed by a *judgment*" hardly describes the phenomenological structure of this sort of experience. Could I be wrong? Could I be wrong in *believing* that it is, specifically, *her* loving touch? Of course I could. What this shows, however, is that there can be genuine *perceptual* mistakes, that is, cases in which the details of belief are in accord with the contents of perception but in which the contents of perception fail to correlate with the external world. Indeed, I'm sure there is at least one possible world in which even Kelsey is mistaken about whose boots those are drying on the back porch.

5. Teresa's Reply to Her Confessor

Return now to the nonsensuous perceptions discussed at length in the third section of this chapter. James's intimate friend claimed to have perceived something entering the room and moving close to the bed. The object perceived was described as a "something" that was "finite, small, and distressful." He claimed to be aware of a "close presence" but added that he did not "recognize it as any individual being or person." A full phenomenological description of Teresa's intellectual vision of Christ might well begin with a similar account. Teresa had a nonsensuous perception of *something* there beside her on her right hand—she, too, called it a "presence."[12] But unlike the experience reported by James's friend, the "presence" Teresa perceived *was* immediately recognized as a specific individual, namely, "Jesus Christ, the Son of the Virgin." The analysis I should like to propose is that Teresa's perception in-

12. See *Interior Castle*, Sixth Mansions, chap. VIII, p. 182.

cluded an "it's Jesus" identification element in addition to the awareness of a presence. And assuming that this analysis is correct, I want now to return to the question left open at the end of Section 3 above—whether there is an intelligible reading of the answer Teresa gave to her confessor when he asked, "If you see nothing, how do you know it is our Lord?" So that we can have her answer before us, I'll quote it again. Teresa replied, "I did not know how [I knew it], but . . . I could not help realizing that He was beside me, and . . . I saw and felt this clearly."

Let's agree that Teresa's intellectual vision consisted of a nonsensuous perception that was, phenomenologically, of the specific individual Jesus Christ standing by her side. Further, let's suppose for a moment that when Teresa told her confessor that she had perceived Christ standing beside her, she meant not only that she had had a perception having this special content but was claiming as well that the perception in question was veridical, that, in fact, Christ had been there by her side. When asked to explain how she knew it was Christ, she then took this to be a challenge of the *second* of these claims. She answered, in effect, that she had no answer. She may even have been saying that she *needed* no answer— the perception was (in Forgie's words) "self-authenticating." Note that unlike the one proposed in the penultimate paragraph of Section 3 above, this analysis of Teresa's reply to her confessor is compatible with the idea that Teresa's perception was phenomenologically and specifically of the particular individual, Jesus Christ. Thus, unlike the former, it does not just reduce Teresa's claim to have perceived Christ to a mere expression of existential belief. Still, I think that this analysis is wrong. And in the course of explaining why I think it is wrong, I shall try to expose the analysis I think is probably right.

Consider again the letter from James's intimate friend—the one in which is reported the nonsensory "sensation" of something next to the bed that was "finite, small, and distressful." Following the pattern established by Teresa's confessor, let's suppose that James writes back to his friend, posing the question, "If you saw nothing, how did you know that there was something next to the bed and (even supposing that you did) how did you know that it was finite, small, and distressful?" Now, to be sure, James's friend might interpret this question as an epistemological inquiry—that is, a call for justification of the claim that something finite, small, and distressful was, in fact, next to the bed. But since no such claim had been made in the original account and since James had specifically solicited this report from his friend as data for his study of what he referred to as "imperfectly developed *hallucinations*," this would probably be the wrong way to understand the question. So what shall we suppose he would be asking? The first thing to notice is that although the friend claimed to have perceived something small and distressful next to the bed, he explicitly denied that the perception contained anything even remotely similar to the kind of content one would antecedently think *essential* to any perception counting as an experience of something next to the bed. This point would hold if the topic concerned ordinary waking-life sense experience. It would hold as well were we discussing dreams or hallucinations. Quite apart from the question of whether the experience was veridical, there is a serious question about how the *phenomenological* account is to be understood. If, phenomenologically, it was a perception of something small next to the bed, how could it be that it lacked the sort of visual, auditory, etc., sense content that one might well suppose is *criterional* of perceptions (whether dreams or waking-life experiences) that count as perceptions of small things next to the bed? James's question would probably best be understood as a reaction to this problem. The point of the inquiry would be to provoke a review of experiential content in the hope that it would reveal some further experiential item—one that would resolve the apparent paradox in the original phenomenological account of the experience. Assuming that the perception included no such item of content, I could imagine James's friend replying to this inquiry using Pike's stratagem: "I don't know how I knew that something small and distressful was next to the bed, but I knew it anyway." He might then add, "The perception was of something small next to the bed and, as confusing as it is, that is just all there is to say about its experiential content."

Returning to Teresa, I think there is reason to suppose that this was the spirit in which she greeted the question posed by her confessor and the spirit in which the reply to her confessor was given. The confessor was obviously interested in the details of phenomenological content—he asked, "What did his face look like?" That, I submit, would have been a strange question had he been trying to determine why Teresa believed that Christ had actually been present. Neither Teresa nor her confessor had ever seen Jesus or even a reliable picture of Jesus. So far as I know, there exists no reliable verbal description of his facial features either. But if this is so, what possible answer could Teresa have given to this question that would have lent any credence to the claim that Christ had actually been at her side?[13] In fact, agreeing with Forgie (as I think we must) that nothing available to Teresa "from the inside, so to speak" could have established the veracity of her perception of Christ, it is hard to see that *any* answer Teresa might have given to *any* question concerning the experiential data included in her vision would have *any* tendency to show that Christ had actually been at her side. It thus makes much better sense to suppose that when Teresa's confessor asked her to tell him how she knew it was Christ, the question was posed not as an epistemological challenge but as a way of prompting Teresa to reflect on the paradoxical nature of her original report. The hope was, I suspect, that she might then be able to add something to her initial description that might help to alleviate its paradoxical ring. Teresa's answer— delivered in response to *this* sort of inquiry—would then be best understood neither as an admission that she had no reason to think her perception veridical nor as the claim that the perception was self-authenticating—both of which would then have been irrele- vant. It is much more likely that the answer would have been intended as a reaffirmation of her original assertion that the vision lacked the sort of sense content ordinarily taken as criterional of experiences counting as perceptions of a person standing by one's side. On this reading, Teresa's answer to her confessor would be fully intelligible though it would have no bearing on the question of whether Christ had actually been present or on the question of whether, and if so why, Teresa believed that Christ had actually been present. It would be a case in which Pike's stratagem had

13. Alasdair MacIntyre makes a point like this in sec. 5 of his essay "Visions." See Flew and MacIntyre, *New Essays in Philosophical Theology,* 258–59.

been used to emphasize a very unusual *phenomenological* feature of her intellectual vision of Christ, namely, that its identification element was not accompanied by the kinds of sensory data ordinarily constitutive of perceptions of a person standing at one's side.

In chapter XXIX of Teresa's *Life* she tells us that she often had intellectual visions of Saint Peter and Saint Paul (271). She says, too, that she had similar visions of Saint Joseph (319) and of Christ's "most glorious Mother."[14] Indeed, even the devil was apparently a frequent object of such perceptions. On this last point, Teresa writes, "I have seldom seem him [the devil] in bodily shape, but I have often seem him without any form, as in the kind of vision I have described, in which no form is seen but the object is known to be there" (292). Further, Teresa suggests that in each of these cases she was aware of a "presence" whom she immediately recognized to be a specific person but that she did not know *how* she knew the identity of the person in question. In *Interior Castle* (Sixth Mansions, chapter VIII) she says: "You will ask how, if this Presence cannot be seen, the soul knows that it is that of Christ, or when it is a saint, or His most Glorious Mother. This is a question which the soul cannot answer, nor can it understand how it knows what it does; it is perfectly certain, however, that it is right" (182). I suspect that in these cases the soul does not know *how* it knows what it knows because intellectual visions *as a kind* lack the sort of sense content usually found in perceptions of specific individuals and upon which the perceiver normally relies when justifying claims concerning the identity of the specific individuals perceived. I call attention to Teresa's accounts of these other intellectual visions because they underscore an implication of the point made in the last paragraph about her intellectual vision of Christ, namely, that if we allow object identification as an "immediate datum" of perception, we shall probably have to allow that experiences can vary in perceptual content even though they contain no ordinary sensory data. On the analysis I would propose, each of these several nonsensory perceptions differed from the others in that it contained its own characteristic identification ele-

14. Teresa, *Interior Castle*, 182.

ment. In these special cases, however, differences in their respective identification elements were in no way correlated with variations in other elements of perceptual content.

6. The Return to Tramper

In the preceding three sections I have tried to clarify Teresa's intellectual vision of Christ in order to use it as a model for understanding Tramper's seemingly theistic religious experience. I turn now to develop the comparison toward which I have been aiming. I'll start by acknowledging two ways in which these two experiences differ.

With respect to Teresa's vision, the purported object of the experience was a physical object—the *man* Jesus. This object had position in physical space at a more or less precise location relative to Teresa's body, namely, just off her right hand. As noted in the first section of Chapter 1, this figure is referred to in the Christian mystical literature as "God (or Christ) in his Humanity." Since Teresa says that the vision persisted for several days, we should probably conclude that she was aware of Christ moving (Teresa says "walking")[15] about from one place to another in and around the convent at Avila. Although some of what Teresa tells us about this experience is reminiscent of what she says about the Prayer of Quiet (for example, nothing was seen with the eyes of the body or with the eyes of the soul), it is clear that her vision of Christ was not a union experience. Again, as stressed in the discussion just mentioned, in union experiences the mystical encounter is between two noncorporeal objects—the soul of the mystic and God *in his Divinity*. God in his Divinity is not a man, but a pure spirit. In union, too, the place of the encounter is not in the physical environment (in the garden or in the chapel) but in some nonphysical setting—either in the soul of the mystic or (in the case of Rapture) in what Teresa calls "another world." That her vision of Christ was not a union experience is a point stressed by Teresa in the third paragraph of chapter XXVII of her *Life* (250).

Now Tramper tells us that in his experience he was aware of

15. Teresa, *Interior Castle*, 180.

"the presence of a *spiritual spirit.*" And although this is a somewhat strange form of words, it seems clearly to entail that the purported object of his awareness was not physical—was not, for example, a man. Further, Tramper says that although he perceived God to be "present," "the feeling of presence was accompanied with no determinate localization." Does this mean that the object was perceived as having no location in physical space? If it does, then given the rest of what Tramper tells us about the experience, it would appear that we are here dealing with a state very much like Rapture. Tramper says that the experience began with "a feeling of being raised above myself" and at its height he was "penetrated" by God's power and goodness. This is rapture talk, as we noted in Section 3 of Chapter 1. On the other hand, maybe Tramper meant, only, that the object of the perception was not experienced as having a *specific* location in the external world—as, for example, off his right hand or directly in front of his face. On this reading, we might still allow that the object was perceived to be out there in space but was not something toward which he could have pointed his finger. I shall not try to decide between these two ways of understanding the text. On either, Tramper's experience differed from Teresa's not only as regards the kind of object allegedly perceived but with respect to the location of the object relative to the body of the perceiver.

With differences acknowledged, I now want to propose that we think of Tramper's experience and Teresa's vision as having at least three features in common.

1. Though these experiences were nonsensory, both were *perceptual* experiences phenomenologically distinguishable from ordinary beliefs or thoughts. We have already looked at the evidence for this in the case of Teresa. In Tramper's report, this appears to be the dominant message of the second passage quoted at the beginning of this chapter. Here Tramper not only says that he "perceived" something but stresses the point that the experience did not involve the apprehension of form, color, odor, or the like. The emphasis on contrast with ordinary sense perception seems clearly designed to mark the experience of interest as being of a special kind *within* the general category of perceptions.

2. Teresa's vision and Tramper's experience were both phe-

nomenologically dualistic, that is, both were experientially of another—of a "not-me." This point is boldly emphasized in Teresa's report, where the object perceived is assigned a place in physical space distinct from, though proximate to, the one occupied by Teresa. Though perhaps less vividly underlined in Tramper's case, the same seems nonetheless clear. Tramper said twice that in his experience he "felt" God to be "present." I take this to mean that Tramper felt God to be near—somewhere in his vicinity. And whether or not "near" is here to be read as a location in physical space (as in Teresa), it seems to me clear that what is felt to be near is felt to be Other. I wouldn't know what to make of the claim that something was felt to be near but was not felt to be other than self.

3. Teresa's vision consisted of a nonsensory perception that was phenomenologically of a nearby Other whom she immediately recognized to be a specific individual, the man Jesus. Similarly, Tramper's experience consisted of a nonsensory perception that was, phenomenologically, of a nearby Other whom he immediately recognized to be a specific individual, God—the omnipotent, omniscient, and perfectly good creator of the universe. This is what Tramper meant when he said, "I felt the presence of God," adding, "I tell the thing just as I was conscious of it." Stated in the terms I have been using in this chapter, this is to say that just as Teresa's experience included an "It's Jesus" identification element as part of its phenomenological content, so Tramper's perception included an "It's God" identification element as part of its phenomenological content. Note that this claim tells us nothing about whether Tramper actually *believed* God was present. Note, too, this analysis in no way precludes the possibility that there were psychological and/or sociological factors working in this case that would be sufficient to *explain* the fact that Tramper immediately recognized the purported object of his perception to be, specifically, God.[16]

Of course, the question remains as to whether this analysis of

16. I mentioned this possibility in the third paragraph of Section 1 above. This topic will be more carefully considered in Supplementary Study 2, where I shall discuss Steven Katz's theory concerning the factors that determine the phenomenological content of mystical experiences.

Tramper's experience is *correct*. And concerning this question my contention in this chapter is, only, that it *might* be right, that is, that Tramper's experience *could* have been so. Forgie's penetrating and provocative argument to the contrary notwithstanding, theistic experience is, I submit, *possible*.

[8]

The Phenomenology
of Union

I am now ready to propose a theory concerning the phenomenological features of the various states of union. The theory will be
developed in the first two sections of the present chapter. The
remaining two sections will contain a defense of the account to be
proposed.

1. Stace's Revised Analysis of "Union"

I shall begin by reviewing a passage from chapter 6 of *The
Teachings of the Mystics* in which Stace comments on what he calls a
"remarkable passage" from chapter III of Jan van Ruysbroeck's *The
Sparkling Stone*. The relevant passage from Ruysbroeck's text reads
as follows (I here quote more of the text than is cited by Stace):

> The union with God which a spiritual man feels, when the union is
> revealed to the spirit as being abysmal, [is one in which the spirit]
> feels itself to be wandering in the breadth, and to dwell in a knowl-
> edge which is ignorance. And through this intimate feeling of
> union, it feels itself to be melting into the Unity; and, through
> dying to all things, into the life of God. And there it feels itself to be
> one life with God. . . . In the transformation within the Unity, all
> spirits fail in their own activity, and feel nothing else by a burning
> up of themselves in the simple Unity of God. . . . In this transcen-

dent state the spirit feels in itself the eternal fire of love. . . . The
spirit forever continues to burn in itself, for its love is eternal; and it
feels itself ever more and more to be burnt up in love, for it is drawn
and transported into the Unity of God, where the spirit burns in
love. If it observes itself, it finds a distinction and an otherness
between itself and God; but where it is burnt up it is undifferentiated
and without distinction, and therefore it feels nothing but unity; for
the flame of the Love of God consumes and devours all that it can
enfold in its Self.[1]

Stace's first comment on this passage is that it is (as he says) a
"direct statement that the [mystical] experience is an undifferentiated unity" (160). Since Ruysbroeck makes clear that he is talking
about a union experience, Stace goes on to claim that this passage
should be taken as further confirmation of his own analysis of the
way "union with God" is used in the Christian mystical literature.
Stace then admits, however, that "an element of doubt is injected
into the matter by the somewhat ambiguous attitude of the passage
on the question of whether there is a duality between God and the
soul or not" (160). And after claiming that the dualistic doctrine
readily detectable in Ruysbroeck's writings generally can be explained by the fact that he (like all Christian mystics) was subject to
what Stace describes as "the overwhelming pressure of the Church
and the theologians, most of whom, of course, had no mystical
experiences," Stace continues his comment on the specific passage
just cited as follows:

If we were to accept Ruysbroeck's statement at its face value, we
should have to hold that sometimes he experiences ("felt" is his own
word) a duality between the soul and God and sometimes a pantheistic unity. The spirit feels the former "when it observes itself"
and the latter when it is "burnt up in the fire of love". Ruysbroeck's
interpretation of this curious situation seems to be that the dualism
is the truth but that the spirit becomes deluded by love into not
noticing the difference between itself and God. This is very difficult
to swallow. It seems to depend on the metaphor of being burned

1. In *John of Ruysbroeck*, 185–86. See Stace, *Teachings of the Mystics*, 160. I should
mention that in Stace's text this passage from Ruysbroeck is wrongly identified as
being from *The Adornment of Spiritual Marriage*.

up. It seems much more likely that Ruysbroeck is reading the doctrine of the Church into his experience. The true explanation would seem to be that when the experience is complete and perfect there is no distinction between subject and object, but that it is possible to stop at a stage at which the experiencer still takes notice of *himself* as an individual and has not achieved complete union. This is the only hypothesis which, accepting Ruysbroeck's introspective account of what he felt was truthful, is still consistent with the hypothesis that the introvertive experience is basically the same in different cultures though it is interpreted differently. (161)

There are a number of things of interest in this passage. I'll comment on them in turn.

First, Stace is no doubt right in his estimate of what Ruysbroeck is saying in chapter III of *The Sparkling Stone* regarding the phenomenological facts connected with experiences of union. There are two distinct phenomena to consider. One has subject-object structure and the other does not. This is what we found, too, in Section 3 of Chapter 2 when studying the materials from chapters XI and XII of Ruysbroeck's *Book of Supreme Truth*. Second, Stace is right again when he interprets Ruysbroeck as holding that "dualism is the truth but that the spirit becomes deluded by love into not noticing the difference between itself and God." Although Ruysbroeck does not really say this in the passage just cited, again, this is something we discovered earlier in Section 3 of Chapter 2. For Ruysbroeck, and for Christian mystics generally, the moment of experience in which the soul detects no distinction between itself and God is a kind of experiential fiction—appearance only—and is not to be thought of as indicative of reality. Still, one comment Stace makes on this point seems to me to be peculiar. He says that in accepting dualism as the truth, it is likely that Ruysbroeck is "reading the doctrine of the Church into his experience." This suggests that Ruysbroeck is somehow misdescribing his experience—that he is letting Church doctrine determine what he says about felt content. Assuming that this is what Stace had in mind, I'm sure he is wrong. As we saw earlier, for Ruysbroeck (and for Christian mystics generally), doctrine is taken as a standard when determining metaphysical, not phenomenological, truth. Thus in the present context, doctrine enters the picture not at the point where the *phenomenological content* of the experience is being *described*, but at the point where the *epistemological status* of the experience is being *assessed*. Of course, this might be what Stace meant when he said that Ruysbroeck was reading doctrine into his experience. Since Stace was not a Christian, this might be, too, what he found so "difficult to swallow."

This brings me to what I take to be the center of Stace's comment on the passage cited above from *The Sparkling Stone*. It is the sentence in which Stace offers what he refers to as the "true explanation" of the Ruysbroeck case. Interpreting liberally, Stace seems here to be allowing that in some cases, at least, union experiences unfold in two intervals or moments—he calls them "stages." The second stage—referred to here as "complete union" and two paragraphs later as "the highest degree of mystical consciousness"—is the introvertive mystical state discussed above in Section 1 of Chapter 5. It lacks subject-object structure. The first stage, however, is clearly not the introvertive mystical state. It is, *phenomenologically,* dualistic. Of course, this is precisely the picture we got in Section 3 of Chapter 2 in our study of chapters XI and XII of Ruysbroeck's *Book of Supreme Truth*. Looking at what was probably a case of Rapture, Ruysbroeck there told us that the experience begins with an interval in which the soul "feels a distinction and otherness between itself and God" and proceeds to a moment in which the felt distinction is lost in the "union without distinction." Stace says that this way of reading the present text serves what would appear to be Ruysbroeck's intention and is also "consistent" with Stace's hypothesis that mystical experience is the same in all cultures. The claim that this reading of Ruysbroeck is "consistent" with Stace's general hypothesis trades on the fact that when framing that hypothesis Stace claimed only that "fully developed" mystical experiences are all of the introvertive sort.[2] This, then, left room for the idea here being exploited, *namely,* that there might be some genuine—though other than "fully developed"—mystical experiences not of the introvertive sort.

2. See Stace, *Teachings of the Mystics,* 14. See also the first passage quoted from Paul Elmer More in the opening paragraph of Chapter 5.

Though I have not had occasion to mention it before, in *Mysticism and Philosophy* and again in the introduction to *The Teachings of the Mystics,* Stace's mystical typology included two types of mystical experiences: (1) the introvertive experience (of course) and (2) a kind referred to as "extrovertive" mystical experience. According to Stace, the extrovertive experience is one in which the mystic sees objects such as trees and peas. The objects detected, however, are perceived to be one, and the one in question is not distinguished from the experiencing subject. Regarding the status of extrovertive experience, Stace said that it is an "incomplete version" of the introvertive state. This is so because, while the mystic is aware of the "all in one" and is thus on the way to an undifferentiated unity, the extrovertive experience still involves sensory awareness of a multiplicity of natural objects. Unlike the introvertive state, the extrovertive experience thus involves both sense perception and the awareness of multiplicity.[3] In the passage before us, Stace now seems to be ready to allow a *second* kind of "incomplete" mystical experience into his scheme. This second member of the "incomplete" class differs from the first on two counts: (1) it is devoid of ordinary sensory data, and, more interestingly, (2) it is phenomenologically *dualistic*—the first such experience to be admitted by Stace into the class of the mystical. Further, since Ruysbroeck is obviously claiming that the Other experienced in the dualistic stage of union is, specifically, God, one might even suppose that Stace is here allowing *theistic* experience a place in his mystical typology! But, of course, this stands in open contrast to his never-failing criticism of Zaehner for suggesting the existence of a dualistic, to say nothing of a theistic, mystical experience. It also conflicts with Stace's earlier insistence that the dualistic phrase "union with God" *always* occurs in the Christian mystical literature as what I have called an "expanded description" of the introvertive state. Though obviously reluctant (indeed, struggling all the way), Stace here seems to have made a major revision in his earlier position. And using this revised Stacean analysis as a point of departure, I now want to make a suggestion as to

3. See Stace, *Mysticism and Philosophy,* 61–62 and 132–33.

how the phenomenological features of the several states of union might be understood.

2. A Phenomenological Proposal

Let us think of the paradigm union experience as one that unfolds through a dualistic stage into a state in which the distinction between subject and object is lost. In the dualistic stage the mystic perceives an Other via a set of sensory-like perceptions referred to in the tradition as "spiritual sensations." Though spiritual sensations come in a variety of types, they are always phenomenologically and specifically of a particular individual, namely, God, the omnipotent, omniscient, and perfectly good creator and sustainer of the universe. In the final stage, the mystic's perceptions of the Other cease. Here the experience peaks in a moment vacant of sensory as well as sensory-like content. Since this climax moment is one in which the mystic is not aware of another, it is also one in which the experiencing mystic ceases to be aware of self. Like the dualistic moment from which it emerges, however, the climax moment is a specifically theistic interval of experience.

Union experiences come in three basic varieties.

The Prayer of Quiet. Traditionally, this state is included in the union class, though it does not include the final stage and is thus not a paradigm union experience. Here, the experiencing mystic is aware of God's being "in the soul"—"in here" as opposed to "out there" in the external world. This is to say that, phenomenologically, God is located in that place within the body where one normally experiences oneself to be. Further, in the Prayer of Quiet, the Divine Other is sensed to be close to the perceiving subject but not so close as to preclude being closer. "Sensed to be close" is here interpreted to mean that the operating spiritual sense faculties are all analogues of ordinary distance senses. More specifically, the spiritual sensations involved are akin to ordinary auditory and olfactory perceptions as well as to ordinary perceptions of heat. They do not include sensations akin to those associated with inside or outside touch or to those connected with taste.

The Prayer of Full Union. Full Union is similar to the Prayer of

Quiet in that God is located "in the soul," that is, "in here," where the experiencing mystic finds herself to be. In this state, however, God is perceived to be in direct contact with the experiencing subject. This is to say that the experience involves perceptions akin to those one has when one is touched by another. Full Union allows of variations. In the typical case, the mystic has touchlike sensations akin to those one has when enwrapped and penetrated by another. In intense cases, the mystic may also perceive God by spiritual sensations of taste. Perceptions said to be like ordinary olfactory, auditory, and visual perceptions may also be involved. In some cases, Full Union develops into a paradigm instance of the union experience. This is to say that it works into a final stage where the mystic is no longer aware of God as Other and which is also vacant of the spiritual perceptions characteristic of its dualistic stage.

Rapture. The identifying mark of the Rapture experience is that it begins with an awareness of the self departing its normal place in the body. Rapture is thus always a so-called out-of-body experience. In some cases, this prelude experience involves a sense of being violently and urgently raised into the air. In other cases it is an awareness of peacefully "flowing" out of the body. A dualistic stage, which then follows the prelude experience, is, in most respects, a repeat of an especially intense instance of the dualistic stage of Full Union. Unlike Full Union, however, spiritual sensations akin to ordinary visual perceptions usually play a dominant role. God is "seen" in a variety of figures, for example, as the Trinity, as God the Father, or as God the Son. Individual attributes of God (for example, omnipotence) are also detected via perceptions akin to sight. Characteristically, the Rapture experience matures into a paradigm instance of the union experience. Here, as in the paradigm version of Full Union, the dualistic stage peaks in a monistic interval lacking subject-object structure as well as all sensory and sensory-like content.

I have two sets of remarks to add. The first set connects with the Prayer of Quiet and the dualistic stage of the paradigm union experience. The second relates exclusively to the union without distinction.

1. With respect to the dualistic moments of the various union experiences, the analyses just proposed put principal emphasis on

the mystic's putative awareness of the place where the encounter occurs ("in the soul" or "out of body") and on the spiritual sensations by which the mystic detects the relative position of the Divine Other vis-à-vis the experiencing subject within the relevant place. Regarding the first set of awarenesses (call them "domain perceptions") I have nothing special to say. I assume that most people reflective enough to read this book with understanding will have little trouble identifying the experiential import of the descriptions involved. Spiritual sensations, however, are another matter. What follows in the next paragraph is offered as an effort to brace this concept against some of the weight that has been placed upon it in the present context.

Spiritual sensations are said to be "like" or "akin" to ordinary sense perceptions of physical objects. This point is strengthened by the fact that spiritual sensations are divided into five distinct types in accordance with the scheme traditionally used to categorize ordinary sense perceptions. It is further reinforced by the fact that each of the types is named after a kind of ordinary sense perception. Spiritual sensations of a given type are said to "correspond to" the ordinary sensory type from which it takes its name. For the most part, these claims are mirrored in the spatial terms used to describe the relative positions of God and the experiencing mystic in the various encounters. God is said to be "close" when the spiritual perceptions involved are restricted to the spiritual counterparts of ordinary distance senses, for example, olfactory or auditory sensations. God is said to be "enwrapping" or "penetrating" the soul of the mystic when the spiritual counterparts of ordinary contact senses come into play, for example, when God is said to be "felt" or "tasted." Apart from highlighting this network of integrated metaphors, however, I have made no effort to define the spiritual perception terms used in the literature on union. It is at this point, I think, that the distinction made by Frits Staal between the study "from without" and the study "from within" comes fully into play.[4] I suspect we have reached the limits of what can be said about the various states of union "from without," that is, via the

4. This distinction is made in the passage I cited from Staal's *Exploring Mysticism* in the second paragraph of the Preface.

study of descriptions offered in the mystical literature. Further insight will require a study "from within"; that is, it will require that we take up the life of contemplation and find out for ourselves. Following Staal on a second point as well, I suspect that the same would have to be said at about the same point in the proceedings were we here discussing the phenomenological features of bodily sensations by which are detected physical objects in physical proximity to the perceiver. Useful though they might be, there is just so much to be gained from descriptions. Full understanding would finally require that one put aside descriptions and acquire the perceptions for oneself.

2. Though I have followed Ruysbroeck and Stace in allowing that union without distinction is an "undifferentiated unity," I have added that this vacant experience is, itself, phenomenologically theistic. This, I think, is required if my account is to square with what I take to be the intentions expressed in the primary mystical literature. But this provision calls for further comment. If a moment of experience is devoid of subject-object and thus involves no awareness of either oneself or another, it is not at all clear how it could be a theistic experience, an experience phenomenologically and specifically of the individual God. An explanation follows:

Consider the following two cases. *Case 1:* I am sitting on a park bench reading a magazine when I am unexpectedly hit on the forehead with a baseball. Upon awakening, I am asked to describe the experience. I say, in effect, "Stun-stars and fading consciousness." I am later told what happened. Thereafter I describe the experience as one of being hit on the head with a baseball. *Case 2:* I am playing baseball and an infield fly is hit to my position at second base. I follow the ball carefully as it arches over the pitcher's mound. I move under the ball, raise my glove, but at the crucial moment I misjudge the catch and the ball hits me on the forehead. Again, I experience stun-stars and fading consciousness. Upon awakening I do not have to be told what happened. I describe the experience as one of being hit on the head with a baseball.

In case 1, when I later describe the experience as one in which I was hit with a baseball, "hit with a baseball" records something I *believe* about the physical circumstances that caused the experience. It does not record something that could be counted as phenomenological content. That I was hit *with a ball* is not something I perceived. In fact, that I was *hit* by something or other is not something I perceived either. Given only stun-stars and fading consciousness, nothing I experienced would lead me to deny that I had been the victim of an internal change—perhaps a blood clot in the brain. In case 2, however, when I later describe the experience as one of being "hit with a ball" the description in question identifies something I directly experienced. Prior to the interval I described as "stun-stars and fading consciousness," I *saw* the ball leave the bat, arch into the air, and descend just over the top of my outstretched glove. The ball loomed large just before I felt the blow. As I say, when I awakened, I did not have to be told what had happened.

Now let's study the two experiences described above as "stun-stars and fading consciousness." We will suppose that they were phenomenologically indistinguishable in that they involved the same kind of stun, the same kind of stars, and the same closedown of consciousness amid the sparkle and roar of perceptual confusion. Still they are phenomenologically distinct. "Hit with a baseball" describes the phenomenological content of the second experience. It does not do so with respect to the first. Why? The answer resides in the fact that in case 2, the experience of stun-stars and fading consciousness occurred as the closing interval of a phenomenological sequence—a sequence made up of perceptions that were phenomenologically of a recognized baseball making its way to a point of contact with my forehead. This is where it differs from the experience of stun-stars and fading consciousness in case 1. Although in both cases, stun-stars and fading consciousness came parceled together with other experiences, it is the *phenomenological ancestry* in case 2 that accounts for the fact that it was, *phenomenologically,* of being hit with a ball. Analogy: Contrast the case of Jones pictured alone and the case of Jones pictured as a member of the graduating class standing in the front row on the steps of College Library. We can suppose that the two pictures of Jones are the same in one respect—the first picture was simply cropped from the group photograph. But unlike in the first, in the second case Jones is pictured as standing third from the left in the front row. This is a difference in pictorial content. In the group picture, Jones has *pictured neighbors* and it is by virtue of this that the photograph is, *pictorially,* of Jones-standing-third-from-the-left-in-the-front-row. In case 2, stun-stars and fading consciousness had experiential (pictured) ancestors that *made* it an experience (picture) of being hit on the head with a ball.

Case 3: I see a spot of light projected on a screen. *Case 4:* I see two spots of light projected on a screen, and as I watch, the spots come closer and closer together until they merge into a single visible spot. Case 3 is an instance of perceiving a single spot. But even if the final stage of case 4 is an instance of perceiving a spot having the same spatial dimensions, brightness, and so on, as the one perceived in case 3, it differs from case 3 in that the awareness involved is not just a perception of *unity* but a perception of *identity*—not just a perception of *one* but a perception of *two* that have *become one.* The difference here stems from the fact that the final stage of case 4 is preceded by the perception of gradually diminishing duality. With respect to this final moment of awareness, one might say that its phenomenological ancestry has survived as an ingredient in its phenomenological content.

Now, let's modify case 4 and suppose that as the two spots encroach upon one another they gradually eclipse or, better, neutralize each other, leaving only a blank screen. This modification will allow case 4 to function as a model for the paradigm union experience where, it is supposed, awareness of two is required if there is to be awareness of any. In the final stage the screen is empty just as the final stage of a paradigm union experience is empty of sensory and sensory-like content as well as empty of awareness of another and thus empty of an awareness of self. What I should now like to suggest, however, is that this negative description fails to capture an element of positive content that results from the fact that the climax moment of the paradigm union experience is preceded by a specifically theistic experience having dualistic structure. Given this context, while the final stage might still be characterized as "empty," it would be more to the point to describe it as we did when dealing with the final stage of case 4 in the preceding paragraph, that is, as an awareness of *identity* or, more specifically, as an awareness of *God-soul identity.* Of course,

here the phrase "God-soul identity" is meant to carry phenomenological import—it is not a Stacean interpretation. It is also meant to
carry *only* phenomenological import—it is offered as a description
of the *appearance* only and is not meant to extend to the real world.
"God-soul identity" expresses a *lack* of experiential content. But it
is not *just* a lack: it is a very specific lack. This is to say, something
very specific is lacking, namely, the felt distinction between oneself
and God. It is like the moment of silence just before the last measure of the *Hallelujah Chorus.* Experientially, this is not *just* a silence. By virtue of its auditory ancestry, it is (as Saint John might
say) a *sounding silence,* more deafening and overwhelming than the
ancestors that make it sound. So also with respect to the experience
of God-soul identity. Phenomenologically, it is an experience of
identity-with-*God,* bearing, if anything, *more* specifically theistic
import than did the phenomenological ancestors that make it so.

   It is interesting to note that on the analysis just proposed, it
would be possible for a mystic to have an experience of Stace's
undifferentiated unity that would *not* count as a theistic experience,
that is, would not count as an experience of there being no distinction between oneself and *God.* This would be an experience in
which the undifferentiated unity occurs by itself, or at least does
not occur as the climax moment of an experience having theistic
ancestry as it does in the paradigm union experience. It is possible
that this is the experience reported by Buddhist and Hindu mystics
and is also the one discussed by Plotinus in the *Enneads.* Lacking
the ancestry that would make it so, such a phenomenon could not
be classified as a theistic experience. This would be like the experience of stun-stars and fading consciousness in case 1 above. It
would also be like the perception of the single spot of light in case
3. Of course, it would be a mistake to suppose that because the
introvertive mystical experience does not have theistic content in
these instances, it also lacks theistic content when occurring as the
mystical peak of a paradigm union experience. Allowing the term
"content" to work in a very permissive way (for example, as we
might say that the silence before the last measure of the *Hallelujah
Chorus* is part of the *content* of the auditory experience), this is a
case where phenomenological context *determines* phenomenological content. More than that, this is a case where phenomenological

context determines the *whole* of phenomenological content. This is so because in the special case of the undifferentiated unity, there is no other content to consider.

3. Phenomenography

In the first two numbered paragraphs of the preface to its first edition, Augustin Poulain writes as follows concerning the enterprise undertaken in *The Graces of Interior Prayer:*

> 1. *Aim.* I had often dreamed of writing a quite small and purely practical treatise on Mysticism. I wished as far as possible to give very clear and very accurate *descriptions,* as well as very plain *rules of conduct.* Have the mystics always achieved this? Have we never suffered from their obscurity, their vagueness? . . .
> 2. *Course Adopted.* It will be seen that I have followed what may be called the *descriptive school.* There is another, the *speculative school,* which endeavors to systemize all facts theologically by connecting them with the study of grace, of man's faculties, or the gifts of the Holy Spirit, etc. The first is that of the saints, or great contemplatives who have observed the extraordinary graces which they have found in themselves. The second has been created by eminent theologians, and it requires a profound knowledge of scholasticism. (XIII)

At the other end of his text, in a chapter entitled "Scientific Methods in Descriptive Mysticism" (chapter XXX), Poulain offers some closing remarks on method that connect importantly with the project outlined in the opening paragraph of the preface. Here he tells us that "descriptive mysticism," like all "sciences," begins with "observations of facts" (539). The task of the theologian is then, at least in part, to clarify and organize—to construct what he calls "classifications" that provide easy and accurate access to the facts in question (546–49). This is at least part of the task that Poulain thinks of himself as having undertaken in his text.

Question: What are the "facts" to which Poulain is referring when claiming that descriptive mysticism begins with the observation of facts? The answer is suggested in the passage quoted above from paragraph 2 of the preface and is developed in more detail in the first few pages of chapter xxx. The facts in question are the mystical states, the "graces" that the great contemplatives have "found within themselves." The facts, in other words, are *phenomenological* facts—facts that have been "observed" by such people as Teresa of Avila and Bernard of Clairvaux. This, then, brings us to a second question: How shall those of us (like Poulain) who are not contemplatives but who are interested in mysticism proceed when investigating these facts? In numbered paragraph 3 of chapter xxx Poulain says this:

> 3. *Sources* of descriptive mysticism. This science relies on two kinds of documents: (1) The descriptions that are found in classical and approved writers; (2) those that can be supplied by living persons from their own experience. These two kinds of information are indispensable; each one throws light upon the other. There are many passages in the old writers, the real sense of which is only grasped when it is commented on by the living voice of a person who has passed through similar states, and the converse is also true. (542)

Regarding the descriptions found in "classical and approved" writers, Poulain warns that the task of unearthing the facts is difficult. Descriptions are often buried in what he calls "a host of accessories: digressions, pious reflections, literary developments, useless repetitions, commentaries on Scripture, etc." He says that "all this extraneous matter must be eliminated and only the *residue* that is based on experience left" (542). On the other hand, materials supplied by living contemplatives will, Poulain thinks, provide at best only "minor facts," or points of detail—he calls them "crumbs from the table." This is true, he thinks, because all the important observations were made long ago by classical contemplatives and thus have already been reported in the abundant primary Christian mystical literature (545).

Stepping back from this discussion, I want first to identify a methodological point of some importance. If we think of descriptive mystical theology as a "science" dealing with "observed facts," we must think of it on the model of, for example, history— that is, as an enterprise in which the facts of primary interest are of the observable sort (they were, or at least could have been, directly observed) but in which the investigator (the "scientist") does not (usually) have *direct* access to them. Paradigmatically, the investigator is not the one who makes the key observations. *His* sources are, as Poulain says, "documents" in which the key observations are *reported* by those who have observed the facts of primary interest.

If we think of phenomenology as the enterprise of describing the experiential content of conscious states, then descriptive mystical theology must be regarded as a branch of phenomenology. Unlike a phenomenological inquiry that proceeds via direct inspection of the conscious states it investigates, however, descriptive mystical theology proceeds via the analysis of *writings* in which those phenomena are reported. In order to mark this very special feature of its procedure, descriptive mystical theology might then be called "phenomeno*graphy*"—the study of *phenomena* by way of *reports* thereof. As the name now suggests, descriptive mystical theology, phenomenography, is a branch of *hermeneutics*. It is what might be called the "hermeneutics of experiential biography." As such, of course, phenomenography is subject to the criteria of adequacy that govern hermeneutical inquiries generally.

Why should one undertake the phenomenographical study of mysticism? Poulain explains his motives in the preface to his text as follows:

> I am writing especially for those souls who are beginning to receive the mystic graces and who do not know how to find their way in this new world. And I address myself to those also who are *drawing near* and who have entered into the adjacent states. The same difficulties present themselves to these souls also.
>
> Now such persons require something really practical. They wish for very exact pictures—I was about to say photographs—in which they can recognize themselves *immediately*. They also require rules of conduct reduced to a few striking formulae, easy to *remember and to apply*.
>
> Certain theologians would require more than this. They will perhaps see in this little book a mere manual, resembling those treatises on practical medicine which do not lose themselves in high biological theory, but merely teach us how to make a *rapid diagnosis* of each

disease and *lay down proper treatment*. But alas! I confess that I should
think myself very happy to have attained such a difficult end! (xiii)

Like many primary mystical texts (for example, Teresa's *Way of
Perfection*), Poulain's text is written with a practical aim in view. It
is offered as a "manual" for would-be or budding contemplatives
who do not know how to "find their way" along the mystical
path. Poulain thinks of his text as providing a set of "exact pictures" of the various mystical graces by reference to which the
novice (or, perhaps, an adviser) can "diagnose" the graces they
have already received or can expect to receive in the future. In his
text, Poulain also provides advice both to mystical practitioners
and to their advisers as to how to regard and react to various
mystical graces.

Like Poulain's, the book I am here beginning to bring to a close
is offered as a study in "descriptive mysticism"—that is to say, a
study in the *phenomenography* of Christian mysticism. In the spirit
of Poulain, the theory proposed in the last section consists of series
of pictures. In this case, however, the pictures are hung from a
single wire by virtue of the fact that they are integrated around a
paradigm. The individual pictures are also considerably more detailed than the ones sketched in Poulain's text. As regards the
theory as a whole, since it is intended to describe the experiential
content of a class of mystical phenomena, it can be regarded as a
phenomenological account. It is proposed, however, in the context
of a phenomenographical inquiry and is thus recommended on
phenomenographical grounds. Accordingly, if it is to be evaluated it
must be so not by direct examination of the facts it purports to
describe (which only a living contemplative could do), but by a
study of the *literature* used as data for the phenomenographical
inquiry of which it is the product. It's like this: if the task is to
formulate a theory about the color of apples using only classical
writings on apples, then even though "apples are red" describes
apples and would thus count as a pomological theory, the question
of whether it is true or false will not be settled by observing apples
but by studying the relevant writings on apples. This last might be
called "pomo*graphy*."

My interest in the inquiry has not been stimulated by the "practical" concerns that motivated Poulain. My concern has been more narrowly academic—to achieve clarity for its own sake as well as to provide some hedge against the possibility that the subtleties of the Christian mystical literature on union might go undiscovered and thus unappreciated in the philosophical discussion of mysticism now in progress. Of course, this does not reflect a difference between Poulain and myself as regards the method of our inquiries or the criteria by which each should be judged.

So what about the theory—is it correct? I'll close with some reflections intended to support the contention that it probably is, or, at least, that something very much like it probably is.

4. The Phenomenography of Union

Question: With respect to a given experience description encountered in the mystical literature, under what conditions should one conclude that it is a Stacean interpretation rather than a mere descriptive report? I shall begin this closing section of the present chapter by considering two answers to this question that have been given in the contemporary philosophical literature on mysticism.

In section 4 of "Interpretation and Mystical Experience," Ninian Smart suggests that a given experience description is to be regarded as interpretive as opposed to merely descriptive in proportion to the degree to which it contains what he calls "doctrinal ramifications" (79). Concerning the doctrinal ramifications contained in a given experience description, Smart says: "Their degree can be crudely estimated [in a given case] by asking: How many propositions are presupposed as true by the description in question?" (79–80). So, for example, if a Christian mystic claims to have had an experience of union with God, this would count as what Smart refers to as a "highly ramified" experience description. This is true, Smart tells us, because in this context the term "God" gains part of its meaning from Christian doctrinal statements such as "God created the Universe," "Jesus Christ is God," and "God acted in history." Thus when describing his experience in the way indicated, the Christian mystic is, in effect, telling us that his mystical encounter involved the presence of the individual who created the universe, is the Christ, acted in history, and so on. And these things, Smart continues, are not "guaranteed by the experience itself" (80). In other words, the truth of the experience description here depends, in part, on the truth of Christian doctrine rather than on the experiential content of the experience described. As a general principle, a given experience description counts as a Stacean interpretation to the extent that its truth rests on facts or factors other than those that can be directly verified by reference to the content of the experience so described.

Return once again to the pictures discussed in Section 2 of Chapter 5. Consider the case in which someone uses caption C to describe picture 2—he says: "This is a picture of a man walking on State Street." We noted earlier that in this case the picture description would not be expanded but might be either extended or not extended. This is to say that we could imagine circumstances in which the description would carry the implication that there is (or was) a real man walking on a real street and that the picture bears the relation to these items marked by the intentional indicator "of"; and we could also imagine circumstances in which precisely the same form of words ("This is a picture of a man walking on State Street") would carry no such implication but would describe *only* the content of the picture itself. Referring to the categories of picture descriptions itemized in Section 2 of Chapter 5, in the first case the description would be in category 3 and in the second it would be in category 4. The point made in that earlier discussion was that the words, by themselves, will not tell us which it is. It depends entirely on the intentions of the one offering the description.

I now want to make a second point about the case in which someone uses caption C to describe picture 2. Suppose the case is one in which the picture description is extended—the description is intended to carry existential import. The description could *also* function as a nonextended description of the pictorial content. Though it tells us something about the world independent of the picture, it *also* tells us something about the content of the picture that has nothing to do with the world independent of the picture. Were we interested in doing so, we *as commentators* could disregard the existential import intended by the describer. This is to say, we could *bracket* its existential import even if it were not so bracketed by the one originally offering the description. The result would be a picture description in category 4 rather than in category 3. Of course, this conversion would, in a sense, mutilate the original. Still, this procedure would be legitimate if the task of the commentator were to call attention to just those implications of the original that relate exclusively to the facts as pictured in picture 2.

It seems to me that Smart's way of separating Stacean interpretations from mere descriptive reports suffers from the fact that it does not take the possibility just mentioned into account when dealing with experience descriptions. For example, suppose that a Christian mystic claimed to have experienced union with God and meant thereby to be communicating the idea that she had actually encountered the omnipotent, omniscient, and perfectly good creator of the universe. The description would then carry full existential import and would thus be a Stacean interpretation. But this would not rule out the possibility that the original description was *also* descriptive of experiential content. This last would be true if, when bracketed, the description reduced to a mere descriptive report. As a procedural principle of phenomenography, therefore, Smart's program for distinguishing interpretations from descriptive reports is too crude to be useful. Having identified a given experience description as a Stacean interpretation, the phenomenographer must consider the possibility that it is, nonetheless, *in part* a purely descriptive report. The part in question is the part remaining when the *phenomenographer* (not the mystic) brackets the original description.[5]

The following passage is from an article published in 1972 by Bruce Garside entitled "Language and the Interpretation of Mystical Experience."

In general, I should think that it is only justifiable to regard an account of a mystical experience as an interpretation rather than a

---

5. This point connects with the one made in Section 4 of Chapter 7 concerning the message conveyed in ordinary conversation by expressions such as "it's a coffee maker." The fact that it expresses a belief about the contents of the external world does not preclude the possibility that it *also* expresses a phenomenological element of the speaker's present perception.

description when there is some biographical evidence to that effect, i.e. when one can see from the mystic's remarks or a biographer's that he is reflecting upon the experience and attempting to see it in some context instead of merely relating it to us. (100)

Illustration: Christian mystics claim that union without distinction is appearance only—it is not indicative of reality. They argue that this is so because to think otherwise would be to fly in the face of orthodox Christian doctrine.[6] Here the mystic is "reflecting" on the God-soul identity experience and attempting to "see it" in the context of *doctrine*. Further, that this is what is happening is something *we* can see via a sympathetic and theologically informed study of the texts. We thus have "biographical evidence"—I would prefer to say *phenomenographical* evidence—which backs the claim that this is an interpretation of the God-soul identity experience and not a mere descriptive report. In this case, I think Garside would allow, we would thus be justified in so concluding.

Considered as an answer to the question posed at the beginning of this section, the principle Garside proposes in the passage quoted above seems to me too restrictive to be adequate. Suppose, for example, that Forgie had been successful in showing that no experience could be, phenomenologically, of some specific individual and thus could not be phenomenologically and specifically of the omnipotent, omniscient, and perfectly good person who created the universe. We would then have to conclude that when used with standard Christian meaning attached to the word "God," the experience description "union with God" is always a Stacean interpretation and not a descriptive report. And in this case, the judgment would be justified on epistemological grounds—that is to say, without consulting phenomenographical data of any sort. My point, of course, is not that Forgie's claim about phenomenological content is correct. It is, rather, that Garside's formula for identifying Stacean interpretations needs to be broadened to allow a wider range of circumstances under which a given experience description could be legitimately classified as an interpretation. With this thought in mind, consider the following revised version of Garside's principle:

6. See Section 3 of Chapter 2 for a full discussion of this point.

Garside's Revised Principle: With respect to a given experience description encountered in mystical literature, count it as an interpretation not descriptive of phenomenological content only if there are adequate phenomenographical or conceptual (including epistemological) reasons to do so.

As a general metalevel principle governing procedure in phenomenography, this principle articulates a presumption concerning experience descriptions encountered in the primary mystical literature. Although the principle allows that the presumption in question is defeasible, it requires that it be defeated if the original description is to be classified as an interpretation not descriptive of experiential content.

I'm not sure whether Garside's Revised Principle should be used when analyzing mystical literature generally. It could be that there are whole traditions in which mystics do not attempt to relate the phenomenological content of their various experiences but are interested only in communicating metaphysical conclusions presumably based on mystical experiences. It could be, too, that even within a tradition where phenomenological descriptions are sometimes offered, great chunks of the literature are intended only to communicate metaphysical, rather than phenomenological, truth. Still it seems to me that when one confronts the literature from which the materials analyzed in the first four chapters of the present book have been extracted, these possibilities do not come into play. As a general remark, I would say that the Christian mystical literature on union is phenomenologically oriented. This is especially evident in that part of the literature devoted to discussions of spiritual sensations. It is evident as well in discussions of union cast in the spatial vocabulary of mutual embrace. As regards the latter, whether framed in first-person language or as third-person descriptions of what "the soul" encounters in union, emphasis is repeatedly placed on what the mystic sees, feels, is aware of, is conscious of, and so on. These accounts are often accompanied with negative addenda obviously intended to direct attention to subtle aspects of positive content—for example, Teresa's claim that in the Prayer of Quiet nothing is seen with the "eyes of the body" or with the "eyes of the soul." As a consequence, I am inclined to think and will therefore assume that Garside's Revised Principle should govern procedure in the study of the literature occupying the center of attention in this book.

I know of only three lines of argument that have been used to support the claim that the descriptions of the several states of union reviewed and analyzed in the first four chapters of the present book are Stacean interpretations rather than mere descriptive reports. These are the ones offered by Stace in chapter 2 of *Mysticism and Philosophy,* Forgie in "Theistic Experience and the Doctrine of Unanimity," and Smart in "Interpretation and Mystical Experience." Formulated in the language of Section 2 of Chapter 5, the first two of these arguments seek to establish that experience descriptions of the sort just mentioned are *expanded* descriptions of mystical experience. The third takes note of the fact that in the context of interest these descriptions are obviously *extended*.[7] In Chapter 6 I cited reasons for thinking that the argument developed by Stace for his position on this topic is not only highly implausible, but, as I put it, "evidentially bankrupt." Though considerably more subtle and interesting than Stace's, Forgie's argument was also found deficient and was thus dismissed in Chapter 7. As regards Smart, in the present section I have argued that even if he is right in thinking that union descriptions usually carry metaphysical import when offered in Christian mystical texts, this fact provides no reason for thinking that they are not also descriptive of experiential content. Given that Garside's Revised Principle governs procedure in this case, my conclusion is that the proposal advanced in Section 2 of the present chapter is probably an accurate (or, at least, nearly accurate) phenomenographical account. This is to say that when judged on the basis of the materials provided in the primary literature of the Christian mystical tradition, the proposal in question appears to describe (or nearly to describe) the phenomenological content of the several states of union.

---

7. Stace also argues that "union with God" is extended, but this is obviously not the thrust of his argument. See Section 2 of Chapter 5 above.

R. C. Zaehner on Theistic
Mystical Experience

Within the contemporary literature on comparative mysticism, the idea that there is a kind of mystical experience that is phenomenologically theistic is usually associated with R. C. Zaehner and his book *Mysticism, Sacred and Profane* (1957). As I pointed out in the introduction to Chapter 5, this was the text both Walter Stace and Ninian Smart criticized when they rejected the claim that theistic mystical experience constitutes a distinct phenomenological type. Let me add at this point that contemporary philosophers (such as I) who separate themselves from Stace and Smart on this issue usually think of themselves as partisans of the Zaehner tradition. It is perhaps not too much to say that Zaehner's considerable and continuing impact on the contemporary philosophical discussion of mysticism is due in large measure to the position he held on theistic mystical experience. In this study I want to examine Zaehner's reasoning on this topic in some detail. As I look at the matter, Stace and Smart were right in thinking that Zaehner failed to distinguish theistic experience as a separate phenomenological category. But the conclusion, I think, is not that there is no such thing as a theistic mystical experience. Zaehner's failure, I believe, stemmed from a mistake he made when selecting a case to exemplify the category of theistic mystical experience. I shall suggest

that is was a feature of Zaehner's argument format that accounts
for the mistake in question.

1. Zaehner's Default on Theistic Experience

In *Mysticism, Sacred and Profane,* Zaehner divides mystics into
three basic types: "nature mystics," "monistic mystics," and "theistic mystics." On Zaehner's account, these distinctions rest on a
correlated three-way distinction between the kinds of preternatural
experiences each of these three kinds of mystics enjoy—labeled
(appropriately enough) "natural," "monistic," and "theistic" mystical experiences, respectively. As regards the first of these kinds,
Zaehner says, in effect, that the natural mystical experience has
sensible content but is nonetheless devoid of subject-object structure. Here the mystic is sensibly aware of the external world but
experiences no distinction between various external objects or between the world as a whole and the self. This is the experience
Stace later called the "extrovertive mystical experience." Zaehner
says that the natural mystical experience is "a vision of nature
transfigured" (21). "It is," he says, "the experience of all as one and
one as all" (28). Turning then to the monistic mystical experience,
Zaehner tells us that it, too, lacks subject-object structure but is
devoid of all perceptual content and is thus different from the
natural mystical experience. In fact, Zaehner says that the monistic
experience is vacant not only of perceptions but of thought and
feeling as well. This appears to be the "undifferentiated unity"
Stace referred to as the "introvertive" mystical state. Zaehner says
it is at least akin to "dreamless sleep" (155–56)—a phrase reminiscent of Paul Elmer More's tag "unconscious oblivion."[1]

What, then, of theistic mystical experience? In the discussion
occupying the early part of Zaehner's text, one is led to think that it
will be defined in terms of its distinctive experiential content and
will thus be distinguished from natural and monistic experience on
phenomenological grounds, just as the latter are distinguished
from one another. So, for example, at the end of chapter 2, where
Zaehner makes his first attempt to pinpoint contrasts between the

1. See the opening paragraph of Chapter 5 above.

three types of mystical experience, theistic experience is characterized as an awareness in which "the soul feels itself to be united
with God in love" (29). The reader is here encouraged to think that
when the details are added, the theistic experience will be identified
as one that is phenomenologically of God. And although perhaps
reluctant to anticipate how this idea will be handled in the text, one
surely expects that theistic experience will at least be distinguished
from natural and monistic experiences on the grounds that it has
subject–object structure. Given that theistic experience is a state in
which, in Zaehner's words, "the soul *feels* itself to be united to God
in *love*," such an experience will have to be phenomenologically
dual, since, as Zaehner rightly says when commenting on the lack
of love themes in the monistic mystical literature, "love implies
duality, and what is 'One without a second' can neither love nor be
loved" (188).

This does not happen, however. As the inquiry continues, Zaehner seems clearly to hold that the root of theistic mysticism is an
experience like the monistic experience in that it lacks subject-
object structure and is also devoid of the ordinary contents of
consciousness, such as sensory data. And, of course, this immediately raises the question of whether theistic experience can be
distinguished at all from the monistic state. Unfortunately, instead
of answering this question directly, Zaehner shifts attention away
from the distinction between monistic and theistic *experiences* and
focuses, instead, on the distinction between monistic and theistic
mystics. He differentiates the latter not by noting differences between their respective mystical experiences but by calling attention
to two kinds of extraphenomenological contrasts: (1) differences
between monistic and theistic mystics with respect to *beliefs* they
hold about God, about themselves, and about their mystical encounters; and (2) differences between monistic and theistic mystics
as regards the way they *react* to their respective mystical experiences. Since this shift is surprising, I'll pause here to provide some
documentation.

After defining "mystical experience" as a "unitive experience,"
that is, "a sense of union or even identity with something other
than oneself," in the fourth paragraph of chapter 3 Zaehner asks
whether the monistic experience expressed in the Hindu Vedanta

by the words "I am Brahman" (the so-called experience of "advaita") should be classified as a mystical experience. Zaehner then explains the point of asking this question. "The difficulty is that in this case it is not strictly proper to speak of union at all; for according to the proposition 'I am Brahman', which means that I am the sole unqualifiable Absolute, One without a second, I cannot logically speak of being united to Brahman, since I am already He (or It)" (32). Zaehner claims, however, that this difficulty does not arise with respect to experiences reported by Christian mystics. Why not? The reason is that "the Christian mystic, if he is orthodox, will not go so far as to say that he actually *is* God in any absolute or unqualified sense" (32). Although Zaehner allows that the Christian mystic may actually think that "I am God" would be a true description of what is actually felt, he adds that this is "a manner of expressing the ineffable experience which Christian mystics normally avoid." Zaehner says that this is because monism was the view held by Meister Eckhart, who was roundly condemned by the pope. From these reflections Zaehner draws the following conclusion:

> Strictly sticking to the letter, then, for the moment a distinction must be drawn between the Christian experience in which the individual is united or "oned" with God, to use the expression of the *Cloud of Unknowing,* and the Vedāntin experience which is one of absolute identity with Brahman,—"I am Brahman" and "What thou art, that am I." (32–33)

Note that the discussion appears to center on the distinction between monistic and theistic *experiences.* But this is appearance only. The real contrast has been located in a difference between Hindu and Christian *mystics* and concerns the *beliefs* they hold about the epistemological status of their respective mystical experiences. Zaehner formulates this point in a baffling sentence at the beginning of the fifth paragraph of chapter 3. Here he says that the difference just identified is a difference "between the Vedāntin and Christian ways of defining the unitive experience," adding that "the difference may well be only one of terminology" (33). And although I find it impossible to believe that the difference described in the last-quoted passage might turn out to be "only one of terminology," the point to be gleaned is that it is *not* to be understood as a phenomenological contrast between monistic and theistic mystical experiences. On this last point Zaehner readily admits that a monistic formula such as "I am God" might well express what the theistic mystic actually *feels*. I should add that this shift in chapter 3 from phenomenological to doctrinal grounds for the distinction between monistic and theistic mysticism does not appear to be a momentary lapse. The same point is anticipated in the closing paragraph of chapter 2 and is also repeatedly emphasized in the closing portions of the text. For example, in the penultimate chapter (chapter 9) Zaehner writes as follows concerning his own insistence on the idea that there is a fundamental difference between theistic and monistic mystics:

> The proof, it seems to me, that I am not talking pure nonsense is in the complete difference of approach which separates the theistic from the monistic mystic. The latter achieves liberation entirely by his own efforts since there is no God apart from himself to help him or with Whom he can be united. In the case of the theistic mystic, on the other hand, it is always God who takes the first step, and it is God Who works in the soul and makes it fit for union. (192)

And, again, summarizing his position on the distinction between monistic and theistic mysticism in the concluding chapter of the book (chapter 10), Zaehner says:

> Here, then, are two distinct and mutually opposed types of mysticism—the monist and the theistic. This is not a question of Christianity and Islam *versus* Hinduism and Buddhism: it is an unbridgeable gulf between all those who see God as incomparably greater than oneself, though He is, at the same time, the root and ground of one's being, and those who maintain that the soul and God are one and the same and that all else is pure illusion. (204)

The differences, in other words, are clearly *doctrinal*, not *phenomenological*. Monistic and theistic mystics differ as regards the beliefs they hold about the nature of God and about God's relation to the individual soul.[2] They also hold different beliefs about the causal origins of the mystical encounter itself.

In the last five pages of his chapter 8, Zaehner develops at length his view concerning the second of the nonphenomenological contrasts mentioned at the beginning of this discussion. Here he maintains that monistic mystics come away from their mystical experiences with a sense of indifference toward the mundane world and disdain for both virtue and sin. On the other hand, for the theistic mystic, Zaehner tells us, "emptiness is the prelude to Holiness" (173). One inspired by love via contact with God will "show this to the world by the holiness of his life and by an abiding humility in face of the immense favours bestowed which he will see to be God's doing, not his own" (193). Zaehner points to Teresa of Avila as a clear illustration of one so affected. He says that Teresa's mystical encounters resulted in "a total transformation and sanctification of character which no merely preternatural agency could bring about" (105). Again Zaehner distinguishes the theistic mystic from the monistic mystic by pointing to something other than phenomenological differences between their respective mystical experiences. Although this time the focus is on behavioral *reactions* rather than on doctrinal beliefs, in neither case is the distinction provided with a bona fide experiential ground.

The upshot is, then, that except for a few very sketchy remarks in the first two chapters of his text, Zaehner's discussion conveys the impression that the theistic mystic is one who *interprets* his *monistic* experience in theistic categories and is thus prompted to lead a humble and virtuous life. But, of course, this is essentially the position defended by Stace in chapter 2 of *Mysticism and Philosophy* and by Ninian Smart in "Interpretation and Mystical Experience." In chapter 1 (section 5) of the first-mentioned text, Stace makes note of the fact that Zaehner failed to specify a phenomenological ground for his distinction between monistic and theistic mysticism. Smart develops the same point more fully in section 6 of his essay. On the basis of my reading of Zaehner's text, I think

2. This way of framing the distinction between monistic and theistic mysticism had already been used by Zaehner in the closing paragraph of chap. 2.

that Stace and Smart are right on this point. Although Zaehner insists to the end that mystical experiences come in three distinct varieties (168), it seems to me plain that he simply fails to exhibit theistic experience as a distinct phenomenological type.

In section 3 of this study, I shall try to identify the feature of Zaehner's discussion that accounts for the failure just identified. As a necessary preliminary to this effort, however, in the next section I shall trace what I take to be the basic line of argument developed in *Mysticism, Sacred and Profane*.

2. Zaehner's Worries about Mescaline

In a book first published in 1954 entitled *The Doors of Perception*, Aldous Huxley reports and discusses a number of the experiences he had while spending a day under the influence of mescaline. In several places Huxley describes his experiences using language carrying specifically religious import. The following are two such passages as quoted by Zaehner in chapter 1 of his text. I quote them here because I want them before us. They will figure importantly in the discussion to follow.

I continued to look at the flowers, and in their living light I seemed to detect the qualitative equivalent of breathing—but of breathing without returns to a starting-point, with no recurrent ebbs but only a repeated flow from beauty to heightened beauty, from deeper to ever deeper meaning. Words like Grace and Transfiguration came to my mind, and this of course was what, among other things, they stood for. My eyes traveled from the rose to the carnation, and from that feathery incandescence to the smooth scrolls of sentient ame-thyst which were the iris. The Beatific Vision, *Sat Chit Ananda*, Being-Awareness-Bliss for the first time I understood, not on the verbal level, not by inchoate hints or at a distance, but precisely and completely what those prodigious syllables referred to. And then I remembered a passage I had read in one of Suzuki's essays. "What is the Dharma-Body of the Buddha?" [The Dharma-Body of the Bud-dha, Huxley is good enough to explain, "is another way of saying Mind, Suchness, the Void, the Godhead."] The question is asked in a Zen monastery by an earnest and bewildered novice. And with the prompt irrelevance of one of the Marx Brothers, the Master answers: "The hedge at the bottom of the garden". "And the man who realizes this truth", the novice dubiously inquires, "what, may I ask, is he?" [To which he receives the disconcerting reply,] "A golden-haired lion."[3]

But as I looked, this purely aesthetic, Cubist's-eye view gave place to what I can only describe as the sacramental vision of reality. I was back where I had been when I was looking at the flowers—back in a world where everything shone with the Inner Light, and was infinite in its significance. The legs, for example, of that chair—how miraculous their tubularity, how supernatural their polished smoothness! I spent several minutes—or was it several centuries?—not merely gazing at those bamboo legs, but actually *being* them—or rather being myself in them; or, to be still more accurate (for "I" was not involved in the case, nor in a certain sense were "they") being my Not-self in the Not-self which was the chair.[4]

Focusing on these and a number of other like comments, in the opening chapter of *Mysticism, Sacred and Profane* Zaehner takes Huxley to be claiming that under the influence of mescaline he had achieved a state of consciousness comparable to those reported in the texts of the world's great religious mystics. Zaehner then says that if Huxley is right about this, "it can only be said that the conclusions to be drawn are alarming" (12). Why alarming? Zaehner answers, "Obviously, if mescaline can produce the Beatific Vision here on earth—a state that we had hitherto believed to have been the reward for much earnest striving after good—the Christian emphasis on morality is not only all wrong but also a little naive" (12–13).[5] Zaehner concludes that mescaline presents us "with a theological problem of great magnitude," adding that "Mr. Huxley is to be thanked for having set the problem." And in succeeding chapters of the text, Zaehner goes on to argue that although experiences of the sort Huxley reports are "unitive" and thus can be classified as genuine mystical experiences ("natural"

3. Huxley, *Doors of Perception*, 18, quoted in Zaehner, *Mysticism, Sacred and Profane*, 5.
4. Huxley, *Doors of Perception*, 22, quoted (with slight changes) in Zaehner, *Mysticism, Sacred and Profane*, 6–7.
5. This point is expressed more fully in chap. 4, p. 124.

mystical experiences), they differ importantly from two other kinds of mystical states: "monistic" and "theistic" mystical experiences. Zaehner claims that natural mystical experiences are not uncommon and have no special connection with religion (xiii). In fact, natural mystical experiences are frequently reported by those suffering the manic stage of schizophrenia.[6] Zaehner maintains, however, that monistic and theistic experiences have a very different status. These are the ones that have worked at the roots of the great religious mystical traditions. The upshot is, presumably, that Huxley was wrong in supposing that he had a mystical experience that could be classified as a beatific vision or as an instance of the Hindu "Being-Awareness-Bliss." Zaehner emphasizes several times in his text that Huxley was misled on this point because he supposed, erroneously, that all genuine mystical experiences are the same.[7]

Having sketched the broad format of the text as a whole, I now want to focus on the argument Zaehner advances in chapter 2. This is the part of the book in which he strikes the distinction between natural mystical experience on the one hand and monistic and theistic mystical experiences on the other. As should be clear from the review just supplied, this is the structural center of the book's basic argument.

Following is a passage from Henry Suso's *The Little Book of Truth*. Zaehner tells us that this passage is "fairly typical of Christian mysticism" and thus can be used as an illustrating instance of a report describing the kind of experience underpinning theistic mysticism.

> It happens, no doubt, that, when the good and faithful servant enters into the joy of his Lord, he becomes intoxicated with the immeasurable abundance of the Divine house. For in an ineffable manner, it happens to him as to a drunk man, who forgets himself, is no longer himself. He is quite dead to himself, and entirely lost in God, has passed into Him, and has become one spirit with Him in all respects, just as a little drop of water that is poured into a large quantity of wine. For, as this is lost to itself, and draws to itself and

6. This point is developed at length in chap. 5 of Zaehner's text.
7. See, e.g., Zaehner, *Mysticism, Sacred and Profane*, ix–xi, 27, and 99.

into itself the taste and color of the wine, similarly it happens to
those who are in the full possession of blessedness. In an inexpress-
ible manner all human desires fall away from them, they melt away
into themselves, and sink away completely into the will of God. If
anything remained in man, and was not entirely poured out of him,
then Scripture could not be true that says: God is to become all
things to all things. Nevertheless, his being remains, though in a
different form, in a different glory, and in a different power. And all
this comes to man through his utter abandonment of self.[8]

Zaehner argues that in the natural mystical experience the mystic
loses track of the distinction between self and Other and thus
becomes one (phenomenologically) with the whole of the objective world. Zaehner takes Huxley's experience of becoming one
(phenomenologically) with the bamboo chair legs as a diminutive
instance of such an experience. In the case of Suso's experience, on
the other hand, the mystic loses track of the distinction between
self and Other and thus becomes one (phenomenologically) with
God. Zaehner says that although both of these experiences lack
subject-object structure, there is an obvious difference between
them. In the first experience, the distinction lost is between self and
(some part of) the sensibly detected objective world. In the second
case, the distinction lost is between self and "the Deity Who is felt
and experienced as being something totally distinct and other than
the objective world" (22). In the second case, too, although "something" is "felt and experienced," nothing is perceived by the
senses—the experience is completely devoid of sensory content.
Returning to Huxley with this case in hand, Zaehner then asks:

> How is it possible for a sane man seriously to maintain that such an
> experience which excludes all sensation of the external world is the
> same as "not merely gazing at those bamboo legs, but actually *being*
> them . . . "? In the first case we have "deification" of a human soul
> in God, the loss of consciousness of all things except God; in the
> second we have identification of the self . . . with the external world
> to the exclusion, it would appear, of God. . . . The sensation that

8. After citing this passage in the middle of chap. 2 (p. 21), Zaehner uses it in the
rest of chap. 2 and on into chap. 3 to support his claims about theistic mystical
experience as a kind.

the individual human being and his external surroundings are not really distinct is not so uncommon as is normally supposed. . . . It is, however, unusual to find a serious author identifying this experience . . . with the Beatific Vision. (22)

Turning next to the monistic mystical experience, Zaehner notes that the mystical state described in the key texts of the Vedanta is one that is captured in the formula "*Atman* is *Brahman*." Zaehner explains this so:

> *Brahman* is the word used to represent the Absolute: it is the sole truly existing and eternal reality, beyond time and space and causation and utterly unaffected by these which, from its own standpoint, have no existence whatever. *Ātman* means "self", the individual soul. The proposition, then, that "*Ātman* is *Brahman*" means that the individual soul is substantially and essentially identical with the unqualifiable Absolute. From this it follows that the phenomenal world has no true existence in itself: from the point of view of the Absolute it is absolutely non-existent. Therefore, the soul which realizes itself as the Absolute, must also realize the phenomenal world as non-existent. This, then, is to experience one's own soul as being the Absolute, and not to experience the phenomenal world at all. (28–29)

Zaehner claims that on this analysis Huxley's mystical experience must be distinguished from the monistic state. "For what sort of sense does it make to say that to experience oneself as actually being three chair legs which represent a minute portion of the phenomenal world, is the same as to experience oneself as the Absolute for which the phenomenal world is simply non-being?" (29). And adding this point to one already made when contrasting Huxley's experience and the theistic experience reported by Suso, Zaehner is now ready to issue his final conclusion. The conclusion in question is initially stated in the closing paragraph of chapter 2 but is not fully articulated until the fifth paragraph of chapter 3. Following is the passage from this last-mentioned source, in which Zaehner claims to be identifying what he calls the "radical difference" between Huxley's experience under mescaline and the experiences that connect with theistic and monistic mysticism.

For in strictly religious mysticism, whether it be Hindu, Christian or Muslim, the whole purpose of the exercise is to concentrate on an ultimate reality to the complete exclusion of all else; and by "all else" is meant the phenomenal world or, as the theists put it, all that is not God. This means the total and absolute detachment from Nature, and isolation of the soul within itself either to realize itself as "God", or to enter into communion with God. The exclusion of all that we normally call Nature is the *sine qua non* of this type of mystical experience: it is the necessary prelude to the further experience of union with God in the Christian and Muslim sense, or to the realization of oneself as Brahman in the Vedāntin sense. To state, then, or to imply, as Huxley does, that his own experience is either identical with, or comparable to, either the Christian Beatific Vision or to what the Hindus call *Sac-cid-ānanda* (*Sat Chit Ananda*) "Being-Awareness-Bliss" is to state or imply an obvious untruth. (33)

Note that in this passage monistic and theistic mysticism are lumped together into a single category called "religious mysticism." Correlatively, monistic and theistic preternatural states are also grouped together as a single type of mystical experience. Although Zaehner attaches no name to the single type of mystical experience in question, the basic thesis of his text would suggest that he might well have called it "religious mystical experience."[9]

3. Zaehner's Use of the Data on Union

Consider the following criticism. Like the monistic mystical experience, the theistic experience lacks the ordinary contents of consciousness and is also devoid of subject-object structure. But if it lacks subject-object structure, then how can Zaehner say that the theistic experience is an awareness of "the Deity who is felt and

9. Note that in the preceding discussion I have restricted myself to a review of Zaehner's critique of Huxley. In particular I have refrained from any consideration of substantive issues connected with the question of whether mystical experiences can be produced by the ingestion of psychedelic substances such as mescaline and, assuming that they can, what consequences should be drawn about the cognitive status of mystical experiences or about their value in the religious life of practicing mystics. So far as I can see, these are three distinct questions, no one of which has an obvious answer. For a helpful discussion of some of these topics I suggest that the reader consult chap. 2 of William Wainwright's *Mysticism*.

experienced to be something totally distinct from the external world" or that it is a case in which "the soul feels itself to be united with God in love"? An experience lacking subject-object structure could not be an awareness of the Deity nor could it be a feeling of oneself united to another in love. This is because an awareness lacking subject-object structure could not be *of* the Deity or *of* oneself or *of* another, nor, for that matter, could it be *of* anything at all. In fact, if the theistic experience lacks subject-object structure and is also devoid of the ordinary contents of consciousness, then it must be the undifferentiated unity Zaehner refers to as the "monistic" mystical experience. Thus, as Stace and Smart have very clearly seen, what Zaehner is calling the "theistic" mystical experience can only be the monistic mystical experience theistically interpreted.

Utilizing the analysis suggested above in Section 2 of Chapter 8, I would respond to this criticism of Zaehner as follows. The claim that the theistic mystical experience lacks subject-object structure must be very carefully qualified. Taking the paradigm union experience as the illustrating case, this experience begins with a dualistic stage and progresses to a peak in which the distinction between subject and object is finally lost. In its dualistic stage the paradigm union experience is a clear case of theistic experience, because the dualistic stage is an interval of awareness that is phenomenologically and specifically of the particular individual God, the omnipotent, omniscient, and perfectly good creator of the universe. Thus, it is only with respect to the climax moment of the paradigm union experience that its theistic content is in any way problematic. And the problem here (as the critic points out) is that it lacks subject-object structure and thus cannot be said, in any straightforward way, to be *of* God, or, in fact, *of* anything at all. Still, by virtue of the fact that it is preceded by a specifically theistic interval of awareness, the climax stage of the paradigm union experience can be described as an experience in which the mystic loses track of the distinction between self and a very specific Other—God. In this special sense, then, it is *of* God. In the language of the *Cloud of Unknowing,* it is an awareness of having become "oned" with God. Stated negatively, it is an experience involving a very specific lack, the lack of awareness of a previously detected distinction between

self and God. It is, in other words, an experience of *identity*—what
I have called "God-soul identity." Of course, this analysis requires
that the mystical peak be a state in which the subject-object distinction is *lost* after having been established in a preceding interval. The
analysis thus makes essential use of the fact that the paradigm
union experience has a progressive structure in which the mystical
peak has dualistic experiential ancestors.

I want now to return to the passage from Henry Suso's *Little
Book of Truth,* which Zaehner first described as "fairly typical of
Christian mysticism" and then used to supply his teaching case of
theistic mystical experience. With respect to this passage, I would
agree with Zaehner on two important counts: (1) it is "typical" of
accounts often found in Christian mystical texts; and (2) it should
be counted as a *theistic* mystical experience. Regarding this second
point, Suso describes the experience as one in which the mystic
"becomes intoxicated with the immeasurable abundance of the
Divine house" and is thus like a "drunk man" who is "quite dead to
himself, and entirely lost in God." Of course, these descriptions
are by now familiar to us. They are standard ways of characterizing the God-soul identity experience. But given just this passage to
draw on for data, how would one explain the idea that this is the
description of a genuine theistic experience and not just a case in
which Suso is *interpreting* the monistic experience in theistic terms?
Since it is devoid of subject-object structure, one could not say that
the experience Suso relates in this passage is (phenomenologically)
of (in Zaehner's words) "the Deity Who is felt and experienced as
being something totally distinct and other than the objective
world." One could not say, either, that it is a state in which the
soul "feels itself to be united with God in love." As mentioned
above, these descriptions require that the experience under discussion have dualistic structure, and this is precisely what Suso is
denying in the passage Zaehner cites from his text. In short, it seems
to me that while this passage from Suso reports a genuine theistic
experience, it is singularly ill-suited to serve as the source of a
teaching case. The God-soul identity state has theistic content only
because it occurs as part of a complex phenomenon in which it is
attended by *dualistic* antecedents. It is in the dualistic antecedents
that the mystic detects *the Deity* who is *felt* and *experienced* as some-

thing distinct from the objective world and in which the mystic *feels himself* to be united with *another* in the double embrace of the mystical hug of *love*. Since this passage from Suso is completely silent regarding the existence and nature of a dualistic interval of awareness *preceding* the God-soul identity state, it does not contain the data needed to explain what it is about this state that *makes* it an awareness of *God*-soul identity and thus *gives* it its specifically theistic content.

Returning, then, to Zaehner's failure to identify theistic mystical experience as a distinct phenomenological kind, I suspect that the losing die was cast in chapter 2 of Zaehner's text, where he presented the passage from Suso as descriptive of a clear, exemplifying case of theistic mystical experience. As I pointed out above, it was in chapter 2 that Zaehner established his categories of mystical experience. The case used in chapter 2 as the illustrating case of the theistic category was therefore bound to have a controlling effect on what could be said about theistic experiences in the rest of the text. And given only this passage from Suso as material for analysis, Zaehner simply could not find a bona fide phenomenological difference between theistic and monistic experience. What Zaehner needed, I think, was an unmistakably *dualistic* experience as his teaching case of the theistic state. Teresa's description of the Prayer of Quiet or some classic description of double embrace in the dualistic stage of the Prayer of Full Union would have provided such a case. With a clear phenomenological difference between their respective experiences then firmly in hand, Zaehner would not have had to rely on nonphenomenological differences when striking the basic distinction between monistic and theistic mystics. My suggestion is, then, that Zaehner's muddle about theistic mystical experience was a consequence of the case he chose to exemplify this category. Given only the God-soul identity state as a point of departure, it is not hard to see why he was led to say, in effect, that theistic experience is just monistic experience theistically interpreted.

Of course, this raises the question of why Zaehner proceeded as he did with respect to the passage chosen from Suso. And on this topic let me say straight out that I have no very firm opinion. Still, I have an idea that may be worth some consideration.

Recall that the primary thesis of *Mysticism, Sacred and Profane* was
that Huxley's experiences under the influence of mescaline could
be sharply distinguished from the preternatural experiences of
central importance in the great religious mystical traditions. The
basic contrast stressed in the book was thus between natural mystical experience on the one hand and monistic and theistic experiences on the other. As I pointed out in the closing sentences of
Section 2 above, this contrast is especially evidenced in the conclusion formulated in chapter 3. There, Zaehner distinguished nature
mysticism from the composite monistic-theistic mysticism, which
is called "religious mysticism." He also contrasted natural mystical
experiences with monistic-theistic mystical experiences, which he
grouped together as a single experiential type. Now as noted
above, Zaehner defined "mystical experience" as a "unitive" experience, characterizing the latter as "a sense of union or even identity
with something other than oneself." And although, by itself, this
definition would be permissive enough to allow a range of mystical phenomena to qualify, Zaehner proceeded as if this definition
required that the extension of the class be restricted to just those
experiences lacking subject-object structure. Why? Surely the answer is not that, as ordinarily understood, the qualifier "mystical"
applies to experiences only when they lack subject-object structure. If this were so, most of the phenomena included in this class
by Christian mystical theologians would simply not count as mystical. My suspicion is that Zaehner restricted the extension of this
class in order to focus attention on a subclass of classical mystical
experiences that share one rather stunning feature with Huxley's
perception of the bamboo chair legs. This restriction provided the
kind of context necessary for fruitful comparison—not like apples
and oranges. And it also allowed contrast to be struck by noting
just one crisp difference between the members of the class so constituted. While Huxley's experience involved a sense of identity
with the sensibly detected external world, Zaehner took the *exclusion* of such a world as the sine qua non of the other, specifically
"religious" kinds of "unitive" experience. Of course, the God-soul
identity experience cast in the role of the exemplifying case for
theistic mystical experience fit nicely into this unfettered format.
And, indeed, the very simplicity of the format itself added elegance

and clarity to the basic argument of Zaehner's text. Still, if this is the real story behind Zaehner's choice of the passage from Suso, then I think it is fair to say that Zaehner was ultimately hoisted on his own artificially limited petard. After all, it is only insofar as a union experience has dualistic structure and is thus *not* a member of Zaehner's "unitive" class that it can be displayed as a genuine instance of a specifically *theistic* kind of mystical experience.

Steven Katz on
Christian Mysticism

One of the more important contributions to the contemporary philosophical literature on mysticism is a set of twenty articles published in two books (ten articles each) entitled *Mysticism and Philosophical Analysis* (1978) and *Mysticism and Religious Traditions* (1983), both edited by Steven T. Katz. In two of the articles contained in these volumes (one in each), Katz himself provides at least the beginnings of a phenomenological analysis of the union experiences reported in Christian mystical texts. He also offers a causal explanation of why these experiences have the particular content they have. These are the items I want to examine in this study. I shall begin by placing Katz's comments on Christian mysticism within the context of the general epistemological theory that undergirds the whole of his discussion.

1. The Construction Theory of Mystical Experience

Why do mystical experiences have the experiential content they have? This, in effect, is the question posed at the beginning of Katz's essay "Language, Epistemology, and Mysticism" (1978) and to which the discussion in that essay is primarily addressed.[1]

---

1. This essay is Katz's contribution to *Mysticism and Philosophical Analysis;* the generative question just formulated is framed by Katz on pp. 25–26, at the beginning of part 2.

Preparatory to answering this question, Katz assumes the following epistemological principle:

> *There are NO pure* (i.e., *unmediated*) *experiences.* Neither mystical
> experience nor more ordinary forms of experience give any indica-
> tion, or any grounds for believing, that they are unmediated. That is
> to say, *all* experience is processed through, organized by, and makes
> itself available to us in extremely complex epistemological ways.
> The notion of an unmediated experience seems, if not self-contra-
> dictory, at best empty. This epistemological fact seems to me to be
> true, because of the sorts of beings we are, even with regard to the
> experiences of those ultimate objects of concern with which the
> mystics have intercourse, e.g., God, Being, nirvana, etc. (26)

Given that all experience is, as he says, "mediated," Katz argues
that all experience is "pre-formed" or "preconditioned" by a complex, culturally acquired, sociopsychological mold consisting of
concepts, beliefs, and expectations that the experiencing subject
brings to experience. Since the phenomenological content of all
experience is thus "shaped" (that is, in part *caused* [40]) by this
mediating experiential frame, we can see already how the question
with which we started is going to get answered. Mystical experiences have the content they have because mystics come to the
experience with certain religious concepts and beliefs, which, together with the symbol systems they employ and their expectations concerning what they will experience, partially create the
content of the mystical experiences they have. So now let us ask:
What content do mystical experiences have? What kinds of experiences are so created? Katz answers that Hindus have experiences
that are, phenomenologically, of Brahman, and Christians have
mystical experiences that are, phenomenologically, of a supreme
person called "God." In fact, as regards their phenomenological
content, there are as many different kinds of mystical experiences
as there are cultures in which they occur. The content of mystical
experience is, Katz says, "contextual" (56–57). Mystics have the
experiences their culturally acquired (call them) "forms of intuition" *condition* them to have (see 26–27, 46, 58–59, 62–64). I import the phrase "forms of intuition" because the theory just outlined is openly and explicitly Kantian (59). It is, one might say, a

"socio-psychological version" of Kant's mind-construction theory of human experience applied to the special case of mysticism.

Prior to assembling the evidence that presumably establishes the truth of his construction theory, as I shall call it, Katz traces its implications for Stace's distinction between experience and interpretation.[2] Katz claims that as formulated and applied by Stace in *Mysticism and Philosophy*, this distinction is "naive" and "simplistic"—indeed, even "simple minded" (28, 29, 31). Why so? Well, according to Katz, Stace's distinction between experience and interpretation stemmed from a failure on Stace's part to consider the "fundamental question" that must be asked about the relationship between the religious experiences and the religious beliefs of the mystic. Having so failed, Stace then failed to realize that the relationship in question "contains a two-directional symmetry: beliefs shape experience, just as experience shapes belief" (30). Thus, Stace was led to think that if a mystic describes an experience in accordance with a previously held religious belief, the description is the product of a *judgment* about the experience made *after* the fact rather than a description of content indigenous to the experience itself. This, Katz tells us, was a mistake—a mistake that is revealed as soon as we realize that the experiential content of a mystical experience is, in part, *caused* by the very beliefs to which Stace refers. We can thus see that Stace's employment of the distinction between experience and interpretation in the study of mysticism turned on a fundamental misunderstanding. What Stace classified as "interpretations" of mystical experiences should have been regarded as direct reports of phenomenological content.[3] Katz adds that although Zaehner's inquiry in *Mysticism, Sacred and Profane* was in some ways more sophisticated than Stace's, it, too, suffered from a failure on Zaehner's part to appreciate the causal impact of the mystic's beliefs on the phenomenological content of mystical experience. Stace impaled Zaehner on the distinction between experience and interpretation only be-

2. What follows in this paragraph are the highlights of Katz's critique of Stace and Zaehner in *Mysticism and Philosophical Analysis*, 27–32.
3. Katz makes this point several times in the discussion after his initial criticism of Stace. See, e.g., Katz, *Mysticism and Philosophical Analysis*, 35, 36, 39–40, 46, 65–66. See also Katz, *Mysticism and Religious Traditions*, 13–14, 41.

cause Zaehner developed his tri-part typology for mystical experience without first undertaking what Katz describes as "the necessary inquiry into the logical and social-contextual conditions of mystical experience which would justify rejecting Stace's simplistic distinction" (31). Katz concludes, "This failure to investigate or to consider . . . the *conditions of experience* in general and the specific conditions of religious/mystical experience in particular is a deficiency which skews [Zaehner's] entire discussion in ways which distort any and all conclusions or suggestions made" (32).

We are now ready for the proof, the "demonstration" Katz claims to supply for the construction theory by reference to what he describes as the "empirical evidence" (46). I'll focus here on just two of the three blocks of evidence Katz develops in detail.

Start with the case of the Jewish mystic—used by Katz as what he calls his "opening gambit" (33). From childhood, this individual learns a host of doctrinal truths, for example, that a personal God created the universe, that God enters into covenants with men, that God and man are ontologically distinct, and so on. These beliefs have been put together into a theological picture that, together with an array of religious images, symbols, values, and ritual behaviors, defines, "*in advance,* what the experience he *wants to have,* and which he then does have, will be like" (33). He thus has an experience that is, phenomenologically, of a personal God, of the Divine Throne, of the hidden Torah, or the like. Katz assures us, however, that one thing the Jewish mystic does *not* experience is identity with God; that is, the Jewish mystic does not have the kind of experience that Ruysbroeck called the "union without distinction." Why not? Katz explains it so:

In the Jewish tradition the strong monotheistic emphasis on God's uniqueness is understood to entail not only his numerical unity and perfection but also his qualitative, ontological, distinction from his creations. . . . As a consequence, Jewish mystics envision the ultimate goal of mystical relation, *devekuth,* not as absorption into God, or as unity with the divine but rather as a loving intimacy, a "clinging to" God, a relation which at all times is aware of the duality of God and mystic, i.e. which *experiences* God as Other rather than Self. All Jewish mystical literature reflects this teaching of *devekuth* as a goal to be sought and, even more importantly, all Jewish mystical testimonies conform to this pattern. (35–36)

The "unavoidable conclusion," Katz tells us, is that the "complex pre-experiential pattern" of beliefs, expectations, and so on, precondition the Jew's mystical experience. This, he says,

> can be ascertained clearly in the Jewish mystic's experience or perhaps a better way to describe it might be to refer to the Jewish mystic's "non-experience". That is to say, the Jewish conditioning pattern so strongly impresses that tradition's mystics (as all Jews) with the fact that one does *not* have mystical experiences of God in which one loses one's identity in ecstatic moments of unity, that the Jewish mystic rarely, if ever, has such an experience. (34)

Moving to the Christian tradition for contrast, Katz begins his account as follows:

> In Christian mysticism we have two types of mystical experience, the non-absorptive type which is reminiscent of Jewish mysticism and its doctrine of *devekuth,* though still with a difference, and the absorptive (or unitive) type in which the goal sought and experience reached is a transcendence of the distinction between self and God and the absorption of the self into God in an all-embracing unity. (41)

A contrast is evident. Unlike Jewish mystics, some Christian mystics have "absorptive" mystical experiences, that is, experiences in which no distinction is discerned between God and the soul of the experiencing mystic.

In his second article on this topic, published in 1983 and entitled "The 'Conservative' Character of Mysticism," Katz emphasizes a second difference between Jewish and Christian mystical experiences, which seems to me to be at least as interesting as the one just identified.[4] After a long and detailed discussion of the sexual imagery from the Song of Songs utilized by both Jewish and Christian mystics, in section 1 of the article Katz claims that while Jewish

4. This article is published in Katz's *Mysticism and Religious Traditions.*

mystics experience God as lover, "they do not experience him in those most intimate and absorptive terms used by so many, especially female, Christian mystics." He then continues so: "Then again, Jewish mystics know only of, and thus experience what Christians call 'God the Father'. On the other hand, Christians do not generally experience 'God the Father' as their lover but rather Jesus. Thus Bonaventure can write: 'There is no other path [to God] but through the burning love of the crucified'" (14). Expanding on the claim that in their mystical experiences, Christian mystics, as he says, "almost always see, feel, touch, love, in short, experience Jesus as the Christ, rather than 'God the Father'" (16), Katz cites a passage from Catherine of Siena as his first illustration (12). The passage relates a vision in which Catherine was wed to Jesus. In the vision Jesus took a gold ring adorned with a magnificent diamond and red emeralds from the ring finger of his left hand and placed it on the index finger of Catherine's left hand. He then kissed her on the mouth. As further illustration, Katz quotes a long and very powerful passage from the works of Lukardis of Oberweimar in which the mystic reports having seen Christ fastened to the cross, dripping with blood. Lukardis tells us that at one point she raised her eyes and saw Christ's right arm "loosened from the cross and hanging feebly down." The passage ends with an account of Lukardis placing her hands against Christ's hands, her feet against Christ's feet and her breast against Christ's breast. She thus "felt interiorly the most bitter pain of the wounds both in her hands and in her feet and in her breast" (15). Returning to this same theme in section 3 and again in section 4 of the same article, Katz cites a vision from Suso (34) as well as a portion of Julian of Norwich's intense and highly complex vision of Christ's bloody passion (46–47) as yet further illustrating instances.

Given Katz's construction theory of mystical experience, one can see why a Christian (though not a Jewish) mystic would have a vision of Christ's passion or of a wedding in which Jesus takes the mystic as his bride. Returning to the first difference noted between Jewish and Christian mystical experience, however, why should it be that Christians have absorptive mystical encounters while Jewish mystics do not? In *Mysticism and Philosophical Analysis*, Katz explains this interesting discrepancy as follows:

What permits, perhaps even encourages, this unitive, absorptive mysticism of the divine he and the finite I found in Christian mysticism, though absent from its Jewish counterpart, is, I believe, the formative influence of the essential incarnational theology of Christianity which is predicated upon an admixing of human and divine elements in the person of Jesus which is outside the limits of Judaic consciousness. Thus, an essential element of the model of Christian spirituality is one of divine-human interpenetration on the ontological level which allows for a unity of divine and human which Judaism rules out. (41)

Katz adds that the influence of Plotinus on some Christian mystics must also be included as an explanatory factor.

The unitive Christian mystics are invariably those such as Eckhart, Tauler and Suso, who have been schooled on Plotinus, Dionysius the Areopagite and Augustine, i.e. the strong Neoplatonic current in Christian intellectual history. Book VI of Plotinus' *Enneads* provides the inspiration for this conceptualization of the final ascension of the soul into unity . . . with the Good. (42)

Katz concludes that "the study of Plotinus and the Neoplatonic mystical tradition shaped the mystic's 'mind's eye' so that his experience conformed to it" (42). Like their Jewish counterparts, Christian mystical experiences are thus, in part, products of the beliefs and expectations of the experiencing mystic.

After arraying considerations presumably showing that the Buddhist mystic's experience of nirvana is also conditioned by culturally acquired beliefs, expectations, language, and the like, Katz closes this part of his discussion by drawing a general conclusion from the evidence surveyed in the three cases considered.

This much is certain: the mystical experience must be mediated by the kinds of beings we are. And the kinds of beings we are require that experience be not only instantaneous and discontinuous, but that it also involve memory, apprehension, expectation, language, accumulation of prior experience, concepts, and expectations, with each experience being built on the back of all these elements and being shaped anew by each fresh experience. Thus experience of x—be x God or *nirvana*—is conditioned both linguistically and cognitively by a variety of factors *including the expectation of what will be experienced*. Related to these expectations are also future directed activities such as meditation, fasting, ritual ablutions, self-mortification, and so on, which create further expectations about what the future and future states of consciousness will be like. There is obviously a self-fulfilling prophetic aspect to this sort of activity. (59)

2. A Note on Procedure

Katz claims to have "demonstrated" the truth of his construction theory of mystical experience by reference to something he refers to as the "empirical evidence." And insofar as I have been able to follow the thread of the reasoning, the "demonstration" in question has the form of an argument that begins with the description of a fact and proceeds to its conclusion via a Kantian-like abductive inference, that is, via the contention that the circumstance mentioned in the conclusion is the only (or at least the best) explanation of the fact described at the outset. Thus, in this case, the argument begins with the (alleged) observation that the phenomenological content of mystical experience varies directly with the doctrinal content of the experiencing mystic's antecedent beliefs. The conclusion drawn is that the construction theory is true, that the content of the experiencing subject's doctrinal belief "shapes" the content of that subject's mystical experience. The inference is presumably justified on the grounds that the construction theory is the only (or at least the best) explanation of the fact that the experiential content of mystical experience is tightly correlated with doctrinal beliefs antecedently held by the experiencing mystic.[5]

Focus for a moment on the last-mentioned fact—the one from which the argument begins. Katz attempts to document its status by drawing on materials from the primary mystical literature. In some cases these materials are actually quoted in the text. More frequently they are presented in the form of digests, or, let's call them, "data

5. This seems to be the point of the reference to Kant and the need for a "transcendental deduction," which, Katz says "reveals *both* conditions of knowing in general as well as the grounds of its own operation and which is thematized according to specific possibilities" (Katz, *Mysticism and Philosophical Analysis*, 59 and n. 84).

summaries," of what is said in the primary literature on a given point. In whatever form they are introduced, however, these materials appear to be the things Katz has in mind when speaking of the "empirical evidence" marshaled in his text in support of the construction theory of mystical experience. Now, among the data summaries used along the way in "Language, Epistemology, and Mysticism," two appear to me to be especially provocative. The ones in question are formulated as two general claims: (1) that Jewish mystics have dualistic experiences in which they are aware of themselves in the mystical relation of *devekuth*, and (2) that some Christian mystics have dualistic, "non-absorptive" experiences of God. Why provocative? Well, think for a moment about the passages in the primary mystical literature (I'll call them "datum passages") of which these two claims are supposed to be summaries. Although Katz fails to tell us exactly what they are or where to find them, it is probably safe to assume that they are passages that say, in effect, that the mystical moment is one in which the soul "clings to" or is "united with" a distinct individual, God. But, of course, these are precisely the kinds of passages Stace would classify as theistic *interpretations* rather than purely descriptive reports. And with respect to data summaries 1 and 2 above, therefore, Stace would reject Katz's claim that they tell us anything about the phenomenological content of the experiences reported by either Jewish or Christian mystics. Thus the appearance of these two data summaries under the heading of "empirical evidence" offered in support of the construction theory must surely provoke the following question: What reason does Katz have for thinking that the datum passages from the mystical literature summarized in 1 and 2 are purely descriptive phenomenological reports rather than items that should be classified as doctrinal interpretations?

It might be thought that Katz already addressed this question when he rejected Stace's distinction between experience and interpretation as "naive" and "simple-minded." One might argue that since Stace's distinction has been effectively dismissed, the question before us has been emptied of import. This response to the question just posed, however, would reflect an important confusion. Katz's only argument for the claim that there is anything wrong with Stace's distinction between experience and interpretation rests on the premise that the construction theory is true. Paraphrased in a nutshell, Katz's critique of Stace is as follows:

> Since antecedently held doctrinal beliefs condition the content of mystical experiences, we must conclude that experience descriptions from primary mystical texts that are classified by Stace as postexperiential doctrinal interpretations are, in fact, purely descriptive phenomenological reports.

Thus, if we were now to be told that Katz's argument for the truth of the construction theory *presupposes* his derivative criticism of Stace, we should have to conclude that the argument as a whole is boldly and uninterestingly circular. So what is the answer to the question posed at the end of the preceding paragraph? The truth, I think, is that there is no answer. As a general rule, Katz seems to proceed on the assumption that Stace's distinction between experience and interpretation can be safely neglected when dealing with the datum passages from the primary mystical literature implicitly employed in his text to establish the (alleged) fact from which his basic argument begins.

Is this all right? In one place Katz seems to excuse this procedure on the grounds that a Stacean account of the relevant datum passages would amount to little more than "*a priori* theorizing."[6] The point seems to be that since Stace could give no reason for regarding these passages as doctrinal interpretations, we are free to assume that they are, instead, straightforward experiential reports. But if this is the point, then I think Katz's reasoning is methodologically muddled. After all, it is Katz who has claimed that the evidence collected in his articles "demonstrates" the truth of the construction theory. Pointing to the data, he is the one who has said that the construction theory is the "unavoidable conclusion." Given that Katz is working in a context of inquiry in which Stace's distinction between experience and interpretation must be treated as a serious contender, it seems to me clear that claims like these must be backed by more than a mere *assumption* concerning the status of the would-be "evidence." What we need here, clearly, is a *reason* to think that a Stacean analysis of the relevant datum pas-

6. Katz, *Mysticism and Philosophical Analysis*, 35.

sages would actually be *wrong*. Whether Katz is right in thinking that such an analysis would constitute only "*a priori* theorizing" is not to the point. In fact (and alas), given that he provides no argument for the claim that a Stacean analysis would be incorrect, Katz's analyses of these datum passages seem clearly subject to the very same charge.

I should add that the preceding negative reflections are intended to apply only to Katz's argument procedure. They are not intended to show, or to suggest, that his construction theory is false. In similar fashion, they are not intended to show, or to suggest, that there are no reasons for rejecting a Stacean reading of the relevant datum passages. Indeed, on this last point, my own view is that with respect to the Christian mystical literature, at least, there *are* such reasons. I have made an effort to articulate some of them in Chapter 6 above.

3. Katz and the Data on Union

I turn now to the items in Katz's essays of most immediate concern to me, namely, the various theses advanced in these texts that deal, specifically, with experiences reported in the Christian mystical literature. Three theses in particular seem to me to stand in need of scrutiny. In the numbered paragraphs following I'll deal with each of them in turn.

1. The suggestion that there are two kinds of Christian mystical experiences and that experiences of the "absorptive" kind were enjoyed by only the subset of Christian mystics who were subject to Neoplatonic influence (for example, Eckhart, Tauler, and Suso) seems to me to be an unfortunate way to organize the data. Though it is hard to say who among the classical Christian mystics were "influenced" by Plotinus, Dionysius, and Augustine (I would bet all), even if some such category could be identified I cannot see how this would bear on the question of whether a fruitful distinction can be made between those who had and those who did not have mystical experiences of the absorptive variety. Of course, Katz is right in claiming that Eckhart, Tauler, and Suso reported experiences of the absorptive kind. But, as we saw above in Section 3 of Chapter 2, so did Ruysbroeck, John of the Cross, Bernard of

Clairvaux, Blosius, and Francis of Sales. All of these, as well as Suso and Tauler, also reported experiences of the nonabsorptive kind. I suspect that Katz's separation of the Christian mystical tradition into camps using Plotinus as the principle of division has little connection with materials actually found in the Christian mystical literature. Let me add that in Chapter 8 I have tried to defend an analysis that seems to me to be more closely tied to these data. Although the analysis in question provides for a variety of subtypes within the general category of union states, it does not connect basically different kinds of mystical experiences to different cultur- ally determined subgroups within the Christian mystical com- munity.

2. Although Katz is right in noting that Christian mystics make abundant use of love imagery taken from the Song of Songs when describing their mystical encounters, he is, I am sure, badly confused about who it is, in these experiences, whom Christians meet in mutual embrace. The one who placed the brightly deco- rated ring on Catherine's finger and then kissed her on the mouth was (as is said in Christian mystical texts) God, or Christ, *in his Humanity*. This is also the one whom Lukardis and Julian saw bleeding on the cross. As noted above in Section 1 of Chapter 1, however, God in his Humanity has physical form—he is a man. And as we also saw in the same discussion, the individual encoun- tered in the various states of union is not God in his Humanity; it is, rather, God *in his Divinity*—a pure spirit who does not have physical form. Thus, God in his Divinity does not have a finger on his left hand from which he could take the ring given to Catherine. Neither does God in his Divinity have hands, feet, or a breast against which Lukardis could press her body. Shall we say that God in his Divinity is "God the Father"—the same one whom Jewish mystics encounter in their mystical moments? Well, except in the literature on Rapture, where they often describe spiritual sensations of sight as being specifically of God the Father, or of God the Son, etc., Christian mystics generally do not identify God in his Divinity with any specific member of the Trinity. A look at the texts reveals that God in his Divinity is usually referred to, simply, as "God," though one can find cases in which this figure is called "Christ," "Our Father," "Our Lord," "His Majesty," "The

King"—indeed, "The Spouse" is, perhaps, the phrase preferred above all others after "God." Of course, this is not to deny that God (Christ) in his Humanity enters importantly into Christian mystical experiences. The visions cited by Katz from Catherine, Lukardis, and Julian are cases in point.[7] But these are instances of experiences generally classified as "mystic apprehensions"—a class of experiences carefully distinguished in the Christian mystical theological tradition from the States of Infused Contemplation, that is, from the states of union. Thus, insofar as the topic concerns the states of union—which are, after all, the Christian counterparts of the Jewish mystic's experience of "God the Father"—it is simply false to say that Christian mystics "almost always" encounter Jesus. Though Katz might be right in suggesting that there are important differences between Jewish and Christian mystical experiences, this, I am sure, is not one of them.

3. I do not know what to make of Katz's contention that Christian mystics (as opposed to Jewish mystics) are susceptible to mystical experiences of the absorptive sort because they are steeped in a tradition that allows for an "admixing" of divine and human elements in the person of Jesus. Is Katz here suggesting that because Jesus is, as he says, "the model of Christian spirituality" and because Jesus is portrayed in Christian doctrine as being both God and man that the Christian mystics are taught to expect that they will become identical to God in the mystical encounter? Surely, this would be a perverse understanding of the beliefs and expectations of most orthodox Christian mystics. Christian doctrine and tradition—no less than Jewish doctrine and tradition—emphatically affirms the ontological distinction between God and his creatures. As we saw in Section 2 of Chapter 2 above, even *after* having an absorptive mystical experience, the orthodox Christian mystic does not believe that at the mystical moment the soul was, in fact, identical to God.

Of course, it could be that Katz had some other point in mind. Try this: because the Christian mystic antecedently believes that

7. In the scheme usually employed by Christian mystical theologians, all three of these experiences would be classified as "corporeal visions." Corporeal visions are usually distinguished from what are called "imaginary" or "imaginative" visions, and both types are distinguished from (so-called) "intellectual visions," such as the one discussed earlier in Section 3 of Chapter 7.

Jesus was both man and God and also longs to be (in the words of Thomas à Kempis) an "imitation of Christ," the Christian mystic aspires to a state of consciousness in which she is not *aware of* the distinction between herself and God. Of course, this is not to say that the Christian mystic expects the mystical experience to be a state involving (in Katz's words) "a divine-human interpenetration on the ontological level." Being an orthodox Christian, she believes that God and her soul are distinct metaphysical entities that neither are nor could become numerically one. Her aspirations are thus confined to what she will *experience;* they do not include some hope about what she will *become.* Still, it seems to me that although this idea is interesting, it has dubious value when considered as an explanation of why specifically Christian mystics have absorptive mystical experiences. A case to consider is the Muslim mystic Al Ghazali, who had mystical experiences of the absorptive kind and, being an orthodox Muslim and thus a committed metaphysical dualist, denied that the God-soul identity experience is veridical.[8] Like Tauler, John of the Cross, Bernard of Clairvaux, and most other Christian mystics, Ghazali said, in effect, that the experience is *appearance* only.[9] The point is, however, that although Ghazali and, for example, John of the Cross both had absorptive mystical experiences and evaluated them in the same way, Ghazali's experience could not be explained by pointing to some belief of his concerning the divine-human nature of *his* "model of spirituality." In Islam, Muhammad is thought of as perfect man but is not usually assigned divine-human status of the sort Christians traditionally assign to Jesus. Given Katz's causal explanation of the absorptive mystical experience in a Christian context, therefore, one could no more expect such an experience in a Muslim setting than one could in a Jewish setting. Thus, insofar as Christian mysticism and Jewish mysticism differ as regards the occurrence of the absorptive mystical encounter, I can't see that Katz has provided any reason to regard this discrepancy as the product of differences in the religious beliefs and/or acquired expectations that "precondition" mystical experiences in these two cases.

8. This case is discussed at length by Zaehner in *Mysticism, Sacred and Profane,* 157–58.
9. See Section 3 of Chapter 2 above for an elaboration of this point.

Walter Stace on the Metaphysics of Union without Distinction

In Section 3 of Chapter 2 we discussed a state that I described as the "mystical peak" of Full Union and Rapture—a state in which the mystic loses track of the distinction between God and the soul and thus comes to experience what I referred to in Section 2 of Chapter 8 as "God-soul identity." This is what Ruysbroeck called the "union without distinction." Further, in the discussion in Chapter 2 I took note of the fact that Christian mystics generally regard union without distinction as appearance only; it is not taken as an index into the nature of reality. This verdict is based on the fact that orthodox Christian doctrine precludes the possibility of God and the soul of the mystic either being or becoming numerically identical. I pointed out that the assumption underlying the reasoning is one made by most Christian mystics prior to any consideration of the epistemological status of religious experience, namely, that orthodox doctrine delivers metaphysical truth. Now, with respect to the propensity of most Christian mystics to interpret their mystical experiences in accordance with standard Church doctrine, Walter Stace writes as follows in section 3, chapter 4, of *Mysticism and Philosophy:*

> It is plain from all the evidence which we have collected throughout this book that the disappearance of the division between subject and object is an essential part of the introvertive mystical experience.

> But the Christian mystics do not carry the conception of the unitary
> consciousness to its logical conclusion when they come to the intel-
> lectual interpretation of their experiences. Their own mystical expe-
> rience impels them to claim the identity of subject and object, the
> identification of God and the individual self. . . . Eckhart, because
> he is the greatest and most original and audacious *intellect* among the
> Christian mystics, expresses this boldly and—from the point of
> view of worldly caution—rashly. So do several of the Sufis. But
> when it comes to the point, the majority of them draw back from
> taking the last step towards which the momentum of their com-
> bined experience and logic is carrying them. They balk at asserting
> what is obviously the dictate of their own consciousness. They fail
> to implement in full the notion of unity. They take the step back-
> ward into dualism. (233-34)

In comments made both before and after this passage, Stace says
that dualism is a "mistaken" (230) or "incorrect" (237) interpretation of mystical experience. In the passage itself, however, the
point seems to be that evidence for this negative conclusion can be
gathered from a study of the very experiences reported by the great
Christian mystics. That God and the soul of the mystic are numerically identical is the conclusion, Stace says, toward which "their
own mystical experience impels them." It is the conclusion toward
which "the momentum of their combined experience and logic is
carrying them." Stace seems to be saying that given the nature of
the God-soul identity experience, when Christian mystics take the
"step backward into dualism" they are somehow involved in a
logical error. Picking up on this theme elsewhere in his text, Stace
claims that there is a "flat contradiction" between dualism considered as a metaphysical theory and, as he says, "the nuclear common characteristic of all mystical experience, *viz.,* that it is an
ultimate unity which is 'beyond all multiplicity'" (230-31). Stace
says that most Christian mystics fail to draw what he calls the
"proper conclusion" from their own fund of data. Their own mystical experience actually "implies" the identity of subject and object.

> The undifferentiated unity which is the mystical experience implies
> that there are no distinctions within the One, or the Universal Self,
> that there is no distinction between object and object, and finally

that there is no distinction between subject and object. Dualism overlooks or denies the last of these three propositions. It is therefore a form of mystical theory which is stunted and undeveloped. It stops half way and fails to carry through the concept of unity to its proper conclusion. (236)

How could it be that most Christian mystics have been guilty of this (alleged) error in reasoning? As I mentioned very briefly in Section 3 of Chapter 5, Stace attributes the mistake less to intellectual failure on the part of practicing mystics than to admonishments and threats received by the mystic from various officials connected with the Church. Stace claims that if left to their own "spontaneous" inclinations, most Christian mystics would affirm metaphysical identity between God and the soul (14).[1] He says, "They are only prevented from doing it by the menaces and pressures of the theologians and ecclesiastical authorities" (232). Dualism, in other words, is *imposed* on the mystical community from an outside force. This point is emphasized in chapter 6 of *The Teachings of the Mystics*. Here Stace says, for example:

> In Christianity the Roman church was so powerful that in general it succeeded in enforcing its will upon the mystics. An Eckhart may tend toward heretical language and get himself into trouble. But the vast majority of great Catholic mystics were submissive and managed to give an interpretation of "union with God" which could be accommodated to strict orthodoxy. And even Eckhart in his defense defers to the Church and attempts to explain away his pantheism. (128)

I should add that there are passages in Stace's discussion of this topic that paint a somewhat softer picture. In one place he says that dualism is a metaphysical theory the individual Christian mystic accepts because of "his own wish to be a law-abiding person within the framework of the ecclesiastical institution." Still, even here Stace includes a factor of external force. He says that the wish on the part of the individual mystic is no doubt "reinforced" by the threat of punishment for heresy.[2]

1. Stace develops this point in more detail on pp. 232–35.
2. Stace, *Mysticism and Philosophy*, 234–35.

I have two things to say about this line of thinking in Stace.

1. Insofar as Stace would have us believe that Christian mystics are somehow guilty of a *logical* error when adopting a dualistic interpretation of the union without distinction, I think we can safely discard the suggestion with no further ceremony. If anything is to be learned from the study of modern philosophy since Descartes, it is that no description of the phenomenological features of any given experience entails anything about the nature of extraexperiential reality. Thus, for example, when Stace says that "the undifferentiated unity which is the mystical experience *implies* that . . . there is no distinction between subject and object" (my italics), we can agree to this if we take it to mean that the undifferentiated unity is, essentially, a state in which the mystic is not aware of a distinction between subject and object. This would be to say that *phenomenologically* the undifferentiated unity lacks subject-object structure and that this is one of the defining features of this experience type. But, of course, this is not to say that the undifferentiated unity (or the description of the undifferentiated unity) implies metaphysical dualism, that is, implies that there is, *in reality,* no distinction between subject and object. The latter implication would hold only if we could make no distinction, in principle, between appearance and reality. I think we must assume that on this point Stace is just whistling in the proverbial dark. Though dualism may be an incorrect interpretation of the God-soul identity experience, we cannot suppose that this conclusion follows from a mere description of its experiential features.

2. Consider the magic show in which I "perceive" the magician pulling quarters out of the air. Of course, I know that the perception is deceptive. Further, I know it is deceptive not because I perceive something at the show that gives it away. Rather, I know it because I come to the show possessed of a fund of background knowledge about the way the world is and about the way it works. Although this fund is partly a product of my own experience, it is mostly acquired through years of both formal and informal instruction from others. Further, this fund provides me with a basic world picture by reference to which I organize and evaluate my day-to-day experiences. This picture dictates that I dismiss the very possibility of pulling quarters out of the air. Does the judg-

ment that my perception is deceptive reflect my own "spontaneous" reaction to the experience? That depends on how spontaneous a "spontaneous" reaction must be. To be sure, while watching the magician I am at first inclined to think he is actually pulling quarters out of the air. That is the way it *looks*. But, on the other hand, my judgment concerning the status of the appearance is made with no hesitations or complex calculations about the consequences of holding an alternative opinion. It is not as though I am being pressured by an outside force (for example, public opinion) into suppressing my own real view on the matter and assigning the standard interpretation to my experience. Of course, were I to claim that the magician actually did pull quarters out of the air I would probably be chastised by my family and friends— "naive" they would say, perhaps even "stupid." But that fact plays no role in my thinking. The point is that although my judgment concerning the epistemic status of my perception is based on a fund of background information acquired mostly from others, the information in question is *mine*—the world picture involved is *my own*. So we might say that my judgment is the "spontaneous" consequence of *my* visual perception judged against *my* basic picture of the way in which the world is put together. Let me add that this kind of spontaneity is one of the things that mark my reaction as *rational*. No thinking person scraps a deeply ingrained and otherwise well-working world picture just to give credence to a single recalcitrant phenomenon.

It is possible, I suppose, that Christian mystics assign a dualistic interpretation to the God-soul identity experience only because they are threatened by ecclesiastical authorities or, more generously, because they wish to be law-abiding participants within the community governed by the ecclesiastical institution. It could be that if left to decide the matter entirely on the basis of their own inclinations, their mystical experiences would lead them to affirm actual, metaphysical identity of God and the individual soul. This hypothesis, however, must be weighed against another. It could be that most Christian mystics measure their mystical experiences against a culturally acquired though personally deep-seated world picture having theistic structure and that also includes items mirroring most of the details of orthodox Christian doctrine. We might allow that the initial reaction to the God-soul identity experience on the part of the experiencing mystic is to think that God and the soul are actually one. We add, however, that this reaction is automatically corrected when judged in the context of firmly rooted Christian beliefs. On this hypothesis, neither the threat of punishment for heresy nor the wish to be a law-abiding person within the framework of the ecclesiastical institution plays any role in the outcome. Christian mystics adopt the dualistic interpretation of the God-soul identity experience because this is the *rational* thing to do. As I said above, no thinking person scraps a deeply ingrained and otherwise well-working world picture just to give credence to a single recalcitrant phenomenon.

My own opinion is that the second of these hypotheses is closer to the truth than is the first. Even if this opinion is wrong, however, I should think that the burden would be on Stace to show it is wrong. I take it as a general principle of behavioral explanation that unfriendly accusations are not to be multiplied beyond necessity.

Works Cited

Angela of Foligno. *The Book of Divine Consolations*. Translated from the Italian by Mary G. Steegmann. Introduction by Algar Thorold. New York: Cooper Square, 1966.

Aquinas, Thomas. *Summa Theologica* (first complete American edition in 3 volumes). Literally translated by the Fathers of the English Dominican Province. New York: Benzinger Brothers, 1947.

Bernard of Clairvaux. *Treatise on Loving God*. In *Bernard of Clairvaux: Selected Works*. Trans. G. R. Evans. Introduction by Jean Leclercq. Preface by Ewert H. Cousins. New York: Paulist Press, 1987.

Blosius, Ludovicus. *A Book of Spiritual Instruction (Institutio Spiritualis)*. Translated from the Latin by Bertrand A. Wilberforce (of the order of Preachers). Edited by a Benedictine of Stanbrook Abbey. Westminster, Md.: Newman Press, 1955.

Buber, Martin. *I and Thou*. A new translation with a Prologue, "I and You," and Notes by Walter Kaufmann. New York: Scribner's, 1970.

Butler, Dom Cuthbert. *Western Mysticism: The Teachings of Augustine, Gregory, and Bernard on Contemplation and the Contemplative Life*. With "Afterthoughts" and a new foreword by David Knowles. London: Constable; Sheffield: Loxley Bros, 1967.

Capitan, W. H., and D. D. Merrill, eds. *Art, Mind, and Religion*. Pittsburgh: University of Pittsburgh Press, 1965.

Farges, Albert. *Mystical Phenomena (Compared with Their Human and Diabolical Counterparts): A Treatise on Mystical Theology* (in agreement with the principles of Saint Teresa set forth by the Carmelite Congress of 1923 at Madrid). Translated from the 2d French edition by S. P. Jacques. London: Burns, Oates and Washbourne, 1926.

Flew, Antony, and Alasdair MacIntyre, eds. *New Essays in Philosophical Theology*. New York: Macmillan, 1955.

Forgie, William. "Theistic Experience and the Doctrine of Unanimity." *International Journal of the Philosophy of Religion* 15 (1984): 13–30.

Francis de Sales. *Treatise on the Love of God*. Translated into English by the Reverend Henry Benedict Mackey, O.S.B. Westport, Conn.: Greenwood Press, 1971.

Garside, Bruce. "Language and the Interpretation of Mystical Experience." *International Journal of the Philosophy of Religion* 3 (1972): 93–102.

Hartmann, Franz. *Personal Christianity: The Doctrines of Jacob Boehme*. New York: Ungar, 1958.

Hochberg, Julian E. *Perception*. Foundations of Modern Psychology Series. Englewood Cliffs, N.J.: Prentice-Hall, 1964.

Huxley, Aldous. *The Doors of Perception*. New York: Harper and Row, Colophon Books, 1963.

Inge, William Ralph. *Studies of The English Mystics*. London: John Murray, 1921.

——. *Christian Mysticism*. London: Methuen, 1948.

James, William. *The Varieties of Religious Experience*. New York: Random House, Modern Library, 1936.

John of the Cross. *Ascent of Mount Carmel*. Translated and edited by E. Allison Peers from the critical edition of P. Silverio de Santa Teresa, C.D. Garden City, N.Y.: Doubleday, Image Books, 1958.

——. *Dark Night of the Soul*. Translated and edited by E. Allison Peers from the critical edition of P. Silverio de Santa Teresa, C.D. Garden City, N.Y.: Doubleday, Image Books, 1959.

——. *Spiritual Canticle*. Translated and edited by E. Allison Peers from the critical edition of P. Silverio de Santa Teresa, C.D. Garden City, N.Y.: Doubleday, Image Books, 1961.

——. *Living Flame of Love*. Translated and edited by E. Allison Peers from the critical edition of P. Silverio de Santa Teresa, C.D. Garden City, N.Y.: Doubleday, Image Books, 1962.

Julian of Norwich. *Revelations of Divine Love*. Translated into modern English and with an Introduction by Clifton Wolters. Baltimore: Penguin Books, 1966.

Katz, Steven T., ed. *Mysticism and Philosophical Analysis*. London: Sheldon Press, 1978.

——, ed. *Mysticism and Religious Traditions*. New York: Oxford University Press, 1983.

More, Paul Elmer. *Christian Mysticism: A Critique*. London: Society for Promoting Christian Knowledge, 1932.

Poulain, Augustin. *The Graces of Interior Prayer [Des Graces D'Oraison]: A Treatise on Mystical Theology*. Translated from the 6th edition by Leonora L. Yorke Smith, with a Preface by the Reverend D. Considine, S.J. London: Kegan Paul, Trench, Trubner, 1910.

Ruysbroeck, Jan van. *John of Ruysbroeck.* Translated from the Flemish by C. A. Wynschenk Dom. Edited with an Introduction and Notes by Evelyn Underhill. London: John M. Watkins, 1951.

Smart, Ninian. "Interpretation and Mystical Experience." *Religious Studies* 1 (1965): 75–87.

Staal, Frits. *Exploring Mysticism: A Methodological Essay.* Berkeley: University of California Press, 1975.

Stace, Walter T. *Mysticism and Philosophy.* Philadelphia: Lippincott, 1960.

——. *The Teachings of the Mystics.* New York: New American Library, 1960.

Suso, Henry. *The Exemplar: Life and Writings of Henry Suso.* Vol. 2. Translated from the German by Sister M. Ann Edward, O.P. Edited by Nicholas Heller. Dubuque: Priory Press, 1962.

Teresa of Avila. *The Life of Teresa of Jesus* [The Autobiography of Saint Teresa of Avila]. Translated and edited by E. Allison Peers from the critical edition of P. Silverio de Santa Teresa, C.D. Garden City, N.Y.: Doubleday, Image Books, 1960.

——. *Interior Castle.* Translated and edited by E. Allison Peers from the critical edition of P. Silverio de Santa Teresa, C.D. Garden City, N.Y.: Doubleday, Image Books, 1961.

——. *The Relations or Manifestations of Her Spiritual State Which St. Teresa Submitted to Her Confessors.* In *The Life of St. Teresa of Avila.* Translated from the Spanish by David Lewis, with an Introduction by David Knowles. Westminster, Md.: Newman Press, 1962.

——. *The Way of Perfection.* Translated and edited by E. Allison Peers from the critical edition of P. Silverio de Santa Teresa, C.D. Garden City, N.Y.: Doubleday, Image Books, 1964.

——. *Conceptions of the Love of God.* In *The Complete Works of St. Teresa of Jesus,* vol. 2. Translated and edited by E. Allison Peers from the critical edition of P. Silverio de Santa Teresa, C.D. London: Sheed and Ward, 1973.

Underhill, Evelyn. *Mysticism: A Study in the Nature and Development of Man's Spiritual Consciousness.* New York: Noonday Press, 1955.

Wainwright, William J. *Mysticism: A Study of Its Nature, Cognitive Value, and Moral Implications.* Brighton: Harvester Press, 1981.

Zaehner, R. C. *Mysticism, Sacred and Profane: An Inquiry into Some Varieties of Praeternatural Experience.* New York: Oxford University Press, Galaxy Books, 1961.

Index